BIKINI-READY MOMS

SUNY series in Feminist Criticism and Theory
Michelle A. Massé, editor

BIKINI-READY MOMS

*Celebrity Profiles,
Motherhood,
and the Body*

LYNN O'BRIEN HALLSTEIN

Cover art: Bikini © Shutterstock.com/Boykung

Published by State University of New York Press, Albany

For information, contact State University of New York Press, Albany, NY
www.sunypress.edu

Production, Diane Ganeles
Marketing, Michael Campochiaro

Library of Congress Cataloging-in-Publication Data
Hallstein, Lynn O'Brien.
  Bikini-ready moms : celebrity profiles, motherhood, and the body / Lynn O'Brien
Hallstein.
      pages cm. — (SUNY series in feminist criticism and theory)
  Includes bibliographical references and index.
  ISBN 978-1-4384-5900-4 (pbk. : alk. paper) — ISBN 978-1-4384-5901-1
(hardcover : alk. paper) — ISBN 978-1-4384-5902-8 (e-book) 1. Motherhood.
2. Celebrities. 3. Body image. 4. Women—Identity. I. Title.
  HQ759.H1866 2015
  306.874'3—dc23
                                          2015001461

10 9 8 7 6 5 4 3 2 1

To my family—Michel, Jean-Philipp, and Joshua—but most especially for Michel for working hard—sometimes with good cheer and sometimes only because he is trying to enact what he says he believes—to resist creating our own neotraditional family.

CONTENTS

ACKNOWLEDGMENTS

This is an original manuscript. However, my initial work on celebrity mom profiles appeared in my 2011 essay titled, "She Gives Birth, She's Wearing a Bikini: Mobilizing the Post-Pregnant Celebrity Mom Body to Manage the Post-Second Wave Crisis in Femininity," *Women's Studies in Communication* 34.2 (November 2011): 1–27. An updated and revised version of that essay appears in chapter 3. My initial thinking about contemporary motherhood at the epicenter of the post-second wave and neoliberal turns appeared in my 2014 book chapter "When Neoliberalism Intersects with Post-Second Wave Mothering: Reinforcing Neo-traditional American Family Configurations and Exacerbating the Post-Second Wave Crisis in Femininity," *Mothering in the Age of Neoliberalism*, edited by Melinda Vandenbeld Giles, Toronto: Demeter Press, 2014: 297–314. A small section of that essay has been integrated in chapter 1 of this manuscript.

I acknowledge and thank Boston University and the College of General Studies for granting me a sabbatical to work on this book. I also acknowledge and thank the Waad family for a research grant that allowed me to work with Allyson English as my undergraduate research assistant. I will forever be in debt to Allyson for her enthusiasm for this project and her excellent research work. Even more important, however, is the fact that, when I was literally on my back recovering from a serious leg injury, her energy and enthusiasm for this project reenergized me and helped me sit up and just do the work to complete the manuscript, leg brace and all. I will be forever grateful for "catching" her excitement when I needed it most.

Introduction

New and Changing Celebrity Mom Profiles: Theoretical Grounding and Interdisciplinary Rhetorical Approach and Method

The celebrity mom profile was probably the most influential media form to sell the new momism, and where its key features were refined, reinforced and romanticized.

—Susan J. Douglas and Meredith Michaels, 113

There is no question about it – celebrity baby stories sell. But recently post-baby body reveals have become such a big magazine staple, they'll stop at nothing to scoop the story.

—Amber James *Popeater.com* par. 2

Beyonce opines, "You can have your child, and you can still have fun, and still be sexy, and still have dreams, and still live for yourself."

—Quoted in Lauren Shutte, "Beyonce Reveals" par. 6

After months of speculation about whether or not she was pregnant with her third child, in January 2014, singer and celebrity Gwen Stefani finally confirmed her third pregnancy with an Instagram selfie. In the selfie, Stefani is clad in an all-black, form-fitting long shirt, miniskirt, tights, and black stilettos. First and foremost, the photo highlighted Stefani's slender pregnancy: pregnant only in her belly and slender everywhere else, still. Noting the new convention of celebrity moms as pregnant in "bump only," a January 22, 2014, *USA Today* online headline about the photo reads, "Gwen Stefani 'bumps it' in stilettos," which is accompanied with a reprint of the selfie Stefani posted on Instagram the day before (Oldenburg). Slender pregnancy is not the only requirement for celebrity moms today; indeed, quickly slender, even bikini-ready, postpartum bodies are also the new norm. Three days postpartum and posing in a bra and underwear reminiscent of a bikini, which highlighted her already-flat six-pack abs three days after giving birth, Norwegian celebrity Caroline Berg Eriksen, a blogger who is married to a professional Norwegian soccer player, also posted a selfie on Instagram. The picture engendered much controversy, including an online article by Beth Greenfield about Eriksen that begins with the following question: "Is the postpregnancy body the new weapon of choice among superfit women?" (par. 1). In a follow-up interview about her posting, Eriksen explained, "People kept telling me that my body would never be the same," Eriksen told ABC News ("New Mom's"). In another report about the controversy and the notion that her postpartum body would never be the same, Eriksen also said, "I wanted to show everyone that's not entirely true. Right after birth— like three minutes after—I felt like myself again" (quoted in Greenfield pars. 15–16). Feeling like herself again, or returning to her prepregnant self postpartum, as if pregnancy was just a small bump in the road, Beyonce also opines about her life and postpartum body after becoming a first-time mother, "You can have your child, and you can still have fun, and still be sexy, and still have dreams, and still live for yourself" ("Beyonce Reveals" Schutte par. 6).

In *Bikini-Ready Moms: Celebrity Profiles, Motherhood, and the Body*, I argue that celebrity moms Stefani, Eriksen, and Beyonce all understand the mothering rules and norms embedded and promoted in these new and second iteration of celebrity mom images and profiles. These images and profiles make the case that mothers can "have it all": contemporary mothers can now slip in and out of pregnancy and motherhood without losing their body—sometimes even improving the postpartum body—as if pregnancy is just a "small bump in the road" in their newfound gender-equitable place in the workplace and public sphere, while also suggesting that mothers can still have fun, be sexy, have their own dreams, and live for themselves after becoming mothers, as long as they continue to be "good" even-more intensive mothers, mothering within neotraditional family configurations. Moreover, I also show that this is the case because celebrity images and profiles work rhetorically to erase the difference that maternity makes in women's lives by encouraging mothers to engage in a third shift of body work; and this third shift is also now a new fourth core principle in the contemporary ideology of good mothering and is the energizing solution to ensure that mothers remain primarily responsible for childrearing and family-life management. Thus, and finally, I conclude that celebrity mom profiles now suggest that, if mothers are having difficulty managing "having it all," then rather than being the "weapon of choice" among women, the maternal body is also a new weapon of choice in the profiles to persuade mothers that maternal body work is the now-specific privatized solution and management tool to energize their ability both to have it all and "do it all" within neotraditional family structures in the private sphere.

Intellectual and Theoretical Foundations

Before I begin to lay out the intellectual and theoretical foundations that inform both my thinking about and analysis of celebrity mom profiles, it is crucial to acknowledge the various forms of privilege they reinforce and further entrench. Doing so is important because, if nothing else, intersectional theorists (Chávez and Griffin; Crenshaw; Hill Collins) have shown that women's lives are shaped differently based on intersecting factors of race, class, and sexuality; and the same is true for mothers. As is already apparent and the analysis that follows will confirm, both celebrity moms generally and their slender-pregnant and quickly slender, even bikini-ready, bodies specifically are thoroughly ensconced in economic, racial, cisgender (a neologism that refers to people whose assigned gender is congruent with their gender identity, or people who are not transgender), and heterosexual privileges. It is clear, in fact, that celebrity moms' lifestyles and the kind of maternal body they embody assume and necessitate privilege because both require vast economic resources to maintain those lifestyles and to buy childcare, so that celebrity moms have the necessary time to engage in the extensive fitness training required for slender-pregnant and quickly slender postpartum bodies. Also essential are the personal trainers and chefs necessary to train so vigorously and for the rigorous food management also promoted in the profiles.

As with most privileged social locations, however, this privilege is almost never stated nor acknowledged in the profiles nor by celebrity moms. In fact, in their own work on celebrity mom profiles, Susan J. Douglas and Meredith Michaels note that the "invisible" labor and various forms of privilege that celebrity moms have are rarely acknowledged in the profiles and, sadly, the analysis that proceeds will show that the same remains true today of the second iteration of profiles. Thus, it is indisputable that celebrity mom profiles promote and reinforce privileged motherhood, primarily by reinforcing white, at-least middle class, cisgender, heterosexual privilege and an even-more intensive ideology of good mothering, what Douglas and Michaels first coined as *the new momism*.

Nonetheless but always with caution and being mindful of the privileged social locations reinforced by celebrity mom profiles, we must continue to evaluate and understand how both the profiles and the new momism work rhetorically, because, as I detail later, all mothers are judged against both.[1] Moreover, although many of us would like to believe that we are somehow immune to both, most of us who are mothers—academics included[2]—are not. In fact, Douglas and Michaels also argue, "Even mothers who deliberately avoid TV and magazines, or who pride themselves on seeing through them [the profiles], have trouble escaping the standards of perfection . . . that the media ceaselessly atomize into the air we breathe" (3). Finally, as the analysis in this book shows, because the new momism is so easy to confuse with feminist or progressive mothering and the neotraditional family configuration that the profiles encourage and promote also appear progressive, it is crucial that we understand the rhetorical dimensions of the profiles that make this the case in order to find effective challenges against it, to continue to "talk back" to the seemingly progressive but ultimately problematic mediated images we are all seduced by at one time or another, and to make visible the privilege entangled with and reinforced in the profiles. Thus, as Douglas and Michaels conclude and I concur: "So instead of dismissing these media images as short-lived (and sometimes even stupid), let's review how they have laid down a thick, sedimented layer of guilt, fear, and anxiety as well as an increasingly powerful urge to talk back" against these mediated images of contemporary motherhood then and now, as Elizabeth Podnieks's book, *Mediated Moms*, also does (14).

The First Iteration of Celebrity Mom Profiles

In addition to situating celebrity mom profiles within the various forms of privilege they promote, the profiles also need to be situated historically to understand how they have changed. In their 2004 landmark work, *The Mommy Myth: The Idealization of Motherhood and How it Undermined Women*, Douglas and Michaels explored early, or what I now refer to as *the first iteration of*, celebrity mom profiles in the chapter "Attack of the Celebrity Moms." They argued these profiles primarily worked to encourage guilt and failure in mothers because the profiles always showed celebrity moms juggling it all—work, family, and mothering—with ease and without difficulty. Douglas and Michaels also argued that these profiles emerged when mothers became a marketing niche and with the rise of celebrity journalism. As they put it humorously, "Beginning in the 1980s, and exploding with a vengeance in the '90s, celebrity journalism brought us a feature spread that spread like head lice through the women's magazines, as well as the more recent celebrity and 'lifestyle' glossies: the celebrity mom profile" (16). The hallmark of these profiles was to show celebrity moms glowing, happy, content, and with their children, often one-to-two years postpartum, while the moms extolled the virtues of motherhood. Douglas and Michaels, in fact, report, and are worth quoting in length, that the celebrity mom:

> had to be photographed displaying a brood toothy grin, her child in her lap or lifted with outstretched arms above her head, an accessory who made her look especially good on her sofa or balcony. Celebrity mothers are invariably surrounded by pastels and suffused in white light; the rooms we often see them in feature white or pastel furniture. Often they are backlit or simply shot against a white backdrop for a nice halo effect. (113)

Moreover, the profiles also conveyed a key message: celebrity mothers found motherhood the best and most important experience in their lives. Indeed, according to Douglas and Michaels, the reports were often accompanied with article and/or cover titles such as, "FROM DESPAIR TO PRAYER: CONNIE SELL-ECA TALKS ABOUT THE MIRACLE OF MARRIAGE AND MOTHERHOOD; MICHELLE PFEIFFER'S BABY LOVE; THE LONGING SHE HAD TO SATISFY (EVEN *BEFORE* THE WEDDING); HOLLYWOOD'S LATEST BABY BOOM MOM-O-RAMA; and THE NEW SEXY MOMS!" (capitalization and emphasis in original 115). Thus, everything about the profile—from the titles, staging, and lighting—highlighted and reinforced the key ideas that celebrity moms loved motherhood, had found their "calling" once they became mothers, and were serene, calm, content, and able to "juggle it all" with ease, while also allowing the moms to show off and/or be pictured with their well-dressed and well-behaved child or children.

Another key pillar of Douglas and Michaels' analysis, however, was their argument that the profiles almost always followed seven rules. Douglas and Michaels reveal these rules by using Princess Diana as the ideal celebrity mom because, as they argue, "Few celebrity mothers were more closely watched, or managed to inspire more points of identification among everyday women during the 1980s and '90s, than the Princess of Wales. The endless profiles of her became the template that would crystallize into the celebrity mom profile" (125). The seven rules of the early profiles are:

> The mom is gorgeous, in clear control of her destiny, and her husband loves her even more once she becomes pregnant and the baby is born (126). They are radiantly happy when they are with their kids (128). They always look and feel fabulous—better than ever—while pregnant, because they are nutrition experts and eat exactly what they should and have the discipline to exercise regularly (128). Whatever your schedule, whatever institutional constraints you confront that keep you away from or less involved with your kids, it must be clear that they are your number-one priority, no matter what (130). There must be some human frailties, some family tragedies, some struggles or foibles that bring the celeb down a peg, make her seem a bit more like us and allow some of us to identify with her (131). The celebrity

mom is fun-loving, eager to jump up and play with the kids at a moment's notice (132). Rule number seven of the celebrity profile insists that truly good, devoted mothering requires lavishing as many material goods on your kids as possible. (132)

Although looking and feeling fabulous were important in the profiles, clearly, when combined, these seven rules primarily worked rhetorically—persuasively—to communicate clear messages and "arguments" about motherhood: that celebrity moms believe that being devoted, attentive mothers is not only the best kind of mothering, being a mother is the best and most important part of who they are *now*, regardless of any success that the celebrities might have had previously. In short, these seven rules worked to promote and persuade mothers to adhere to and enact a very specific ideology of "good mothering."

Indeed, Douglas and Michaels also argued that celebrity mom profiles are at the heart of *the new momism*, a term they coined and the primary topic of the larger book. The new momism is the form of intensive mothering that emerged in the 1980s and continues to be in full force today, albeit in new and more intensive ways. Drawing on Sharon Hays' work, Douglas and Michaels argued that this good mothering ideology rests on three core beliefs and values: "the insistence that no woman is truly complete or fulfilled unless she has kids, that women remain the best primary caretakers of children, and that to be a remotely decent mother, a woman has to devote her entire physical, psychological, emotional, and intellectual being, 24/7, to her children" (4). These three core principles also mean that the new momism requires mothers to develop professional-level skills, such as therapist, pediatrician, consumer products safety instructor, and teacher, in order to meet and treat the needs of children (Douglas and Michaels 6). In addition to creating impossible ideals of mothering, the new momism also defined women first and foremost in relation to their children and encouraged women to believe that mothering was the most important job for women, regardless of any success a woman might have had prior to motherhood; all of which, clearly, are promoted and reinforced by the seven rules of celebrity mom profiles. Thus, Douglas and Michaels concluded, "the celebrity mom profile was probably the most influential media form to sell the new momism, and where its key features were refined, reinforced and romanticized" (113).

The final pillar of Douglas and Michael's argument was that the new momism is also a post-second wave ideology because it both acknowledges and integrates second wave feminist rhetoric and ideas. Indeed, the post-second wave middle-class premise that contemporary women now have the choice to do it all is now entrenched in the new momism. Specifically, first young girls and then young women are taught that they live at a time when women can have it all: education, a career, and a family as long as they make good choices. As Douglas and Michaels put it, embedded in the new momism is the idea that women:

> have their own ambitions and money, raise kids on their own, or freely choose to stay at home with kids rather than being forced to. . . . Central to the new momism, in fact, is the feminist insistence that woman [sic] have *choices*, that they are active agents in control of their own destiny, that they have autonomy. (5; emphasis added)

Douglas and Michaels also argued that this integration of the ideology and rhetoric of choice are vividly apparent in the emergence of the supermom ideal that surfaced as second wave feminism gained prominence in culture.

In fact, Douglas and Michaels, along with Lauri Parker West, argued the classic example of the supermom is the famous 1970s Enjolie perfume ad of a woman who could do it all and make everyone happy. In the ad, the "new modern mom shimmied onto the screen singing, 'I can bring home the bacon, fry it up in a pan, and never, ever let you forget you're a man'" (Douglas and Michaels 79). In short, the new mother could have it all. Situating their discussion of having it all in relation to postfeminism—the idea that feminism is no longer needed because second wave feminism "solved" gender inequity and, as a result, women can now have it all and no longer need feminist action—Douglas and Michaels suggested that the new momism "has become the central, justifying ideology of what has come to be called 'postfeminism'" (24). While they are disdainful of postfeminism, Douglas and Michaels also argued: "Postfeminism means that you can now work outside the home even in jobs previously restricted to men, go to graduate school, pump iron, and pump your own gas, as long as you remain fashion conscious, slim, nurturing, deferential to men, and become a doting selfless mother" (25). Thus, from the beginning, celebrity mom profiles justified and reinforced privileged motherhood, the new momism, postfeminism, and grounded the general solution to having it all within mothers' abilities to make good post-second wave choices.

The New and Second Iteration of Celebrity Mom Profiles

Today, even more so than when Douglas and Michaels' first analyzed the profiles, however, media are saturated with celebrity mom images and profiles like Stefani's, Eriksen's, and Beyonce's in gossip and entertainment magazines (both in print and online), at gossip websites, and even on entertainment television shows. Indeed, one cannot grocery shop, surf the Internet, or watch entertainment television without being bombarded by celebrity mom images and profiles. Indeed, although celebrity mom profiles have always featured fit, in-shape moms, more recent profiles,[3] particularly from 2010 on, have begun to highlight and feature both celebrity moms' slender-pregnant and quickly slender, even bikini-ready, postpartum bodies; and this change in focus is significant.

In addition to the examples that frame the opening of this book, examples abound. Focusing only on the "bump" of pregnancy, for example, a May 2013 *Hollywoodlife.com* profile of Kim Kardashian, exclaims "Kim showed off nearly every inch of her pregnant body in a tiny bikini on her Grecian vacation, and she looked amazing! We love that the mom-to-be is proud of her baby bump and changing shape—she has no reason to cover up!" ("Kim Kardashian Showing Off," Steihl par. 8). Moreover, Kate Middleton, also pregnant at the same time as Kardashian, was featured on a February 2013 *Star Magazine* cover in her blue bikini, and the copy read: "Kate Shows Off Baby Bump!" (February 13, 2013). In yet another example, in an October 2013 *omg! Insider Update* video about Ivanka Trump's third pregnancy and cover photo for the October/November issue of *Fit Pregnancy*, viewers are told that, at six-months pregnant, "Trump slipped into a very stylish, form-fitting dress that displayed her baby bump" (Frazier 0:33). Like Stefani, both Trump's dress and photo first and foremost highlight that Trump is pregnant only in her belly; everything else about her pregnant body has remained slender and fit.

In terms of postpartum profiles, a May 2013 *omg!* entry declares, "Snookie Shows Off Fab Post-Baby Abs" (Shewfelt), while a 2010 *OK Weekly* cover story features Kendra Wilkinson-Baskett in a blue bikini holding her eight-week-old son, Hank (Bass). The title on the cover is, "My Body after Baby," which is followed by "How I Lost 25 lbs in 8 Weeks" and "My Easy Diet Fitness Secrets Will Work For You, Too!" A March 2013 *omg!* entry declares: "Holly Madison Shows Off Slim Post-Baby Body Three Weeks After Giving Birth to Daughter Rainbow," which is accompanied with a picture of Madison in a form-fitting, blue minidress ("Holly Madison Shows Off"). In another March 2013 example and in keeping with her extremely fast weight loss and return to the slender body, *omg!* touted Shakira's fast weight loss two-months postpartum with the following headline: "Shakira Flaunts Post-Baby Body in Skin-Tight Leather Pants" (Stephens). And Eriksen's three-day postpartum selfie noted earlier is one of the speediest postpartum examples.

Unlike early postpartum celebrity mom profiles that featured celebrities one to two years after giving birth, with their children in their lavish but kid-friendly and expensively kid-accessorized homes,[4] and with article titles and stories that focused on the celebrities' mothering, then, contemporary celebrity mom profiles are now beginning earlier—when the celebrity is pregnant—and are also highlighting and featuring the maternal body, almost always sans children, both in terms of the pictures and, especially, in emphasizing the state of the celebrities' maternal bodies rather than emphasizing the state of their mothering experiences and practices. In other words, in this new and second iteration of celebrity mom profiles, the mothers' experiences of mothering, the children, and their expensively kid-accessorized homes are gone or secondary, and, instead, celebrity mom profiles are beginning with pregnancy—rather than postbirth—which means the postpartum features occur far earlier than in the past, and both the pregnancy and postpartum profiles and images make the maternal body the focus of profiles: either via the slender-pregnant or quickly slender postpartum body.

While this book is the first book to explore and detail how and why celebrity mom profiles have changed in the ways just noted, I am not the first scholar to notice a changed and pronounced media focus on celebrities' slender-pregnant and postpartum bodies, nor am I the only scholar exploring how celebrity motherhood is being reshaped today. Other contemporary scholars (Bishop; Jermnyn; "Yummy Mummies" McRobbie; Nash; Podnieks), for example, also suggest that fascination with celebrity moms has only increased, even taking on new "nuances." As Deborah Jermyn argues:

> fascination with celebrity moms has continued since [since 2000] this time, taking on new nuances as it has become focused, first, on new stars (cf. Victoria Beckham and Elizabeth Hurley); has been marked by an intense scrutiny of stars' post-baby weight loss (cf. the cover story photograph montage of scantily-clad "Hot bodies after baby" on the UK's Now magazine, 29 October 2007); and has come to co-exist with, if not actually facilitate, the rise of the "yummy mummy," a kind of linked demograph visible among aspirational "ordinary" women and not merely celebrities. (166)

Moreover, scholars (Bishop; Cunningham; Jermyn; "Yummy Mummies" McRobbie; Nash) also note the growing importance of the maternal body in celebrity motherhood, especially the shift to slender-pregnancy and quickly slender postpartum bodies. Additionally, Angela McRobbie suggests a link between the maternal body, body work, and the market, as do other body scholars (Dworkin and Wachs; Gimlin; Gremillion; Heijin Lee; Jette). McRobbie ("Yummy Mummies") concludes, in fact, that the new focus on the bodies of celebrity mothers is changing the nature of motherhood when she argues, "The tribe of yummy mummies—Sadie Frost, for example, or Davina McCall, or Victoria Beckham—also contributes to a redefinition of motherhood for the nation's young women" (par. 2). Or, as Nash argues by directly linking the pregnant maternal body to "good" motherhood, "in the UK, Australia, and North America, a 'fit, risk-free, flexible, and responsible body' is the mark of a 'good' mother" (169). Thus, although I am not the first scholar to recognize the newfound importance of the maternal body of celebrities in contemporary celebrity mom profiles, I am the first to address how this new focus is changing the rules and structure of celebrity mom profiles and the new momism since Douglas and Michael's groundbreaking work.

The Maternal Body and the Post-Second Wave Crisis in Femininity

Moreover, I am the first scholar to argue that, when the new profiles make the maternal body the central feature of the new profiles, this also reveals that celebrity mom profiles now use the maternal body as the novel postfeminist neoliberal management tool or weapon of choice and solution to what I refer to as a new *post-second wave*[5] *crisis in femininity* that emerges when contemporary women become mothers. Although much has been written about the crisis in masculinity (Brooks; Dworkin and Wachs; Edwards, Tim; Katz; Kimmel; Malin; Messner; "Managing Masculinities" Shugart) as a result of the gains brought about by second wave feminism and the concurrent changes to gender roles and assumptions, little has been written about the contemporary crisis women face as second-wave beneficiaries and mothers: their lives are split between newfound gains as unencumbered women (women without children) in the public sphere and gender-based and problematic family-life roles and formations in the private sphere when women become mothers. Indeed, feminist writers and scholars (Crittenden; Hirshman; "Public Choices" O'Brien Hallstein; "Mother Outlaws" O'Reilly; Orenstein; Warner; Williams; Wood) have all shown that, even though second wave feminism opened up access to educational and professional contexts for many women in the public sphere, women still have primary responsibility for childcare and childrearing in the private sphere once they have children.

Popular writers (Crittenden; Hirshman; Wolf), for example, all argue that this is the case even when women work and across class lines. As Linda Hirshman puts it: "the assignment of responsibility for the household to women applies in every social class" (11). Ann Crittenden also reveals in *The Price of Motherhood* that women's responsibility for childrearing and care also emerges even if a couple shared household labor before the arrival of a child. As she puts it: "Before the arrival of the first child, [professional and educated] couples tend to share the house work fairly equally. But something about a baby encourages the resurgence of traditional gender roles" in heterosexual relationships (25). Ironically, then, many women today, particularly privileged cisgender women who are college educated, middle-class, professional, and in heterosexual relationships, may not actually encounter overt gender discrimination until they become mothers. As a result, Crittenden also argues: "Many child-less women under the age of thirty five believe that all the feminist battles have been won" (88). But, as Crittenden continues, "once a woman has a baby, the egalitarian office party is over" (88).

Contemporary privileged women's lives, then, are split between post–second wave gains in the public sphere and ongoing and prob-lematic gender-based understandings of family life in the private sphere that continue to place the burden of responsibility for chil-drearing and family life on mothers once children arrive. Thus, con-temporary mothers—especially first-time mothers when they face their post-second wave split subjectivity for the first time—must learn how to manage the crisis that emerges when they face the contradictions, challenges, and problems of having it all, of simul-taneously living between post-second wave gains as unencumbered women in the public sphere and problematic and ongoing gender-based responsibilities within the private sphere once they become mothers.

Additionally, the maternal body is also entangled with and tied to contemporary women's post-second wave split subjectivity and ideological understandings of what constitutes "good" femininity, "good" mothering, and "good" post-second wave crisis management. While I detail why this is the case in much more detail in chapter 1, here I suggest that this is the case because today feminine and maternal selves are also now tied to the neoliberal understanding of the body and body work in relation to gender. In fact, feminist and body scholars (Bordo "Reading"; Dworkin and Wachs; Gim-lin; Gremillion; Lee, Sharon; Jette; Pitts-Taylor) argue that, at the same time that the post-second wave era was ushered in, the early 1980s also ushered in a new fitness movement for both men and women. Drawing on Susan Bordo, Shannon Jette contends that the commodification of the hard body, the identification of women as a distinct market segment, and a generation of physically active and fit women beginning to have children all converged such that pregnant women became both a market and a health dynamic that needed to be managed (332). And, similar to the role media play in promoting celebrity mom profiles, as Shari Dworkin and Faye Linda Wachs suggest, "media play a central role in the dissemination and circula-tion of discourses about bodies and health" in ways that shape how contemporary women now understand their relationship to their body and what constitutes a "healthy," "normal," and even "moral" feminine body (12).

One of the most important discourses disseminated and circulating in media, then, is the discourse of healthism, which situates the problem of health and disease at the level of the individual. In fact, drawing on the groundbreaking work of Robert Crawford, who first coined and defined *healthism*, Dworkin and Wachs argue that contemporary capitalist culture is "infused with notions of 'health' and health promotion that reveal assumptions about normality, well-being, and morality (and not necessarily healthy)" (11). Solutions, then, promoted in media for being healthy are formulated at the individual level, particularly via body projects, which focus on "healthy" body management. Or, as Helen Gremillion puts it, contemporary "bodies are imagined as resources for fitness and health, and the fit body is an icon for achieving individualism, productivity, and 'self-actualization' within late capitalist consumer culture in the contemporary United States" (385). Thus, as Dworkin and Wachs also conclude, the appearance of a fit body, "rather than the reality of fitness, has become a critical determinant of social status and a factor that is self-policed by individuals as they negotiate social positions" and self-identity (12).

Entangled with and complicating body projects is the fact that contemporary culture is also infused with a kind of body panic—what Dworkin and Wachs describe as anxiety about attaining an increasingly difficult-to-achieve ideal fit body, a body ideal that is now conflated with good citizenship—that is the confluence of key culture changes, especially in relation to post-second wave gender roles and assumptions, neoliberalism, and healthism. Indeed, as Dworkin and Wachs put it, while also explicitly acknowledging a post-second wave context and drawing on the work of Kimmel: "As has been noted by Kimmel (2000), at the turn of the millennium, men's and women's lives are becoming 'more similar,' at least for the most advantaged. For the privileged, most professions are gender-neutral, and women and men are routinely employed in the same professions, enjoy the same leisure activities, and engage in similar rituals of selfcare" and body management (120). And, as self-care and body work have become equally important for both men and women and more and more entrenched in our neoliberal era, conceiving the body as a project to be worked on has also come to play a

key role in self-actualization and self-identity for all neoliberal subjects, but especially for post-second wave women (Gimlin; Gremillion; Lee, Sharon; Shilling). Thus, summarizing body scholarship,
Nash concludes: "Drawing on Giddens' (1990) concept of 'body
projects', 'postmodernists' and feminists have argued that bodies are
not only sites for self-expression, they are also heavily regulated by
normative standards of feminine performance" (28).

Equally important, body work and body projects have also
become pivotal to and entangled with the maternal body and contemporary women's post-second wave split subjectivity. Nash's work
on the pregnant maternal body, in fact, suggests that the right kind
of pregnant body is now a symbol for the right kind of current and
future motherhood. As she argues, "Having a firm, managed body
for such women is a 'symbol of correct attitude,' particularly in pregnancy: 'working out' suggests that a mother cares about herself and
her unborn child" and has become a normalized prerequisite for
middle-class motherhood (169, 170). As a result, I contend that the
maternal body has become a critical determinant of maternal social
status as mothers also negotiate standards of feminine performance
and their post-second wave split subjectivity today. In other words,
I am the first scholar to suggest that the maternal body is also now
a symbol for contemporary mothers' post-second-wave crisis management: the right kind of maternal body now also reveals the right
or "correct" kind of feminine performance via mothering and post-
second-wave crisis management for contemporary "good" mothers
living in our current postfeminist and neoliberal epoch.[6]

Moreover, based on the analysis done in chapter 2 and chapter
3, I also demonstrate that the structure of celebrity mom profiles
has also changed to include both slender-pregnant and quickly slender, even bikini-ready, postpartum profiles in order to encourage a
two-step process for contemporary women to accept, even embrace,
their post-second wave split subjectivity in ways that also encourage mothers to accept, even embrace, a third shift of body work *as
the energizing solution* to their post-second wave crisis in femininity.
Indeed, based on the analysis that follows, I argue that slender-pregnant celebrity mom profiles *are now the first step* in training post-
second wave women to embrace their split subjectivity and the first
three tenets of the new momism. I then also assert that postpartum
celebrity mom images and profiles *are now the second step* in training

post-second wave women to embrace further their split subjectivity and the even-more intensified new momism that has integrated a new fourth core principle: a third shift of energizing body work. Finally, I suggest that this means that the third shift of body work works rhetorically to erase the difference that maternity makes in women's lives and is also the now-specific energizing solution for mothers to have it all by doing it all themselves, alone and in the private sphere.

If, as Andrea O'Reilly (*Mother Outlaws*) maintains, patriarchal ideologies of "good" motherhood function as culturally constructed practices, ones that are continuously redesigned in response to changing economic and societal factors, then, understanding how and why celebrity mom profiles are now highlighting and featuring the maternal body in the ways just noted can reveal much about how the new momism continues to develop as a sophisticated postfeminist neoliberal ideology. In order to continue to understand the ways that the new celebrity mom profiles are continuing to reshape, refine, and reinforce the new momism and postfeminism, then, requires more than just a chapter in a book or edited volume, and/or a journal-length essay. Rather, what is needed is a book-length study of why and how new celebrity mom profiles are working today to reshape and refine the new momism and postfeminism. In doing so, *Bikini-Ready Moms* is continuing and updating the conversation that Douglas and Michaels[7] initiated and other scholars (Bishop; Podnieks) have continued, while providing the first full-length rhetorical analysis of contemporary celebrity mom profiles that now make the body primary and children and mothering experiences secondary.

Interdisciplinary Rhetorical Approach and Method

I explore how the slender-pregnant and quickly slender, even bikini-ready, celebrity mom profiles work rhetorically to communicate and shape a new set of values, beliefs, and assumptions about contemporary idealized and privileged motherhood and the new momism, while also offering new and problematic postfeminist neoliberal "solutions" to the post-second wave crisis in femininity. To do so and be consistent with much feminist and motherhood-studies scholarship, the theoretical foundations for the analysis are inter-disciplinary, as I draw on and employ ideas and scholarship from the following disciplines: communication, women's and moth-erhood studies, body studies, and sociology. In what I believe is a novel interdisciplinary approach, I bring ideas from these disciplines together by employing McRobbie's ("Post-Feminism"[8]) academic work on postfeminist "double entanglement" in my rhetorical analy-sis of contemporary celebrity mom profiles.

At the center of McRobbie's concept and also at the core of my own theoretical foundations here is the recognition that a "postfemi-nist" understanding of contemporary culture abounds, especially in media. In this context, postfeminism means that second wave femi-nist ideas and rhetoric[9] are both pervasive and assumed, regardless of whether or not any particular person identifies as a feminist. More-over, colloquially and especially in media, *postfeminism* is usually used such that the "post" prefix indicates that feminism is passé, no longer necessary, and/or rejects previous feminisms. Indeed, postfeminism suggests that second wave feminism was so successful there is no longer a need for feminism. Because this kind of understanding both assumes and rejects feminist ideas and rhetoric, McRobbie argues, "post-feminism permits the close examination of a number of inter-secting but also conflicting currents" (255). In her own work, then, McRobbie explores how conflicting cultural changes and ideologies intersect and work together, concurrently. Moreover, McRobbie also explores how second wave feminist ideas and rhetoric are used to indicate gender equality has been achieved for women and therefore feminism is no longer necessary. As McRobbie puts it, "post-femi-nism positively draws on and invokes feminism as that which can be taken into account, to suggest that equality is achieved, in order to install a whole repertoire of new meanings which emphasise that it is no longer needed, it is a spent force" (*Post-Feminism* 255).

Because McRobbie is interested in postfeminism's "doubleness," drawing on the work of Judith Butler, McRobbie also proposes the notion of "double entanglement." McRobbie's specific example of double entanglement is as follows:

This [double entanglement] comprises the co-existence of neo-conservative values in relation to gender, sexuality and family life (for example, George Bush supporting the campaign to encourage chastity among young people, and in March 2004 declaring that civilisation itself depends on traditional marriage), with processes of liberalisation in regard to choice and diversity in domestic, sexual and kinship relations (for example, gay couples now able to adopt, foster or have their own children by whatever means, and in the UK and Canada, full rights to civil partnerships). (255–256)

Analyzing postfeminist "chick" films, McRobbie, explores how double entanglement works in these films, so that the films can appear to be engaging in well-intended and well-informed responses to feminism for young women, while also repudiating a need for second wave feminism. Moreover, McRobbie argues, "Finally it suggests that by means of the tropes of freedom and choice which are now inextricably connected with the category of 'young women,' feminism is decisively aged and made to seem redundant" ("Post-Feminism" 255). McRobbie's interest, then, is to explore how feminist ideas are entangled with conflicting ideologies, how ideologies co-exist in seemingly contradictory currents, and, as a result, how those contradictory currents reshape and reinforce particular postfeminist understandings and ideas.

As is McRobbie's, then, my interest here is to explore how feminist ideas are entangled with conflicting ideologies and how these ideologies co-exist in seemingly contradictory currents in both contemporary motherhood and the visual and written ideas and texts that constitute the new celebrity mom profiles. As a result, in chapter 1 I expand and extend McRobbie's notion of "double entanglement" by also exploring how the post-second wave and neoliberal turns are entangled and now working together—sometimes co-existing and sometimes in contradictory ways—to reshape and refine both contemporary women's post-second wave split subjectivity and contemporary motherhood today, while also exploring in chapter 2 and chapter 3 how the new iteration of celebrity mom profiles work *to persuade* contemporary mothers *to believe and embody* the ideological messages embedded within the more-intensified new momism today at the crosscurrents of the post-second wave and neoliberal turns.

Method: Rhetorical Criticism

While my thinking and approach are interdisciplinary, my method is rhetorical in that I analyze *how* the new celebrity mom profiles work to persuade readers—through both visual images and written texts embedded in celebrity mom profiles—to adhere to and embody the rules and norms promoted in and via the profiles. Although much rhetorical criticism emerges from the field of communication, it is an interdisciplinary activity focused on both analyzing arguments and making interpretive arguments about how artifacts or texts work persuasively. Sonja K. Foss, in fact, argues that rhetorical criticism is "a qualitative research method that is designed for the systematic investigation and explanation of symbolic acts and artifacts for the purpose of understanding rhetorical processes" (6). Equally important, rhetorical analyses are, as Celeste Condit suggests, fundamentally concerned with how symbols influence perceptions and actions, making it especially conducive to the assessment of cultural discourses, including those about the body (14–15). Helene Shugart also suggests the power of rhetorical analyses, particularly in the context of intersecting cultural tensions and the body. As she suggests, writing about obesity discourses, "assessing the rhetorical configurations of such discourse, especially as they are 'written' on and by the body, is enlightening on its own terms, and further illuminating of the intersections and negotiations of broader contemporary cultural tensions and anxieties, as well" ("Consuming Citizens" 110–111).

In *Bikini-Ready Moms*, then, my rhetorical analysis centers on ideological rhetorical criticism of celebrity mom profiles as they are written on and about the maternal body. I also explore how celebrity mom images and profiles work as a postfeminist neoliberal hegemonic ideology[10] of "good mothering." In doing so, I analyze and evaluate *why and how* celebrity mom profiles are now integrating the slender-pregnant and quickly slender, even bikini-ready, maternal body as the central feature of the new celebrity mom profiles, while also continuing to refine, reinforce, and romanticize the new momism in ways that also offer postfeminist neoliberal solutions to the post-second wave crisis in femininity. Along the way, I also ask and answer three other overarching and related questions: How do the new profiles work rhetorically to reshape and refine the new momism? What are the consequences of this reshaping and refining for how we understand contemporary motherhood and the post-second wave crisis in femininity? What are the key features and new rules of celebrity mom profiles? I answer these questions by drawing on and analyzing well over 100 different celebrity mom profiles and images—both pregnant and postpartum—in gossip and entertainment magazines (both in print and online) and at gossip websites from May 2009 through June 2014. Thus, my primary focus is to explore how celebrity mom profiles and images work to persuade readers to adopt and embody the new momism promoted in the new celebrity mom profiles, while also offering problematic solutions to the post-second wave crisis in femininity.

Chapter Previews

Before proceeding to the analysis, in chapter 1, "Contemporary Motherhood at the Epicenter of Intersecting Cultural Changes: The Neoliberal and Post-Second Wave Turns," I answer the "why" question of this book theoretically—why has this iteration of celebrity mom profiles emerged now?—by exploring further how the postfeminist double entanglement is working in relation to the neoliberal and post-second wave turns. I argue that, given the intensification of intensive mothering, the fact that contemporary motherhood now sits at the epicenter of the post-second wave and neoliberal turns, and the rise of neotraditional family configurations as the "best" answer when "good" postfeminist neoliberal mothers face the crisis in femininity, it now makes more sense why the structure of celebrity mom profiles has begun to change. These new profiles are changing in response to the economic and social changes that ground our contemporary postfeminist neoliberal context and the new momism today at the crosscurrents of the post-second wave and neoliberal turns. And this context now undergirds contemporary motherhood and the everyday, privatized, and individualized commonsense solution to the post-second wave crisis at the heart of motherhood today: the neotraditional family.

Moreover, I also further detail the newfound importance of the maternal body as the symbol of correct neoliberal motherhood by also arguing that *the reason why* the maternal body has taken such

prominence in celebrity mom profiles is because today the maternal body has become a critical determinant of maternal social status as mothers also negotiate standards of feminine performance and
subjectivity at the epicenter of our intersecting post-second wave
and neoliberal era. In fact, I argue that the contemporary maternal
body *is the new embodiment* of contemporary motherhood at the epicenter of the intersecting post-second wave and neoliberal turns. I
also suggest that, as the body, body work, and body projects have
all taken a central place in self-identity generally and in terms of
maternal identity more specifically in society, this explains the final
piece of why the maternal body has taken a central focus in new
celebrity mom profiles. As both the new momism and neoliberalism have intensified and continued to be refined as a result of the
intersecting post-second wave and neoliberal turns, celebrity mom
profiles have also shifted to account for the newfound importance of
and connection between the body and maternal identity that exists
today. Equally important, however, I also contend that, as the maternal body has become central to the kind of maternal identity promoted, reinforced, and detailed in the new celebrity mom profiles,
the maternal body—via body management and a third shift of body
work—has also become both the symbol of and *the management tool*
for the post-second wave crisis in femininity.

Chapter 2 and chapter 3 are the analysis chapters, and these
chapters address the "how" question of this book—how are celebrity mom profiles now integrating the slender-pregnant and quickly
slender, even bikini-ready, maternal body as the central feature of
the new celebrity mom profiles? Chapter 2, "Step One—Becoming
First-Time Mothers: Slender-Pregnant Celebrity Mom Profiles," is
the longest chapter of the book, because this chapter also lays the
groundwork to make the case that the second iteration of celebrity mom profiles now works in a new two-step process. Based on
a case study of the ways media pitted celebrity moms Kate Middleton and Kim Kardashian in a battle for the "best pregnancy" during
both women's first pregnancy, I argue that slender-pregnant celebrity mom profiles *are now the first step* in training post-second wave
woman to embrace their split subjectivity and an even-more intensified intensive mothering position and ideology. By focusing on the
maternal body as the symbol for and embodiment of future mothering, slender-pregnant profiles do so by constructing the maternal

body as the weapon of choice in making the case that the measure of a good future mother is tied to *how* she manages her pregnant maternal body—how she manages her weight gain, her maternity style, her comfort and happiness with her pregnant body, and how she prepares for her impending birth and acceptance, even embrace, of both her future post-second wave split subjectivity and an even-more intensified intensive mothering ideology.

In chapter 3, "Step Two—Being Bikini-Ready Moms: Postpartum Celebrity Mom Profiles," I continue to address the how question—how does the quickly slender body work rhetorically?—by unpacking the themes that have emerged in quickly slender, even bikini-ready, postpartum celebrity mom profiles: "bouncing back: faster and better," "the before-and-after format," "the third shift of body work," "debuting the new, even better postpartum body to be a 'sexy' mom," and "not denying women's reproductive capacity: rather, erasing any signs of pregnancy and maternity." I argue that these themes reveal that, in addition to continuing to make the maternal body the weapon of choice, postpartum celebrity mom images and profiles *are now the second step* in training post-second wave women to embrace further their split subjectivity and an even-more intensive mothering position and ideology that now requires a third shift of body work, which is also a new and fourth core principle of the new momism. As such, the new momism now suggests that the solution to mothers' post-second wave crisis in femininity is to engage in more and faster body work to erase any visible signs of maternity on the postpartum body, while also entangling the neoliberal solution of body work with a hegemonic neotraditional family formation that also denies the difference maternity continues to make in women's lives today.

In chapter 4, "Consequences, Rules, and Conclusions about Bikini-Ready Moms," I argue that, when the analyses in chapter 2 and chapter 3 are combined, important new consequences and rules emerge for both the new profiles and new momism, which have notable implications for future scholarship. More specifically, I suggest that the now more-intensive new momism has changed and developed such that the new profiles encourage a new "super-supermom," further entrench mothers' split subjectivity and their acceptance, even embrace of that subjectivity, while also revealing that a new preparatory connection exists between slender-pregnant and postpartum profiles, which also reveals a new two-step process of acceptance of that split subjectivity.

I also contend that, even though the number of rules have not changed—the second iteration of profiles continue to promote seven rules for the profiles—all of these rules are tied to the maternal body and work together to encourage mothers to accept, even embrace, their split subjectivity and maternal body management and body work as the solution to having it all today. Because celebrity mom profiles have a two-step process now, I also suggest, however, that three of the seven rules are connected to slender-pregnant profiles, while four rules are connected to postpartum profiles; although, all seven, ultimately, work together to persuade good intensive mothers that a third shift of body work in neotraditional family configurations is the best and more-specific solution to managing the post-second wave crisis in femininity, while also energizing them so that they can be even more intensive good mothers. This means that, while some of the emphasis of the old rules that Douglas and Michaels first revealed are still embedded in the focus on the maternal body, other components of the old rules have disappeared or are now secondary. In short, in this chapter, I also argue that the old rules connected to beauty ideals and body management have been intensified in the new profile structure, while husbands are gone—they rarely appear and are rarely mentioned—and children have become secondary or "props" to the focus on the maternal body; even though children are still important to good mothering and deserving of both enormous amounts of attention and material goods.

Finally, I end this chapter with a discussion of key theoretical conclusions and issues that emerge as a result of my analysis and findings. I do so to offer some theoretical insights about future research on and about "mediated" motherhood. More specifically, I argue that it is vital that future scholarship recognize just how much motherhood and neotraditional family configurations are "new/old" hegemonic barriers, the importance of the fourth principle of body work both to contemporary motherhood and the profiles, the ways that profiles now cultivate self-blame for mothers, and ground future work at the intersection of the post-second wave and neoliberal turns, if feminist motherhood studies scholars both hope to have a more complete understanding of contemporary motherhood and to begin the work of theorizing the now-necessary mothers' revolution.

As a way to begin less-theoretical and more-practical conversations about resisting being bikini-ready moms, in chapter 5, "Resisting Being Bikini-Ready Moms: Five Strategies of Resistance," I close the book by proposing five strategies of resistance for privileged mothers in heterosexual partnerships and/or marriages suggested by both the theoretical and analytical work done earlier in the book. The five strategies are: Strategy One: Consciousness Raising; Strategy Two: Resist Maternal Body Norms; Strategy Three: Participate in the Now-Necessary Mothers' Movement; Strategy Four: Begin New Feminist Conversations; and Strategy Five: Ask Post-Second Wave Fathers To Do What They Say They Believe.

1

Contemporary Motherhood at the Epicenter of Intersecting Cultural Changes

The Neoliberal and Post–Second Wave Turns

Instead of blaming society, moms today tend to blame themselves. They say they've chosen poorly. And so they take on the Herculean task of being absolutely everything to their children, simply because *no one else is doing anything at all to help them.*
                                    —Judith Warner, par. 22, italicized in original

The position of the body within contemporary culture is indicative of a degree of *reflexivity* towards the body and identity that is, arguable, without precedent.
                                    —Chris Shilling, 2, italics in the original

The Introduction began to make the case that the structure of contemporary celebrity mom profiles has changed: the maternal body is the central feature now and, as a result, this key change also suggests that the new momism—the hegemonic "good" mothering ideology—is also changing.[1] Before proceeding to how this change works rhetorically in actual profiles to discover the norms and rules of the new celebrity mom profiles,[2] this chapter addresses *why* the structure of celebrity mom profiles has shifted in response to changing economic and societal factors associated with the neoliberal and post–second wave turns that are at the epicenter of contemporary motherhood. Thus, this chapter is primarily theoretical and weaves together a variety of conceptual issues and concerns in the service of my contention that the intersecting post-second wave and neoliberal turns are the primary cause for why both the new momism and the celebrity mom profiles that reinforce and romanticize the new momism have both changed.

In fact, after exploring and detailing how the new momism has intensified, I then argue that the conflicting currents now embedded in our post-second wave and neoliberal context are entangled such that the second wave feminist rhetoric of choice is now fundamentally linked to neoliberal choice, individualism, and individual responsibility generally and specifically in the context of contemporary motherhood. Equally important, I also suggest that today the general solution offered for the post-second wave crisis is a neotraditional family configuration: a "new" sophisticated-looking, even progressive appearing, family configuration that continues to place the burden of childrearing on mothers, while also serving as a "foil and a shield" that ultimately erodes many of the gains in the public sphere that unencumbered women enjoy. Finally, I conclude this theoretical chapter by elaborating further on the newfound importance of the body and gendered body panic that have also emerged at these crosscurrents. I do so to substantiate further my argument that the maternal body has become the key symbol and embodiment of contemporary motherhood, and, as a result, celebrity mom profiles now make the maternal body the central feature to further reinforce and promote the newfound role and importance of the maternal body in contemporary maternal subjectivity and contemporary "good" motherhood.

The Intensification of Intensive Mothering

At the same time that celebrity mom profiles are changing, intensive mothering, or what Douglas and Michael's called *the new momism*, is intensifying by becoming even more demanding of mothers; and, these two changes are related. As noted in the Introduction, Douglas and Michaels' understanding of the new momism draws on sociologist Sharon Hays' 1996 work on what she termed *intensive mothering* in her landmark book *The Cultural Contradictions of Motherhood*. As a review, Douglas and Michaels' argued that the new momism is the normative or ideal "good" mothering ideology in affluent Western countries, especially in America. This "good mothering" ideology rests on three core beliefs and values: "the insistence that no woman is truly complete or fulfilled unless she has kids, that women remain the best primary caretakers of children, and that to be a remotely decent mother, a woman has to devote her entire physical, psychological, emotional, and intellectual being, 24/7, to her children" (Douglas and Michaels 4). As a result, the new momism has always been a demanding approach to mothering that is child-centered and requires mothers always to be responsive in terms of their interactions with their children and professional in terms of their concerted efforts to ensure that their children develop into happy, emotionally and physically healthy, and appropriately ethical children and future adults. In addition to being child-centric in that a child's needs are always to take precedence over a mother's needs, from the beginning, intensive mothering expectations (IME) are also expert-guided, emotionally absorbing, labor intensive, and financially expensive. As such, intensive mothering requires mothers to bring professional-level skills to their mothering, while also presuming and promoting at least middle-class economic standing, values, and beliefs. Finally, although not all mothers practice intensive mothering, the intensive mothering ideology and the embedded expectations promote a system of beliefs and values about what "good mothers" ought to do and, as a result, mothers who are unable or unwilling to meet IME risk being labeled as *bad mothers*.

Hays also argued, and Douglas and Michaels concurred, that intensive mothering began in the 1980s to redomesticate women through motherhood as more and more women took advantage of the large-scale social, legal, and gender changes brought about the 1960s and 1970s social movements, particularly by feminist groups advocating for gender equality between men and women. Indeed, as more and more women became educated and entered the labor force, while also delaying motherhood to establish their career, 1980s and 1990s media stories promoted good mothering values and beliefs while warning about the consequences of bad mothering. Indeed, IME were embedded in media representations of mothers, particularly in terms of maternal advice, marketing, and news stories about children being abducted and/or molested while at daycare, and in TV stories and news reports about children being taken away from bad mothers: neglectful, welfare, and/or drug-addicted mothers. Douglas and Michaels suggested, however, that celebrity mom profiles have played the most important role in reinforcing and romanticizing intensive mothering and regulating the behavior of mothers and women into IME.

More recently, however, scholars and writers (Bianchi et al.; Coontz; Lee, Sharon; Nelson; Rosenfeld and Wise; Lovejoy and Stone; Villalobos; Warner; Wolf) are arguing that intensive mothering is intensifying and contemporary mothers are doing even more mothering rather than less, even though more and more American women are working. Indeed, Pamela Stone and Meg Lovejoy suggest that the contemporary reality is "that most college-educated mothers in the USA are working (Boushey 2008) and recent cohorts of college-educated mothers are more, not less, likely to be working than ever before (Percheski 2008)" (632). Drawing on Banchi et al., Ana Villalobos also argues, "There is broad consensus that mothering has intensified during the last four or five decades. Although women's paid work hours have increased during precisely the same decades, mothers paradoxically spend more time with their children now than they did in 1965" (6–7). Working mothers are also far more actively engaged with their children than full-time mothers were in previous generations (Bianchi et al; Lee, Sharon; Lovejoy and Stone; *Mother Outlaws* O'Reilly; Villalobos; Wolf). Moreover, financially, families, especially mothers, are investing in and spending more than ever before on their children, while also being more emotionally absorbed by and in their relations with their children (Coontz; Rosenfeld and Wise). By 2007, the Pew Research Center reported: "There is broad agreement among the public that it is harder to be a parent today—especially a mother—than it was in the 1970s or 1980s. Fully 70% of the public says it is more difficult to be a mother today than it was 20 or 30 years ago, while somewhat fewer (60%) say the same about being a father" ("Motherhood Today" par. 1).

Contemporary sociologists (Lareau; Nelson; Villalobos) suggest that economic changes and anxiety also play key factors in the more recent intensification. In *Parenting Out of Control*, for example, Margaret Nelson proposes that the economy and fears of "downward mobility" are central components of the intensification, especially for privileged middle-class families. For these parents, economic uncertainties and worries, specifically the fear of children not getting ahead and/or maintaining their class position, are fueling a more intensive approach to mothering, especially for privileged middle-class mothers. In fact, Nelson documents how a fear of downward mobility can drive professional parents into "out of control" child surveillance and micro-management[3] to ensure the children have every opportunity to still "get ahead" or maintain their class position. Similarly, Annette Lareau argues that economically privileged mothers respond to this anxiety by taking an intensive "managerial approach" to mothering to ensure a successful future for their children.

The managerial approach is time-intensive and requires finding, securing, scheduling, and shuttling children to the appropriate classes, activities, and/or extra support that experts now deem as necessary for developing healthy children and, equally important, ensuring children's class and economic success. In her own work and also addressing why intensification is happening now, Villalobos suggests another factor is insecurity. As she suggests, "I argue that these historical trends [a culture of fear and economic insecurity] are related and that, as families have felt increasingly under threat (and less and less protected by social safety nets and other forms of support), they have pinned their hopes on intensive mothering as the security solution for their own individual families" (9). In short, even though both Douglas and Michaels and Hays argued that intensive mothering was labor intensive, this more recent scholarship suggests that intensive mothering is continuing to be refined and developed such that *it is even more demanding* for mothers than it was when scholars first named and detailed *intensive mothering*. This intensification does not mean, however, that the three core principles of the new momism have changed. Rather, the core principles have only become more demanding and exacting for mothers and require mothers to devote even more time and energy to their mothering and children in order to be "good" mothers. What has changed, then, is that contemporary motherhood requires mothers to have and utilize yet more energy to meet the even-more demanding requirements of good mothering today.

I maintain that this intensification and the need for even more energy from mothers are at the epicenter of understanding the changing and new landscape of contemporary motherhood and celebrity mom profiles. In particular, though I agree with the

sociological explanations, I also contend that another critical factor in the intensification, which is also fundamentally linked to why
celebrity mom profiles have changed in structure, is that contemporary motherhood is now unfolding squarely at the intersection of
the post-second wave and neoliberal turns. As a result, this intersection is a significant contributing reason why intensive mothering has
intensified and, equally important, is also why the structure of celebrity mom profiles has changed. Villalobos's writing even hints at
the importance of this intersection when she notes that families are
"less protected by social safety nets and other forms of support," and,
as a result, are "pinning" solutions on individual families, requiring
even more from mothers rather than less. I concur with Villalobos
and also suggest that our contemporary intersecting neoliberal and
postfeminist context is a primary cause for the lack of social safety
nets and, equally important, this context is the key reason why solutions—both security and "having it all"—are being "pinned" on individual families. In short, I suggest that another compounding factor
for the intensification, which is also tied to the key economic and
societal changes that O'Reilly suggests ideologies of good motherhood have always been tied to, are the contemporary economic and
social trends that have emerged at the intersection of the post-second wave and neoliberal turns that now undergird both the new
structure of celebrity mom profiles and contemporary motherhood. I
now turn to making this case.

Intersecting Cultural Changes:
The Neoliberal and Post-Second Wave Turns

The Post-Second Wave Turn

Presently, American motherhood is now sitting at the cross currents
of the neoliberal and post-second wave turns such that neoliberal
principles and sensibilities of individualism, individual responsibility, and choice are now entangled with postfeminist rhetoric of and
ideas about reproductive choice and gender equality in ways that,
ultimately, make contemporary motherhood and IME even more
demanding for mothers. In fact, in an American context, neoliberal

principles became entangled with post-second wave feminist ideas, in part because both emerged at the same time historically. Indeed, the neoliberal turn in the United States coincided with a "post-second wave turn": the shift from asking for gender change to living with the results of second wave feminist gains. Although debates remain about how exactly to define second- and third wave feminisms and whether it is appropriate to describe the second wave as "over" or "continuing," I prefer, following Bonnie Dow's lead, to understand the second wave as "history," with both ongoing problems and possibilities for contemporary culture. Indeed, drawing on the work of both Dow and Evans, I understand white second wave feminism as feminism of the 1960s and through the 1970s that was primarily but not exclusively organized by and around white, middle-class women who focused on securing equal rights for women—their "sisters"—with men and is generally marked as ending with the failure of the Equal Rights Amendment in 1982. Moreover, at least within white American feminism, the 1980s through the mid-1990s is viewed as the time when American culture, women, and feminists began to live with the successes of and backlash against second wave feminist gains.

In terms of second wave feminist gains, it is irrefutable that second wave feminisms had many successes that transformed women's lives. As I have argued elsewhere (*White Feminists*), the Women's History section of *The Encyclopedia Britannica* online summarizes these successes succinctly:

Women gained access to jobs in every corner of the U.S. economy, and employers with long histories of discrimination were required to provide timetables for increasing the number of women in their workforces. Divorce laws were liberalized; employers were barred from firing pregnant women; and women's studies programs were created in colleges and universities. Record numbers of women ran for—and started winning—political office. In 1972, Congress passed Title IX of the Higher Education Act, which prohibited discrimination on the basis of sex in any educational program receiving federal funds and thereby forced all-male schools to open their doors to women and athletic programs to sponsor and finance female sports teams. And in 1973, in its controversial ruling on *Roe* v. *Wade*, the United States Supreme Court legalized abortion. (50)

Undeniably, then, by the 1980s and continuing today, privileged women began to live as second wave beneficiaries: women who took advantage of the changes brought about by second wave feminism, whether or not they identified as feminist. At the same time, however, the early backlash against second wave gains emerged, particularly during the 1980s, as Douglas and Michaels and others (Dow; Evans; Hays; Hirsch and Fox Keller; Katzenstein; McRobbie *The Aftermath*) also suggest. One of the primary reasons for this backlash was the conservative political and social climate that were the hallmarks of the Reagan presidency in the 1980s. Mary Katzenstein also summarizes this climate: "The decade of the 1980s was distinctive for ten uninterrupted years of antifeminist, antiliberal, self-identified conservative presidential administrations" (30). Moreover, Marianne Hirsch and Evelyn Fox Keller concur: "no discussion of either feminism or feminist theory in the 1980s can begin without at least acknowledging the hostility of the larger political, economic, and cultural climate which we have had to endure" (1). From the 1980s on, then, the post-second wave context simultaneously acknowledged and refuted second wave gains, while also beginning to be entangled with the 1980s social and economic "Reagan Revolution."

The U.S. Neoliberal Turn

In fact, as a result, I also assert that the post-second wave turn intersected and became entangled with the neoliberal turn in the United States that was first implemented in earnest during the so-called Reagan Revolution. David Harvey marks the beginning of the "neoliberal turn" in the United States in 1979. He argues that it began in 1979 when Paul Volker, "engineered a draconian shift in US monetary policy. The long-standing commitment in the US liberal democratic state to the principles of the New Deal, full employment as the key objective, was abandoned in favour of policy designed to quell inflation no matter what the consequences might be for employment" (23). But, Harvey and other scholars (Bezanson and Luxton; Brown; Craven; Miller, Antonio, and Bonanno; Vavrus) also argue that neoliberal thinking and economic policy took off in earnest with Ronald Reagan's election in 1980. As Harvey puts it, "The Reagan administration then provided the requisite political backing through further deregulation, tax cuts, budget cuts, and attacks on trade union and professional power" (25). These trends gained ground and accelerated through the 1990s, particularly in terms of reducing welfare and social policies (Brown; Lee, Sharon; McRobbie *The Aftermath*). And, this neoliberal turn spread. Thus, as Sharon Heijin Lee argues today, "Globally, neoliberal policies have spread over the last 30 years under the US leadership of the International Monetary Fund (IMF) and World Bank, albeit unevenly" (50).

Within the American context, then, neoliberal rationalities have become pervasive in all parts of society. Wendy Brown, in fact, suggests "Neo-liberal rationality, while foregrounding the market, is not only or even primarily focused on the economy; rather it involves *extending and disseminating market values to all institutions and social action,* even as the market itself remains a distinctive player" (italics in original, par. 7). Writing about contemporary American culture, Kate Bezanson and Meg Luxton suggest that one consequence of this infusion of neoliberal sensibilities is that individuals are now held responsible for their circumstances, even if they are impoverished or unemployed. As they put it: "Neoliberalism emphasizes free markets, decreased state regulation of capital, lower direct taxes, and an approach that sees the individual, rather than the market, as blameworthy for poverty and unemployment" (4). The centrality of individualism is also noted by Kati Kauppinen who argues, quoting Butterwegge et al., "In this respect one of the key features of neoliberalism is individualism, as manifest both in the crucial idea of 'actions of groups and collectives only being reducible to the goals, attitudes and performance of individuals'" (86). Thus, the neoliberal turn represents an ideological shift away from Keynesian economic policies, which saw the state playing an active role in market regulation and social provisions, to an emphasis on free markets, decreased state regulation, and a shift from the "public good" to "individual responsibility."

Two key consequences in the public sphere of the neoliberal focus on individualism and individual responsibility are an emphasis on freedom of choice and the fundamental assumption of the equal capacity of individuals to make fully "free" choices. As Stuart Hall puts it: "Neoliberalism is grounded in the 'free, possessive individual' with the state cast as tyrannical and oppressive. The welfare state, in particular, is the arch enemy of freedom" (par. 3). The language and key idea of second wave feminism that is most often invoked with neoliberalism is *choice*. In fact, recent feminist scholarship on the rhetoric of choice (Craven; Douglas and Michaels; Hayden and O'Brien Hallstein; Stone; Vavrus) also reveals the central role choice—contemporary women's ability to control reproduction such that motherhood is now considered a woman's choice—plays in contemporary women's understanding of femininity and motherhood. Indeed, as I noted in the Introduction, Douglas and Michaels argued that the choice to "do it all" is already embedded in post-second wave understandings of femininity and motherhood.

Social problems, then, are seen as outside the purview of the state and instead individuals need to take responsibility for solving their own "problems" via their own good choices. Or, as Harvey argues:

> each individual is held accountable for his or her own actions and well-being. . . . Individual success or failure is interpreted in terms of entrepreneurial virtues or personal failings (such as not investing significantly enough in one's own human capital through education) rather than being attributed to any systemic property (such as the class exclusions usually attributed to capitalism). (65–66)

Consequently, neoliberalism extends and disseminates market values to all institutions and social action, while also individualizing and privatizing social problems via individual choices. Including, as I argue next, in contemporary motherhood.

Contemporary Motherhood at the Epicenter of the Post-Second Wave and Neoliberal Turns

Contemporary American motherhood is at the epicenter of these post-second wave and neoliberal crosscurrents and sensibilities. Equally important, contemporary American women who came of age at the center of the intersection between the neoliberal and post-second wave turns employ a kind of maternal agency that integrates both neoliberal and post-second wave ideas, especially in relation to individualism, choice, and the assumption of privatizing social problems. One consequence is that many contemporary mothers now believe that family life and the post-second wave crisis in femininity can and should be resolved via their own individual choices in the private sphere, and the next two chapters show that celebrity mom profiles cultivate and reinforce these beliefs.

For now, however, it is important to reveal just how much American motherhood now draws on notions of individualism, choice, and privatization of social problems. Addressing why many contemporary mothers in their thirties and forties are apolitical and assume they must solve any difficulty they face as mothers on their own, Judith Warner's (*Mommy Madness*) work reveals these connections well. Warner argues, "Good daughters of the Reagan Revolution, we disdained social activism and cultivated our own gardens with a kind of muscle-bound, tightly wound, über-achieving, all-encompassing, never-failing self-control that passed, in the 1980s, for female empowerment" (par. 12). Also raised to be independent and self-sufficient and deferring motherhood for a career as post-second wave beneficiaries, many contemporary mothers integrate second wave feminist ideas of female independence and self-sufficiency with neoliberal principles in their contemporary understanding of motherhood. Again, talking about contemporary American mothers, Warner is helpful here when she argues, "They've been bred to be independent and self-sufficient. To rely on their own initiative and 'personal responsibility.' To *privatize* their problems" (italicized in original par. 21).

Another significant consequence of being "good Reagan daughters" and "good second wave beneficiaries" is that contemporary mothers blame themselves and/or hold themselves responsible for any difficulty they experience mothering. Moreover, mothers do so because they have been disciplined to assume that the problems they face result from their own poor choices. As Warner argues, "Instead of blaming society, moms today tend to blame themselves. They say they've chosen poorly. And so they take on the Herculean task of being absolutely everything to their children, simply because *no one else is doing anything at all to help them*" (italicized in original par. 22). Feminist scholars (Kauppinen; Thompson; Vavrus) who explore neoliberalism and contemporary representations of motherhood also suggest mothers blame themselves when women fail to succeed in "juggling it all." As Vavrus puts it, noting how second wave feminist ideas are also entangled with self-blame and the postfeminist fallacy that feminism is no longer needed, "if women fail to succeed under these conditions [postfeminist conditions], they have only themselves to blame (such 'failures' are often explained using the language of Second Wave feminism)" (49).

Contemporary Motherhood's Double Entanglement: The Struggle to "Have it All"

I assert, then, that for many American mothers, especially privileged women who have taken full advantage of the educational and professional opportunities that opened up to already privileged women after second wave feminism, contemporary motherhood now sits squarely at the epicenter of conflicting and intersecting cultural changes and ideologies brought about by the post-second wave and neoliberal turns. Indeed, as the previous discussion suggests, post-second wave beneficiaries have been "bred to be independent," to rely on their own initiative, personal responsibility, and good choices. At the same time, however, once they become mothers, post-second wave neoliberal mothering *now* coexists with *unchanged* values in the private sphere in relation to gender and family-life management and responsibilities that continue to suggest that mothers still have primary responsibility for childrearing and family-life management. Thus, as I noted in the Introduction, many American women fully realize these double entanglements and conflicting crosscurrents when they first begin to struggle to have it all, juggle it all, do it all, and/or find balance between their roles as mothers and professionals. And, as I argued in the Introduction, this is also the moment when the post-second wave crisis in femininity emerges most fully for many contemporary women.

The most obvious place, then, that the having-it-all struggle emerges is within the so-called work-life balance dilemma: the struggle to "juggle" or balance work commitments in the public sphere in relation to childrearing and care responsibilities in the private sphere. Moreover, the issue of balance is also a uniquely post-second wave issue. As Rosemary Crompton and Clare Lyonette note:

> Until the closing decades of the twentieth century, the question of work-life "balance" was perceived as relatively unproblematic because of two widespread assumptions: (a) the "standard worker" was full-time and usually a man, and (b) women were conventionally assigned to the unpaid labour of caring and domestic work (Crompton, 1999). Thus a "balance" between market (employment) and caring work was resolved via the domestication of women, coupled, to varying degrees, with their formal and informal exclusion from market work. At the beginning of the twenty-first century, however, this arrangement is in the process of re-articulation and attitudes to and policy perspectives on women's employment have undergone a profound transformation. (379)

Today many women are now "standard workers," working full time. Unchanged, however, as scholars (Crittenden; Stone; Williams) have shown decisively, is that workplace organizing assumptions continue to be based on a masculine model that assumes that full-time workers—whether male or female—are unencumbered by family responsibilities.

This means that assumption two has not changed: women continue to be assigned to the unpaid labor of caring and domestic work. To put it another way: while attitudes and perspectives on women's employment have transformed as a result of second wave feminist gains, "standard worker assumptions" and women's ongoing domestic and childcare responsibilities have not. Additionally, because women now have even more domestic, childrearing, and childcare responsibilities and affordable, reliable childcare remains elusive in the public sphere, many American mothers find themselves struggling on a daily basis to try to meet their obligations at home and at work and, more often than not, ground solutions in their own individual choices.

The role choice now plays in mothers' lives is confirmed, in fact, by Pamela Stone's recent work. In the context of high-achieving privileged women's lives, for example, Stone notes that many of the 54 women she interviewed relied on what she refers to as *choice feminism*—a form of third wave feminism that emphasizes individualism, personal choices, and personal agency—in describing their decision to quit working when they faced work-life balance issues. As Stone reports, "choice rhetoric—phrases such as 'active choice,' 'professional choice'—studded their interviews, appearing in 70 percent of them and implicit in others" (113). While Stone calls this *choice feminism*, Sharon Lee refers to it as *neoliberal feminism*. As Lee argues, neoliberal feminism equates female empowerment with consumer choice (56). Thus, the second wave rhetoric of reproductive choice has become intertwined with neoliberalism's understanding of choice and individual responsibility generally in the context of motherhood and more specifically within the context of having it all and managing the post-second wave crisis in femininity.

Everyday Conversations about "Having It All"

The preceding argument that the intersecting post-second wave and neoliberal discourses of choice, individualism, and individual responsibility converge such that the only "normal" and "natural" solutions to having-it-all struggles center on women's post-second wave neoliberal choices has primarily been theoretical. The proliferation of the intersecting neoliberal and post-second wave ideologies, however, are also now "common sense" in contemporary culture, particularly in the context of "everyday conversations" about having it all. Harvey argues that, in order to understand fully just how much neoliberal rationalities have proliferated in the United States and become hegemonic or commonsense ideologies, we must "look to . . . qualities of everyday experience" (40–41). Recently, much discussion has emerged in the popular press in the United States about motherhood and having it all, and this discussion reveals just how much post-second wave neoliberal choice, individualism, and personal responsibility are currently common sense and embedded in contemporary American culture and conversations about contemporary motherhood at the intersection of the post-second wave and neoliberal turns.

A June 12, 2012, *New York Times* article, "Motherhood Still a Cause for Pay Inequity," by Edruado Porter, for example, implicitly addresses the post-second wave crisis women face and the ways that individual responsibility and choice are tangled up with contemporary motherhood. Noting ongoing pay inequity for women, while also explicitly recognizing how much more similar men and women's lives are in the public sphere, Porter argues, "Most economists believe the gap between women's and men's wages does not stem primarily from employers paying women less than men for the same job. . . . Much, though, is a result of the constraints of motherhood" (par. 6). Consequently, Porter suggests that obvious or overt gender discrimination is not the primary issue; rather, the primary issue is mothers' choices. As he puts it, "But outright sex discrimination has declined sharply, most economists agree. Today, women's career choices—constrained by the burdens of motherhood and family—account for most of the pay gap between women and men" (par. 11). Moreover, after the recent publication of Anne-Marie Slaughter's *Atlantic Monthly* cover article, "Why Women Still Can't Have It All," where Slaughter argued that American women still cannot have it all due to professional and social barriers, Ellen Galinsky, president of the Families and Work Institute, was asked in a National Public Radio hour-long show devoted to the *Atlantic Monthly* article, why the article was getting so much press attention, particularly because issues of work-life balance have been discussed among women for a long time. Galinsky's response: "Everybody thinks of it as a personal problem[,] and that they have to solve that problem" (Transcript par. 7).

Equally revealing is the way the online responses to Porter's article invoked and used the rhetoric of choice and individual responsibility. While there were some more nuanced and thoughtful responses, most respondents, who addressed issues related to Porter's call for public policy changes to accommodate mothers, rejected the public policy suggestions and did so by drawing on neoliberal and post-second wave understandings of choice and individual responsibility in the private sphere. In addition to being grounded in the rhetoric of choice, "TS," for example, suggests, "If women want more successful careers, they should demand partners who will equally share domestic responsibilities. Dividing the burden of childcare is a personal choice made between the parents, and if one assumes more responsibility than the other, that parent's career will likely suffer. Why should any employer or coworker [sic] have to make up for that?" (June 12, 2012, comment 3). A grammatically incorrect comment by Anne Ingram also concurs that, because motherhood is a choice, professional institutions need not support working mothers. As she puts it: "My feeling is that if you have kids, [sic] that is your business. don't [sic] bring it into the workplace and make other people compensate for you. it's [sic] your choice and your problem" (June 12, 2012, comment 16). These comments are crystal clear and continue to confirm that the general solution to having it all is grounded in contemporary mothers' choices, and, if any individual woman is having difficulty "juggling it all," then, it is her "choice and her problem," her personal responsibility to manage in the private sphere.

As a result, because American motherhood is now founded on an intersecting post-second wave and neoliberal foundation, today, motherhood is understood as a personal, individual choice for women. Among other things, this means that American mothers' relationship to contemporary society has continued to change because of this intersecting foundation. Writing about reality television and neoliberal ideas, Mary Thompson argues, "neoliberal ideologies that rely on notions of the individual, 'free choice,' and individual responsibility, have emerged as a new mode of expressing the changing relationships of the individual to 'neoliberal' society" (337–338). Thompson's ideas also apply to contemporary motherhood: post-second wave women's contemporary relationship to society has fundamentally changed from one of *maternal destiny* to *post-second wave neoliberal maternal choice.* The implications of this shift are both freeing—unencumbered women's lives are more and more similar to unencumbered men's lives in the public sphere—and problematic—women's encumbered lives in the private sphere continue to be shaped by maternal responsibilities, responsibilities that are now viewed as women's "free" post-second wave *and* neoliberal choice.

Contemporary maternal choice that sits at the conflicting and intersecting neoliberal and post-second wave turns, however, primarily works *as a postfeminist neoliberal rationality* because it depoliticizes the second wave feminist politics of choice by suggesting that the public sphere is no longer sexist; and, if the family is, then, it is a result of women's choice to have and/or to make those sexist arrangements. As "TS" suggested: if family life is problematic because women are not getting enough support at home, then, women are to blame for their poor choices, not ongoing gender-power structures in both the private and public spheres. This intersection is also postfeminist in denying any ongoing need for feminist action or intervention in contemporary mothers' struggle to have it all. Thus, the postfeminist neoliberal foci on individual choice, personal responsibility, and privatization all discourage social solutions for work-life concerns—the time when the post-second wave crisis in femininity emerges most clearly—and instead encourage mothers and families to find their own individual solutions in the private sphere, as do "good" Reagan daughters, and, as a result, also continue to intensify intensive mothering.

The Neotraditional Family: The General Solution to Contemporary Mothers' Double Entanglements

Both structurally and at the everyday level, then, intersecting neoliberal and post-second wave rationalities have become so entangled that very few "solutions" emerge when contemporary mothers face the post-second wave crisis in femininity. As they struggle to find the energy to have it all or balance it all, in fact, the individual and privatized solution many mothers find themselves "choosing" is the "new" contemporary commonsense solution: the neotraditional family structure. As I (*When Neoliberalism*) have argued elsewhere and Miriam Peskowitz concurs, neotraditional family configurations appear to be new and even progressive because many contemporary, privileged heterosexual families have both an educated and professional mother and father and are founded on *the idea of gender equity*. This family configuration continues to be problematic, however, because the basic foundation of pre-second wave family roles and responsibilities still hold in the private sphere once children arrive: mothers continue to be primary caregivers of children in this "new" family type, even when they work and are partnered with men who believe in gender equity and equitable caregiving. In other words, while unencumbered women have benefited in real and important ways from second wave feminism, once women become mothers, especially high-achieving privileged women, most of those women adopt neotraditional family configurations because the intersecting post-second wave and neoliberal foundation of contemporary motherhood combine such that the only commonsense solution to the post-second wave crisis in femininity is to "choose" the neotraditional family configuration, which, ultimately, encourages women to have it all by doing it all alone in the private sphere.

As with postfeminism generally, where key feminist principles are simultaneously acknowledged and refuted, then, neotraditional family configurations as the "best" solution to the crisis in femininity is a postfemininst neoliberal solution that simultaneously acknowledges and integrates key features of second wave feminist ideas and rhetoric, while also undoing those ideas and undoing state support or function from social provisions for families. In other words, I am making an analogous argument to Wendy Brown's argument that neoliberalism is a contemporary political condition that simultaneously acknowledges and guts democracy, while also serving as a foil and a shield for the undoing of democracy. As Brown puts it about neoliberalism, "this is a political condition in which the substance of many of the significant features of constitutional and representative democracy have been gutted, jettisoned, or end-run, even as they continue to be promulgated ideologically, serving as a foil and shield for their undoing and for the doing of death elsewhere" (par. 30). I contend, then, that postfeminist neoliberal neotraditional family configurations appear to be new, even progressive, while also making the family the primary location for individual, private-sphere solutions for the choices women and men make in relation to work-life balance issues, which means that this family configuration makes an "end-run" around any social support for family life and work-life balance problems and any perceived need for feminist action. Thus, neotraditional families also serve as a foil and a shield for the undoing of key second wave ideas about reproductive choice.

Why the Structure of Celebrity Mom Profiles Has Changed

Given the intensification of intensive mothering, the fact that contemporary motherhood now sits at the epicenter of the post-second wave and neoliberal turns, and the rise of neotraditional family configurations as the "best" answer when "good" postfeminist neoliberal mothers face the crisis in femininity, it now makes more sense why the structure of celebrity mom profiles has begun to change. These new profiles are changing in response to the economic and social changes that ground our contemporary postfeminist neoliberal context and the new momism today. And, this context now undergirds contemporary motherhood and the everyday, commonsense solution to the post-second wave crisis at the heart of motherhood today: the neotraditional family. In light of the fact that celebrity mom profiles have always been the most influential media form to sell the new momism, it also makes sense that celebrity mom profiles have been redesigned to account for the changing economic and societal factors that are now entangled at the intersection of the post-second wave and neoliberal turns. Moreover, the analysis in the next two chapters reveals that celebrity mom profiles work rhetorically to promote maternal body management in slender-pregnant profiles to encourage contemporary mothers to accept, even embrace, their post-second wave subjectivity and encourage body work in postpartum profiles to energize women's ability to have it all, to support and further re-entrench neotraditional family structures as the commonsense norm, and to erase the difference maternity continues to make in contemporary women's lives.

What has yet to be explained, however, is: Why, in this new context, is the maternal body the key feature of the contemporary celebrity mom profiles? To put it another way, while the preceding theoretical arguments make the case for why celebrity mom profiles have been redesigned, why the new momism is intensifying, and why neotraditional family configurations are the commonsense and more general solution to the post-second wave crisis in femininity, the preceding does not explain fully why the maternal body has become so important and central to the contemporary profile structure. Consequently, before moving on to the analysis *of how the profiles work rhetorically* in the next two chapters to promote the new structure of celebrity mom profiles, I trace the growing importance of the body in general in contemporary culture and specifically to the maternal body. Doing so also allows me to elaborate further my understanding of the contemporary entanglement of the post-second wave and neoliberal turns in relation to the body and body work and to lay the necessary theoretical groundwork to argue in the next two chapters that celebrity mom profiles are also integrating pregnant body management and postpartum body work as the fourth new core principle and value in the new momism and as the now more-specific solution to do it all alone within neotraditional family configurations. Thus, I now turn to detailing current thinking about the body generally in contemporary culture and the maternal body specifically, ultimately, to argue that today the maternal body has become the most important symbol and embodiment of good motherhood.

The Maternal Body at the Intersection of the Post-Second Wave and Neoliberal Turns

Bodies scholars (Dworkin and Wachs; Jette; Shilling; Sweetman; White) and other neoliberal scholars (Brown; Gershon; Gimlin; Gremillion; Lee, Sharon) argue that the body has taken on new meaning as a result of the neoliberal turn. In order to understand why the body has taken on this new meaning, it is important to review contemporary scholarship on the ways neoliberalism has changed cultural understandings of subjectivity, agency, and the embodiment of those changes. Indeed, the shifting focus to neoliberal rationalities has had a profound effect on neoliberal subjectivity and how neoliberal agency is enacted in general and through the body.

After noting that Harvey suggests that the hallmarks of neoliberalism are deregulation, privatization, and state withdrawal from social provisions, Ilana Gershon, for example, reports that "Harvey argues that these shifts from liberal economic policies to neoliberal policies were also necessarily accompanied by relatively successful efforts to promote new conceptions of what it means to be an individual and an agent" (538). Drawing on Foucault's understanding of governmentality—the organized practices (techniques, mentalities, and rationalities) of a government to produce citizens best suited to fulfill the government's policies—Brown also argues that a neoliberal political rationality is emerging as "a mode of governance encompassing but not limited to the state, and one which produces subjects, forms of citizenship and behavior, and a new organization of the social" (par. 2). This neoliberal rationality, Brown also suggests, "reaches from the soul of the citizen-subject to education policy to practices of empire" (par. 7). Or, as Lee puts: "As many scholars assert, neoliberalism does not just shift state functions to the private sector but also functions as a mode of govermentality that shifts strategies of the government to private individuals" (51). Thus, Brown also argues, "Governmentality is a rich term which Foucault defines as the 'conduct of conduct.' The term is also intended to signify the modern importance of *governing* over ruling, and the critical role of *mentality* in governing as opposed to the notion that power and ideas are separate phenomena" (italics in original, endnote 2).

Contemporary neoliberal subjectivity, then, is grounded in a "mentality" or ways of understanding that interpellate subjects as neoliberal entrepreneurial actors. As such, neoliberalism produces subjects who are entrepreneurial actors in every sphere of life and are controlled through their freedom and their choice making (Lee, Sharon 51). In short, neoliberal subjects are disciplined to view themselves as selves to be managed and, as such, self-regulate themselves to adhere to neoliberal rationalities. In this way, neoliberalism, through governmentality, as Brown concludes, "features state formation of subjects rather than state control of subjects; put slightly differently, it features control achieved through formation rather than repression or punishment" (endnote 2). As a result, another consequence of neoliberal subjectivity is that neoliberal subjects must be reflexive managers of both their abilities and sense of self. Or, as Gershon argues, "this is a self that is produced through an engagement with a market, that is, neoliberal markets require participants to be reflexive managers of their abilities and alliances" (538). Subjects as reflexive managers have important implications for neoliberal understandings of agency. In fact, in this context, agency requires a reflexive stance, or what Brown calls a capacity for "self-care," where people are subjects for themselves—a collection of processes to be managed (quoted in Gershon 539). Among other things, this means that neoliberal subjects view themselves as having "improvable assets" that they reflexively manage; they see themselves as a project to be managed and guided toward success through their own personal agency and self-care. Today, then, the body has become a primary location for managing a person's improvable assets.

The Embodiment of Neoliberal and Post-Second Wave Rationalities

As a result, as neoliberal consumption and policies have become more pronounced and intensified in the past thirty years, the body has taken on new meaning, prominence, and even work for neoliberal subjects. Debra Gimlin, in fact, suggests: "In turn, an intensified focus on consumption and the birth of a global system characterized by economic and environmental risk have focused our attention inward, making the body a target of purposeful action in its own right" (700–701). As a result, body scholars (Dworkin and Wachs; Gimlin; Lee, Sharon; Shilling; Sweetman; Turner; White) also now argue the body has become a key symbol and embodiment of both good self-care and "good" neoliberal citizenship. As a result, the body has become a domain of self-management, self-entrepreneurship, and self-care; it is a premier location to enact self-reflexive management, personal agency, and good neoliberal citizenship. Or, as Lee also argues "bodies as domains of self-entrepreneurship, management, and care—the body itself has become a prized commodity and 'regimes of self' work such that people are seeing themselves as enterprising selves actively shaping their lives through choices" and body work (26). Kevin White concludes and, in fact, argues that the body has taken on even more importance today than at the time that Foucault[4] first theorized the relationship between the body and the political field. Indeed, as White argues, with the decline of industrial production since Foucault's death in 1984, "the requirement is that we now possess autonomous bodies which we self-regulate and control" (270). Thus, the body is now seen as a prized commodity, and how one manages their body is also now viewed as symbolic of neoliberal subjects' "healthy" identity (or "unhealthy" identity if not managed well).

Yet another consequence of neoliberalism, then, is that the body is now fundamental to self-identity. Or, as Chris Shilling puts it: "in the current era, there is a particular tendency for the body to become central to the modern person's sense of self-identity" (1) Gimlin also suggests that the body is fundamental to identity within high modernity, arguing a tightening of the relationship of the body to the self is associated with a range of phenomena, including "the prevalence of health education messages portraying well-being as a personal responsibility, the centrality of appearance to a highly visual consumer culture, and the emergence of many new styles of body modification" (700). Indeed, as Paul Sweetman asserts, body projects are "attempts to construct a sense of identity in an era where previous forms of identity are increasingly untenable" (347). Also drawing on the work of both Shilling and Giddens, Sweetman concludes, in fact, that the "body is increasingly mobilized as a plastic resource onto which a reflexive sense of self is projected in an attempt to lend solidity to the narrative thus envisaged. We are, in other words, increasingly responsible for the designs of our bodies and selves (Giddens, 1991: 102)" (348–349).

The importance of the body to neoliberal subjects means that the body has even more symbolic value in terms of confirming what now constitutes good neoliberal citizenship and is now intimately linked to neoliberal subjects' embodied identities. As Shilling argues, "Irrespective of the partiality and unevenness of these processes [modernization], however, the growth of cosmopolitan cities, the spread of global media such as the Internet and satellite television, and the increased internationalization of consumer culture that valorizes the body as a bearer of symbolic value, have encouraged people to become increasingly reflexive about their embodied identities" (4). The body is also symbolically important now because many believe that the body is one of the last sites of control as processes of modernization and social change have taken off and advanced. Also noting the decline in the grand narratives of religion and politics that use to give people meaning in their lives, Gimlin concludes, in fact, "Because such changes have been accompanied by the increasing availability of technology for rationalizing the body, our physical being has come to be understood as one of the last arenas that we are able to control" (700).

As a result, working on the body—doing "body work"—also requires reflexivity or the ability of contemporary subjects to reflect on their bodies in relation to their identity and to reflect on their "embodied identities." As Shilling argues, "By 'reflexivity' I am referring here to the ability of embodied individuals to reflect upon their own biological constitution, appearance, sense of self actions, and relationship with others; to treat themselves as both subjects and objects" (footnote 1, 20). And, this reflexivity is also unparalleled and is a new and significant change in contemporary society. As Shilling also suggests, "the position of the body within contemporary culture is indicative of a degree of *reflexivity* towards the body and identity that is, arguable, without precedent" (italics in original 2). Body work also requires continually negotiating dominant understandings of subjectivity and health, and health and body work are now displays of neoliberal subjects' achievement of good neoliberal citizenship (Gremillion 395, 397).

Finally and equally important, body projects and body work are now also fundamentally linked to post-second wave gender identity. Lee, in fact, argues that "body making"—cosmetic surgery, for example, or body projects—working out, weight control, dieting, and/or attending fitness classes—are also intimately intertwined with gender identity (20). This also means there is now a conflation of self-identity with contemporary gender identity vis-à-vis body management practices like attending to fashion, dieting, and cosmetic surgery in contemporary culture. In fact, "feminine" body making and work and body management practices are now the method for reconciling the separation between the body as "object" and feminine identity construction. Thus, reflexive body making, work, and management have also become a gendered form of neoliberal agency: women's bodies are mobilized via the neoliberal market and neoliberal sensibilities as a means of identity construction, self-empowerment, and as a premier symbol of the good postfeminist feminine neoliberal citizenship.

The Contemporary Maternal Body: The Embodiment of the Intersection

Maternal bodies have not been immune from these developments. Indeed, as I suggested in the Introduction and now should be understood more fully, today the maternal body is also fundamental to maternal identity in contemporary culture. To paraphrase Shilling, maternal body projects allow mothers to reflect on their own biological constitution, appearance, sense of self-actions, relationships with others, and to treat themselves as both subjects and objects, as they try to adhere to and embody the principles and values required of good motherhood today. I also suggested in the Introduction that complicating body projects is the fact that contemporary culture is infused with a kind of body panic—what Dworkin and Wachs describe as anxiety about attaining an increasingly difficult-to-achieve ideal fit body, a body ideal that I suggest is also now conflated with good motherhood; that is, the confluence of key post-second wave and neoliberal culture changes, especially in relation to the post-second wave gender, neoliberalism, and healthism issues just reviewed. Indeed, as Dworkin and Wachs also conclude, the appearance of a fit body, "rather than the reality of fitness, has become a critical determinant of social status and a factor that is self-policed by individuals as they negotiate social positions" (12). Finally, I argued in the Introduction that this means the maternal body is now a critical determinant of maternal status in the context of contemporary motherhood. Thus, today the maternal body has become a critical symbol and determinant of maternal social status as mothers also negotiate standards of feminine performance and maternal subjectivity at the epicenter of our intersecting post-second wave and neoliberal era.

I contend, in fact, that the contemporary maternal body *is the new embodiment* of contemporary motherhood at the epicenter of the intersecting post-second wave and neoliberal turns. I also maintain that, as the body, body work, and body projects have all taken a central place in self-identity generally and in terms of maternal identity more specifically, the newfound centrality of the maternal body explains the final piece of why the maternal body has taken a central focus in new celebrity mom profiles. As the both the new momism and motherhood have intensified and continued to be refined as a result of the intersecting post-second wave and neoliberal turns, celebrity mom profiles have also shifted to account for the new-found importance of and connection between the body and maternal identity that exists today. Equally important, however, I also suggest and show in much more detail in the next two chapters, that, as the maternal body has become central to the kind of maternal identity promoted, reinforced, and romanticized in the new celebrity mom profiles, the maternal body has also become both the symbol of and *the management tool* for both contemporary mothers' need to be even more energized mothers and the mediated "body panic" addressed in the new profiles.

Here, again, I draw on Dworkin and Wachs' understanding of body panic and the relation of body shape as the symbol of both good health and morally good maternal citizenship today. As they put it: "body shape is a corporal metaphor for health" but also body shapes have come to mean "not just medioco-scientifically 'good' but also morally 'good'" (12). They also suggest, however, that "contemporary media produce body panic not only through idealized imagery that invokes individualized feelings about the body, but also though a process of what is included as content inside of media text and representation—what signifiers are used—and what is, by extension, left out" (Dworkin and Wachs 12). Thus, analyzing how the new profiles work rhetorically via both what is "in" and "out" in the profiles also allows me to understand how this second iteration of profiles are making arguments for what now counts as morally good and bad contemporary motherhood at the crosscurrents of the post-second wave and neoliberal turns.

Ultimately, then, the analysis that follows in the next two chapters works to argue that the maternal body—both slender pregnant and quickly slender, even bikini ready, maternal body—serves as a field on which broader anxieties and tensions about the post-second wave crisis in femininity are reflected, negotiated, and rationalized through a two-step process: first, via body management in the slender-pregnancy profiles then, second, via a third shift of energizing and now-necessary body work in the postpartum profiles, all of which, ultimately, reinforce and reentrench neotraditional family configurations as the individualized and privatized solution for the post-second wave crisis in femininity and as a means to erase the difference maternity continues to make in women's lives today. I now turn to fleshing out the two-step process by engaging in a case study of the first step: accepting, even embracing, the values and body-management promoted and reinforced via slender-pregnant profiles.

2

Step One—Becoming First-Time Mothers

Slender-Pregnant Celebrity Mom Profiles

"She's Glowing! Kate Middleton Shows Off Baby Bump in Yellow Coat Dress."

—Headline for *US Weekly Online*, 05/22/13

"Kim Kardashian on Pregnancy Curves: 'How the F-ck Did I Get Like This?'"

—Headline for *US Weekly Online*, 05/22/13

In May 2013, British magazine, *You*, published a cover story photo of then-pregnant celebrities British Princess Kate Middleton and Reality TV star Kim Kardashian. Both women were around six months pregnant at the time and pregnant with their first child. In the cover picture, Middleton is facing forward, smiling broadly, and she is dressed in a black shirt under a red "box" coat that is buttoned across her "barely there" stomach, as she holds a small, black clutch purse. Kardashian is positioned sideways and on the right side of the cover to the left of Middleton. Staring ahead with her mouth tightly closed and looking very unhappy, Kardashian is wearing a "tight" form-fitting teal dress that highlights her small "bump" and large hips and posterior, especially in comparison to Middleton. Near the bottom of the bodies of the two women, across the upper legs of both women, the cover title reads, "Battle of the bumps!," which is followed with a second heading, "Kate the Waif vs Kim the Whale." Finally, two questions are embedded in the image. Immediately below Middleton's purse and positioned near her barely there bump, we see the question "Too Thin?," while, right below Kardashian's posterior, drawing our eyes to her "large booty," we read the question "Too Fat?"

This cover photo and the accompanying text epitomize how the obsessive media coverage of Middleton and Kardashian's pregnancies is crystallizing the template for slender-pregnant celebrity mom profiles. In fact, as I show, media regularly pitted Middleton and Kardashian in a battle between two ends of the post-second wave neoliberal continuum—with Middleton as the "good" "post-second wave neoliberal princess" versus Kardashian as the "bad" "post-second wave neoliberal excessive Reality TV star"—as a way to reflect and negotiate broader gender, race, class, and family anxieties and boundaries between "awful ordinary" and "exemplary ordinary" future intensive mothering to make the case that pregnant women, especially first-time mothers, must train and prepare for good future mothering via restrained and tasteful choices in self-care, pregnancy announcements, pregnant body management, especially via disciplined and controlled eating and weight management, body "skimming" yet still-tasteful and proper maternity wear, and preparing responsibly for impending motherhood, while also making clear that the future mother has fully embraced her post-second wave split subjectivity and the core tenets of intensive mothering.

In doing so, I also begin to answer the second overarching question of the book: *How* are celebrity mom profiles integrating the slender-pregnant and quickly slender, even bikini-ready, maternal body as the central feature of the new celebrity profiles? To answer this question fully, however, I do two case studies: this chapter explores slender-pregnant profiles by analyzing media coverage of the Kate Middleton and Kim Kardashian pregnancies, while the next chapter is a case study of postpartum celebrity mom profiles. Thus, I begin by analyzing how slender-pregnant profiles are the first preparatory step in making the case that good body management is a prerequisite for and symbol of good future intensive motherhood.

"Heavily" Regulated (Pun Intended) Pregnant Body Analysis: The Perfect
Post-Second Wave Princess versus the Awful Excessive Reality TV Star

In their analysis of earlier celebrity mom profiles, Douglas and
Michaels reveal the seven rules of those profiles via their own case
study of Princess Diana. They did so, as they argued, because "Few
celebrity mothers were more closely watched, or managed to inspire
more points of identification among everyday women during the
1980s and '90s, than the Princess of Wales. The endless profiles of
her became the template that would crystallize into the celebrity
mom profile" (125). Like Princess Diana, Catherine (Kate) Middleton's first pregnancy was closely watched by media. Married to
Diana's first son, William, Middleton is also like Diana, as I show
in this chapter, because the endless pregnancy profiles of Middleton
have solidified the template that is crystallizing what now constitutes perfectly good slender-pregnant celebrity mom profiles. Middleton, however, is different from Diana in several important ways.

Unlike Diana, who married Charles after a relatively short court-
ship when she was only twenty and a kindergarten assistant teacher
and then quickly became pregnant two months after her marriage to
Charles, delivering her first son, William, in June of 1982, Middleton married William at twenty-nine on April 29, 2011, after: having dated William for almost ten years; she finished university, and
she had had a professional life to some degree working for her family's mail-order party-supply store, among other jobs. While famous
when she was dating Prince William, Middleton's fame skyrocketed
when she became a "real-life" princess after her marriage to William; the marriage was widely covered by media and was estimated
to cost more than $34 million ("Royal Wedding" Adams). After the
marriage, Middleton's official title became, "Catherine, Duchess of
Cambridge"; although, media continue primarily to refer to her as
Kate or as *Kate Middleton*.

Middleton gave birth to her first child, a son, George Alexander
Louis, at age thirty-one in July 2013. In this way, then, Middleton
is an ideal post-second wave beneficiary: she deferred marriage and
children for an education and career until she was in her late twen-
ties early thirties. As a result, Middleton's journey to becoming a
mother is typical of contemporary women today, as Diana's journey

to becoming a mother was more typical of her generation. Diana, however, as Douglas and Michaels' argue, was the ideal celebrity mom of the old structure: the focus of the profiles was on Diana's actual mothering. Unlike Diana, the media obsession with Middleton was on her maternal body, especially Middleton's slender-pregnant body, and reveals much about how celebrity mom profiles have shifted to obsessive coverage of the maternal body, albeit in this case the pregnant body, as both a symbol and embodiment of future motherhood. And, like the coverage of Diana, the media coverage of Middleton's pregnancy is playing a key role in how the template for slender-pregnant celebrity profiles is crystallizing today.

Unlike Diana, however, Middleton's pregnancy was regularly covered in relation and, often, linked to another celebrity who was pregnant at the same time: American Reality TV star and entrepreneur Kim Kardashian. In fact, almost as soon as Middleton's pregnancy was announced and began to be discussed by media, Middleton's pregnancy was regularly discussed in comparison to Kardashian's pregnancy, as the *You* cover reveals.[1] Kardashian, 32 at the time of her pregnancy, was married but separated from her then-second-husband professional basketball player Chris Humphries, whom she married on August 20, 2011, and was pregnant with African American rapper Kanye West, her boyfriend at the time. While Kardashian and Humphries' marriage was short-lived—lasting only 72 days after a lavish wedding that was broadcast on the E! network as a two-part special titled *Kim's Fairytale Wedding: A Kardashian Event* and was estimated to cost $20 million ("Royal Wedding" Adams)—their divorce took a year and seven months to finalize, primarily because Humphries filed for annulment based on his belief that Kardashian only married him for publicity and, as a result, the marriage was a sham. Kardashian insisted she married Humphries for love, and Kardashian refused to settle until she and Humphries were granted a divorce in early June 2013.

The divorce was finalized before Kardashian gave birth to her first child, a daughter, North West, in mid-June 2013 (five weeks earlier than her mid-July due date), and she and West became engaged in October 2013 on Kardashian's thirty-third birthday and married in yet another lavish and extensively covered-by-media wedding on May 24, 2014. Kardashian's fame first came as a result of a sex tape, but her fame skyrocketed as a result of her Reality

TV shows *Keeping up with the Kardashians*, *Kourtney and Kim Take New York*, and *Kourtney and Kim Take Miami*. However, Kardashian is also an entrepreneur, fashion designer, sometime actress, and even book author with her sisters Khloe and Kourtney (*Kardashian Konfidential*). Unlike Middleton, Kardashian did not attend college and, in 2000, she married for the first time at age nineteen to music producer Damon Thomas, which lasted three years. After her first marriage, however, Kardashian is like Middleton in that she deferred marrying again until she established a career, and Kardashian did not have her first child until she was in her early thirties. So, like Middleton, Kardashian is also a second-wave beneficiary in her focus on establishing a career first prior to having children, while the media coverage of her pregnancy also plays a key role in how the template for slender-pregnant profiles is crystallizing.

Because Middleton and Kardashian are both post-second wave beneficiaries, first-time mothers, and media regularly covered their pregnancies together, I analyze the media coverage of both women in relation to one another to understand better how slender-pregnant profiles are developing today. That Kardashian and Middleton are covered by media in relation to one another is not particularly surprising. Indeed, as Elizabeth Podnieks argues, media and its target audiences often position celebrity moms "in symbiosis, primarily in terms of maternal reputation" (91–92). In addition to being positioned in terms of good versus bad future mothers, however, Middleton and Kardashian are also positioned in relation to one another as "extremes." That Middleton and Kardashian are positioned as extreme ends of the good-versus-bad (future) mothering continuum is also not especially unexpected either. Indeed, Douglas and Michaels argued that because media "traffic in extremes," media have "built an interlocking, cumulative image of the dedicated, doting 'mom' versus the delinquent, bad 'mother'" (5–7). Therefore, positioning Middleton and Kardashian as extremes in relation to one another is also not new or novel.

The "Battle" for the Best Pregnancy

What is fascinating, however, is that even before they were pregnant and from the beginning of the media coverage after both women's pregnancies became public knowledge, the comparison between the two focused on a "battle" between the two rather than just simply holding one of the women up as the "doting" future mom and the other as the "delinquent" future mother. Moreover, it is also interesting just how much and consistently these two celebrities were covered together by media, even though many other celebrities were pregnant at the time. So, for example, Jessica Simpson and Busy Philipps were also pregnant with their second children at the same time Middleton and Kardashian were pregnant with their first children. Even so, media focused primarily on Middleton and Kardashian's pregnancies and at the expense of covering other pregnant celebrities. Philipps, in fact, even noted how grateful she was that media were focused on Middleton and Kardashian instead of her. Covering Philipp's appearance on the *Chelsea Lately* show, Eggenberger reports that Philipps said the following: "'I won the lottery! If you wanna get knocked up as someone on television, you want there to be the princess, Kim Kardashian and Jessica Simpson[2] to also be pregnant, because it just takes all the heat off of you,' the 33-year-old told Chelsea Handler on *Chelsea Lately* on Tuesday" (par. 2).

As a result, two interesting questions emerge about the media focus on Middleton and Kardashian: Why were these two women in particular pitted against one another in a battle and what is the battle about? It is not unusual to pit women against each other in competition; this strategy is a well-worn gender-based strategy. What is unusual, however, as I show, is that Middleton and Kardashian were regularly declared to be in a battle against one another to show "whose pregnancy was the best." So, for example, in addition to the *You* magazine cover story already noted, late in their pregnancies, a June 24, 2013, *US Weekly* cover featured Middleton and Kardashian with a four-line title, all of which were framed around the Middleton "versus" Kardashian theme ("Battle" Grossbart). Line one, in a pink box with white font and all caps reads, "KATE VS KIM," which was followed by line two, written in larger, yellow, font, and reads, "Due the Same Day!" Line three, in pink, smaller font, but all caps reads, "IT'S A ROYALS VS REALITY SHOWDOWN." Finally, the fourth line, in white, is two sentences: "The nurseries, baby clothes, their bump style, & baby weight battles. Inside the exciting last month." Because "versus" always means to be "against," "in contrast to," and/or "in opposition to," when used, "versus" or "vs" are shorthand ways for media to remind readers/viewers that

Middleton and Kardashian are always positioned in opposition to one another, are in battle against one another.

Moreover, the battle metaphor started very early in media coverage of the two women's pregnancies and was quite intense. So, for example, huffingtonpost.com "charted" the battle early in a story titled, "Kate Middleton vs. Kim Kardashian: It's Time for a Pregnancy Battle," written by Leigh Blickley. This story also has an embedded video titled, "Kim Kardashian, Kate Middleton Redefine Maternity Wear," which is accompanied by two side-by-side photos of the women's faces, where Middleton is smiling broadly, facing the camera, and looking happy; while in her picture, Kardashian's head is titled to the left, with her bangs hanging slightly over her eyes, and appearing "sultry." Under these two pictures, the following question appears: "Kate Middleton vs. Kim Kardashian: Both are expecting babies, but whose pregnancy is best?" Then, paragraph one reads, "They may be two of the most talked about women in celebrity news, but Kate Middleton and Kim Kardashian couldn't be more different." Finally, in paragraph five, right above a chart that compares the two women, readers learn, "Well let's focus on other things . . . it's time for a pregnancy face-off."

On the actual chart that accompanies the article, Middleton is in the left column and Kardashian is in the right column. In this order, the chart covers the following twelve facts: age, due date, marriage status, height, where each woman was born, why each woman is famous, how each woman dresses their baby bump, reported pregnancy cravings, the women's experiences with morning sickness, each woman's travel engagements, a description of each woman's belly, and that each woman is reportedly having a girl. In almost every comparison, Middleton comes out the "winner" or is viewed and/or described more positively in relation to Kardashian. So, for example, in answering the question why each woman is famous, the chart reveals: for Middleton: "Famous because she's the Duchess of Cambridge, a princess and in line to become queen consort"; while, for Kardashian we learn, "Famous because of her sizable assets and reality shows, like 'Keeping up with the Kardashians,'" and so on. Thus, while the two women are acknowledged to be "very different," they are viewed similarly in that the media positioned them in an intense battle against one another from early in their pregnancies and throughout the media coverage.

The Battle before the Pregnancies

Intriguingly, however, media used this battle framing between the two women before both were pregnant. In fact, media positioned Middleton and Kardashian as battling or competing to be the "best" female celebrity prior to their pregnancies, which was made clear in the media coverage of their weddings. As noted earlier, both women married in 2011 and had expensive weddings that were covered extensively and comparatively by media both before and after the weddings. Leigh Edwards, in fact, suggests, in her discussion of Kardashian's wedding, "With the lavish, multimillion dollar wedding came media comparisons to the Prince William and Princess Catherine royal wedding (earning the Kardashians sometime satirical analogies to American versions of celebrity as royalty)" (26–27). Media stories also suggested that Kardashian was competing with Middleton in terms of both fame and the wedding. Almost always, however, Kardashian is positioned as competing with Middleton rather than vice versa. So, for example, writing after the weddings and while both women were pregnant, Amy Ess wrote an article titled, "Is Kim Kardashian competing with Kate Middleton for Fame?" In the opening paragraph, readers learn, "Kim Kardashian and Kate Middleton have been hotly compared in the media over the past year. Why, you ask? It appears that the celebrity diva, Kim, has been in the duchess' footsteps when it comes to certain important milestones. Weddings at the same time. Babies due at similar times. One might question, does Kim want to outshine this queen to be, or is this all just simply a coincidence?" (par. 1).

Ess also notes that Middleton and Kardashian's weddings were the most watched weddings of the year. Then, Ess writes, "Flash forward a year later, and both Kim and Kate are now pregnant at the same time. Kim is separated from Kris and is having the baby with beau, Kanye West. Both of these stars (*of a different caliber*) are closing in on their due date, making fans and those who do not love Kim so much, wonder who will have the more fabulous baby" (italics added par. 3). In April 2012, a year after Middleton's wedding, which would have also been near the year anniversary of Kardashian's wedding to Humphries, *huffingtonpost.com* did a "retrospective" titled, "Royal Wedding vs. Kim Kardashian's Wedding: By The Numbers" (Adams). In the article, Rebecca Adams notes that "another nuptial that took television by storm: the short-lived Kim Kardashian-Kris Humphries wedding extravaganza" (par. 1). She then opines, "Although seemingly incomparable at first thought, both weddings turned into enormously expensive celebrity circuses that broke television records. Expectedly, the royal couple delivered the pomp and circumstance of a British affair, while their American counterparts delivered the drama and glitz that we've come to expect from the Kardashian clan. But which wedding was the *most* extravagant?" (italics in original par. 2).

Adams then compares how the two weddings "stack up against each other" (par. 3). The article primarily focuses on the cost of the weddings—the ring, the cake, the venue—and reveals that Middleton's wedding cost $34 million, while Kardashian's wedding cost $20 million (par. 10). Finally, Adams concludes, "While Kate Middleton showed us that good things come to those who wait (going from commoner to princess: priceless), Kim's second attempt at matrimony wasn't so successful. Let's hope Kim K and Kanye make it to the aisle—third time's a charm!" (par. 12). Equally fascinating, Ess describes the two weddings in the following way: "As Kate Middleton made a grand entrance and won the hearts of many on her wedding day to Prince William, Kim's wedding to NBA player, Kris Humphries, was not far behind. These were the two most popular weddings of 2012.[3] While some preferred to watch a classy royal wedding, others preferred to watch an over-the-top reality star wedding" (par. 2).

While Middleton "won our hearts," and her wedding "delivered pomp and circumstance," was "classy," and showed "that good things come to those who wait," Kardashian was not "loved so much," was in Middleton's "footsteps," and Kardashian's wedding "delivered drama and glitz," was considered "over the top," worthy of "satirical analogies," even though Kardashian's wedding cost less than the royal wedding, and, even more important, Kardashian had to defend the "authenticity" of her wedding and short-lived marriage against charges both by the media and Humphries. So, for example, Edwards reports, "When Kim's media spectacle wedding to Kris Humphries ended in divorce 72[4] days later, many journalists and commentators criticized the opulent wedding and questioned whether the marriage had been a sham for the cameras" (27). And, the divorce took almost two years to be granted because, as noted already, Kardashian and Humphries wanted to end the marriage differently: while Kardashian wanted a divorce, Humphries filed for an annulment, claiming that the marriage was a sham or "fake" and that Kardashian only married him for ratings for her TV show.

Media covered this difference between Kardashian and Humphries extensively. So, for example, *Mail Online.com* ran an article about the divorce with the lengthy title, "'I really did love him': Pregnant Kim Kardashian hits back at claims she married Kris Humphries for publicity . . . as she sits through NINE HOUR divorce deposition" (capitalization in the original Saunders). Later, Louis Saunders's reports, "Insisting she didn't tie the knot with the 28-year-old basketball player to boost ratings for her reality show, the raven-haired beauty maintained she 'really did love' the sportsman when he popped the question. . . . Kim 'testified under oath' that her intentions were genuine when she accepted Kris' marriage proposal, despite the union only going on to last for 72 days" (pars. 2–3). In another example, *TMZ* reported that Kris Humphries' relatives are "claiming Kim K's 72-day-marriage to the NBA star was nothing but a 'sham' and it's about damn time she fess up to it. . . . Kris' aunt Dedria—who attended K & K's wedding back in 2011— is adamant Kim duped her nephew into tying the knot as a ploy to boost ratings for 'Keeping Up With the Kardashians'" ("Kris Humphries" *TMZ Online* pars. 1–2). Thus, Kardashian defended herself to "prove" that neither she nor her marriage to Humphries were fake or a sham, and she prolonged divorce proceedings until she was granted a divorce in June 2013.

Why These Two and Battling for What?

The comparisons of the two weddings clearly reveal multiple and intertwined issues in tension and at play in the media coverage and comparison of Middleton and Kardashian, prior to their pregnancy announcements, which also begin to reveal the complex and intertwined issues being reflected and negotiated in the battle between these two women and the slender-pregnancy profiles that emerged. First, the comparison between the two weddings reveals just how much these two women were positioned in contrast to one another and, equally important, began to frame two central questions about the authenticity of each woman: Which fairy-tale wedding was more authentic and which woman is more authentic? Obviously, unquestioned is an underlying gender assumption: even in our post-second wave context, women continue to aspire to fairy-tale weddings and marriages. While that assumption was unquestioned, what was questioned, then, was whose fairy-tale celebrity wedding and which woman was "more authentic"?

Clearly, in the wedding comparisons, media coverage worked rhetorically to assess Middleton's as the authentic and classy wedding, even revealing that "good things come to those who wait," and that it is possible for a "commoner" to become a princess—to become "special" or "extraordinary" as a real-life princess—which, in the end, is "priceless," outside of market evaluation, while media coverage worked rhetorically to assess Kardashian's wedding as "questionably" authentic, over-the-top, and a "media spectacle" that put Kardashian on the defensive about whether or not both the wedding and she were fake or shams and done only for Reality TV. As such and given that both women are contemporary post-second wave celebrity women, the wedding comparisons began to position Middleton and her celebrity, prior to her pregnancy, as an authentic "post-second wave princess," while Kardashian, prior to her pregnancy, was positioned as a "suspect," over-the-top Reality TV star.

Second, the comparisons raised questions about the quality and value of each woman's fame, implicitly for Middleton but explicitly for Kardashian when Humphries and the media raised issues about Kardashian's authenticity. Indeed, both media and Humphries explicitly raise the issue about how Kardashian's relationship to Reality TV and what Su Holmes calls the *discourse of fame*—where ordinary people use Reality TV as an "entrepreneurial bid for media exposure"—are intertwined in the assessment of Kardashian's celebrity (111). Quoting Daniel Boorstin, Holmes suggests the "discourse of fame" is used as shorthand for the "triviality" of Reality TV, which is seen as "shamelessly encouraging (while also epitomizing) the acceleration of a celebrity culture in which people are well known simply for their 'well-known-ness' rather than for 'greatness, worthy endeavours or talent'" (111). And, when Kardashian is compared to Middleton, the discourse of fame that surrounds both—and the questions it raises in terms of the authenticity and worthiness of each woman's celebrity—is important because both women were "ordinary" women made famous.

Indeed, in addition to being first-time mothers, Middleton and Kardashian also share some important similarities in their "prior ordinariness." Both women are ordinary post-second wave daughters of self-made, affluent families. In Middleton's case, in British parlance, she was a commoner prior to becoming a royal through her marriage to William. Kardashian, on the other hand, was an ordinary American woman who was made famous first through a sex tape and then via Reality TV. Clearly, then, fame came in very different ways for these two: Middleton married a real-life "prince charming" or "soon-to-be-king" and became a real-life princess, while Kardashian became famous via Reality TV and her "sizable" assets. Or, as *huffingtonpost.com* put it on the pregnancy-battle chart of the women: Middleton, "Famous because she's the Duchess of Cambridge, a princess and in line to become queen consort," while for Kardashian it reads, "Famous because of her sizable assets and reality shows, like 'Keeping Up With The Kardashians,' etc." (Blickley). Clearly, Middleton's fame is tied up in a real-life, authentic fairy tale, where the "moral" of the fairy tale is that good things come to those who wait, and this is priceless. Clearly, Kardashian's fame, on the other hand, is suspect and tied up in cultural anxiety about Reality TV making ordinary people famous for all the "wrong reasons," and the "moral" of her possibly-inauthentic fairytale is a warning: a warning about over-the-top excess being inauthentic and even, possibly, a sham.

Moreover, the discourse of fame, especially as it is linked to reality television, is always tied to issues of class, cultural, and family values. As a Reality TV star, then, Kardashian's celebrity and the assessment of her—both individually and via the comparisons to Middleton—are also intertwined with the discourse of fame and issues of class, cultural, and family values, and the questions that Reality TV raises in terms of those issues. In particular, as a relatively new cultural phenomenon, Reality TV, in its focus on ordinary people who, often, then become famous because of their time on Reality TV, raises questions about the culture, class, and family values of celebrity culture in general and celebrities like Kardashian specifically. Indeed, because most viewers are now aware that editing and filming are often "scripted" and/or "set-up," questions abound about the reality of Reality TV. Or, as Beverly Skeggs and Helen Wood write, "Critics of the staging of reality television, its emphasis upon narrative editing, the selection of participants, the prominence of personalities and plot, suggest that the 'fakeness' of the reality which it purports to represent is the problem" (23).

As a result, Reality TV raises class questions tied to cultural value, especially in terms of the classiness or trashiness of the ordinary people shown on Reality TV; questions that also implicitly and sometimes explicitly were addressed in the wedding comparisons between Middleton and Kardashian. Su Holmes and Deborah Jermyn, for example, argue, because ordinary people are turned into celebrities who actively participate in celebrity culture, Reality TV still has questionable cultural value and is often referred to as "trash TV" (8). Moreover, because of the neoliberal deregulation of television in the 1990s and the fact that Reality TV is considered "cheap" programming to develop and create and also features ordinary people rather than "legitimate" or "authentic" television stars, questions about the quality and cultural value of Reality TV flourish. One consequence, as Holmes and Jermyn also note quoting Bazalgette, while "Reality TV may have in some ways signalled a broader 'democratisation' of television, criticism of why are 'all these *awful ordinary* people allowed on television' can be seen to represent a response couched in discourses of class" (italics in original 9). In other words, although Reality TV can be seen as democratizing television, because of the "tabloidization and therefore [possible] debasement of contemporary culture" questions of value—both in terms of class and culture—emerge in terms of the taste and class values represented and cultivated in Reality TV shows (Skeggs and Wood 23). As a genre, then, Reality TV raises anxiety and nervousness about its blurring of boundaries between the real and scripted, the authentic and inauthentic, classiness and trashiness and quality and nonquality embedded in and represented on Reality TV, and its relationship to celebrity culture in general and of Reality TV celebrities, like Kardashian, in particular. Thus and equally important, Reality TV "powerfully portrays major anxieties of the era," including tensions about basic social units like the American family, and it "also capitalizes on and raises issues around an underlying worry about cultural change, especially about American families" (Edwards 1, 3).

As a result, the comparisons of the weddings and the previous examples of media coverage of the women's pregnancies also reveal questions about the authenticity, worthiness, cultural value, and classiness of Kardashian's celebrity in general and her maternal position specifically in comparison to Middleton's celebrity in general and maternal position specifically and, even more important, future motherhood. And, as I show in the analysis of the slender-pregnant profiles that emerged after the women's pregnancies became public knowledge, these questions are a precursor of the gender, class-based, cultural, and family values anxieties that are displayed in the "battle" between Middleton and Kardashian's celebrity pregnancies and future motherhood, where the battle is reflecting on and responding to broader cultural anxiety and nervousness about the blurring of boundaries between the real and scripted, the authentic and inauthentic, classiness and trashiness and quality and non-quality of post-second wave neoliberal motherhood today. And, as I also show, because these two celebrity women represent two ends of the post-second wave neoliberal gender continuum, media coverage worked rhetorically to position Kardashian and her maternal body as representing the anxiety and ambivalence about excessive, inauthentic, and "bad" future motherhood that her pregnancy embodies as Kardashian makes all the wrong choices in body management, maternity wear, and failure to prepare appropriately for the impending birth of her child—she is a "warning" about the consequences of awful ordinary future mothering done wrong—while media worked rhetorically to position Middleton and her maternal body as representing the tightly managed, authentic, and exemplary ordinary good future motherhood that her pregnancy embodies as she makes all the right, good choices in body management, maternity wear, and in her prepping well for her impending birth. In short, I suggest that much of what the battle is about and why media focused so extensively on these two pregnant celebrities together and at the expense of other pregnant celebrities is because the slender-pregnant profiles of these two women are also negotiating the boundaries between ordinary and special future mothering, between awful ordinary post-second wave neoliberal future motherhood and exemplary ordinary post-second wave neoliberal future motherhood.

The coverage of the battle between the weddings, then, is a precursor of the battle between the two women and the themes embedded in slender-pregnancy profiles at the crosscurrents of our post-second wave neoliberal context: in both the wedding coverage and the pregnancy profiles, as I show, these two celebrity moms are, indeed, "stars of a different caliber": a perfectly good post-second wave neoliberal real-life princess versus an awfully bad post-second wave neoliberal over-the-top excessive reality star. And, the basic themes revealed in the analysis of the wedding coverage continue to play out in the pregnancy profiles and images that begin, first, in the pregnancy announcements and, second, in the subsequent slender-pregnancy profiles that followed.

Pregnancy Announcements: The "Tight-Lipped Reluctant" versus "Blabbing" Announcements

The pregnancy announcements were starkly different: Middleton's pregnancy was announced reluctantly, while Kardashian's was announced by Kanye West on stage during one of his concerts, and the announcements further entrenched the discourse of fame surrounding both women and maternal subject position of each. Not yet twelve weeks pregnant in December 2012, Middleton was rushed to the hospital because she was suffering from hyperemesis gravidarum, an acute morning sickness that requires supplementary hydration and nutrients. Prior to the hospitalization, Middleton and William were described by Lama Hasan, an ABC News reporter, as "so tightly lipped about the pregnancy, that even some people here at the Palace, including the Queen, Prince Charles, and other members of the Royal Family, reportedly only found out about it today" (Hasan). In other words, Middleton and Prince William had not even told the Royal family yet about Middleton's pregnancy. This is particularly significant given that media had been closely watching Middleton from the moment she was married for any signs of a pregnancy.

Moreover, becoming quickly pregnant was what was expected of Middleton by both the media and the Royal family given the fact that both Princess Diana and Queen Elizabeth II, Prince Charles' mother, had both become quickly pregnant and gave birth early in their marriages: Diana eleven months later and Queen Elizabeth a year later. Thus, the fact that it appears that Middleton and William withheld the information that Middleton was pregnant from both the Royal family and the media is important. Even though they had been and wanted to be tight lipped about the announcement, however, the hospitalization compelled the couple to reveal the pregnancy earlier than they had planned both to the Royal family and the public. Or as Josh Vissar put it, an article titled, "Kate and Prince William announce pregnancy early amid fear news would leak over Internet," "The Duchess' hospitalization forced the couple to go public with the news earlier than planned—they had only told the Queen and Prince Charles earlier today" (par. 3). Indeed, readers were told that Middleton had no choice. Vissar also reports, "The *Daily Mail's* royal correspondent, Rebecca English, reported that the couple had no plans to announce the pregnancy this early but thought they had no other choice given the hospitalization" (par. 15).

In the end, the Palace made the announcement when Middleton was admitted to the hospital, which was something the Palace had made clear they intended to do prior to Middleton becoming pregnant. In fact, before Middleton's pregnancy and because of all the media speculation about whether or not Middleton was pregnant that emerged after the wedding, the Royal family had made it unambiguous that they did not want "Hollywood" to make the announcement when Middleton became pregnant; the Palace wanted to control what and how a pregnancy announcement would be made. When asked who would make a pregnancy announcement when Middleton became pregnant, Christina Ng reported the following: "The palace, which rarely comments on speculation, took the unusual step of saying, 'We would be the ones to make the announcement, not Hollywood'" (par. 16). Undoubtedly, in this context, Hollywood is being used pejoratively in at least two ways: first, the Palace made clear that they wanted to control the announcement and did not want the celebrity media to make the announcement. Also, by using the phrase *not Hollywood*, the palace is using code for "not the entertainment industry," "not the tabloidization and therefore the debasement of an announcement," which also, most often, has negative connotations of being "flashy, vulgar, and/or fake," as in "that's so Hollywood," that is, so fake, tasteless, and/or debased.

The Palace did make the announcement, also reluctantly but because of the hospitalization. The official announcement by St James's Palace read: "The Duke and Duchess of Cambridge are very pleased to announce that the Duchess of Cambridge is expecting a baby. The duchess was admitted this afternoon to King Edward VII hospital in central London with hyperemesis gravidarum. As the pregnancy is in its very early stages, her royal highness is expected to stay in hospital for several days and will require a period of rest thereafter" (Davies pars. 5–6). As a result, Middleton had not announced her pregnancy before she was hospitalized—she had remained tight lipped about it both publicly and privately—but she was forced to tell both the public and the Royal family due to her pregnancy-related illness. Thus, Middleton's pregnancy announcement was done reluctantly and only due to her hospitalization.

Kardashian's pregnancy, on the other hand, was announced live on stage by Kanye West during a concert he was performing when Kardashian was in the audience. Kanye told the audience of 5,000 to "stop the music and make noise for my baby mama," referring to Kardashian, who was in the audience (Sieczkowski). According to Caven Sieczkowski, reporting for *huffingtonpost.com*, Kardashian had no idea West was planning to make the announcement. As Sieczkowski reported, "She and the 35-year-old 'Clique' rapper had not discussed announcing the news and were reportedly going to wait until she started showing, TMZ notes" (par. 6). In fact, *TMZ* revealed, "According to our sources, Kanye was moved to *blab* on stage because Kim's BFF and her mom were at the show—along with several of Kanye's family members. Kim didn't seem to mind the surprise—we're told she was crying tears of joy when Kanye revealed they're expecting, and was especially moved because he did it during one of her fave songs . . . 'Lost in the World'" (emphasis added, "Kim Kardashian had" pars. 2 and 3).

Unlike the Middleton announcement, clearly, Kardashian's announcement could be read as very Hollywood, that is, flashy, over the top, and possibly tasteless. And, unlike Middleton and Prince William who were tight lipped, West "blabbed," let the secret slip, and told that secret Hollywood style: live, on stage, in the middle of his concert, and to his fans. In other words, when compared, unlike Middleton and Prince William who had been able to keep "the secret" from both the Royal family and the public, West seemed unable to control himself and keep to the plan of announcing the pregnancy when Kardashian was further along. Thus, when the pregnancy announcements are compared, Middleton's continues to represent the themes of control, waiting, and good taste, while Kardashian's continues to entrench the themes of excess, being over the top, possibly lack of taste, and lack of control.

Problematic Gender and Racial Discourses

In addition to further entrenching Kardashian's maternal position as the over-the-top Reality TV star, by positioning Kardashian as his "baby mama," West also situated Kardashian within a complex and potentially problematic race and gender discourse. *Baby Mama* is a term that first gained prominence in popular culture in the early 2000s in the lyrics of American hip-hop, rap, and R&B artists. Writing for *Slate Magazine Online*, Julia Turner argues, "The OED lists *baby-daddy* and *baby-mama* as 'colloquial, chiefly African-American' variants of the Jamaican terms *baby-father* and *baby-mother*" (par. 3). In Jamaica, the terms simply mean "the father of the baby" and "the mother of the baby" without judgment or moral valuation. Turner also reports, "By the mid to late '90s, the terms *baby-daddy* and *baby-mama* were appearing regularly in American hip-hop and R&B songs, and the words were consistently used to refer to an ex [girlfriend/wife or boyfriend/husband]" (par. 6). While Turner reports that baby mama is no longer exclusively a negative term, Tia Tyree, citing other scholars' work, argues otherwise, and is worth quoting in length:

> The baby mama is a woman who becomes pregnant to keep a relationship with the father of her child, take his money, or keeps the child as a "part of him" ("Freaks, Gold Diggers" 32–34). She uses "unethical" actions to obtain baby mama status (Stephens and Few 53), and her desire for the father of her child is supposedly so strong that she would sacrifice her personal life plans to have his baby (Wyatt 131). Common representations of baby mamas are usually of young, single, poor urban females, unlike the Black queens who are middle-class and usually have a "king." The baby mama is "frequently cast in sexist, racist, paternalistic, contested, and convoluted notions of the strong, angry, promiscuous, childbearing, wild black woman" (Morgan 427). (52–53)

Although it is now more commonly applied to any woman who is pregnant and unmarried or now single and a mother, a baby mama is still often used negatively with racialized, paternalistic, and sexist connotations.

In fact, colloquially, *The Urban Dictionary.com* defines *baby mama* in the following way:

> A term used to define an unmarried young woman (but can be a woman of any age) who has had a child. As mentioned before in another definition, most of the time it is used for when it was simply a sexual relationship, compared to ex-wife or girlfriend. Usually this has a negative connotation, a lot of baby mamas are seen as desperate, gold digging, emotionally starved, shady women who had a baby out of spite or to keep a man. Sometimes they may act like this because of missed child support payments, unfulfilled promises by the father, or convenient sex by the father. Either or both may exist in any situation. (Entry 2)

Moreover, and also in popular culture, *Wiktionary* suggests that baby mama is "Often considered pejorative, particularly if applied to unmarried black parents—if used by one parent of the other, can imply 'child in common but no meaningful relationship,' while if used by outsiders, can imply disapproval of children born out of wedlock" ("Baby Mama" par. 3). However, as does Turner, *Wiktionary* also notes, "These days, the terms no longer seem 'chiefly African-American'—they're everywhere, the latest bits of hip-hop lingo to gain widespread use" (par. 8).

While Kardashian is not African American—her mother is white and her father was Armenian—by using the term *baby mama*, West, who is African American, racialized Kardashian as "other," especially in relation to Middleton. And, it is important to note that Middleton's pregnancy was widely expected, anticipated, and Middleton is a white "someday queen" with a real-life soon-to-be king, while Kardashian's pregnancy with West was unexpected, even a bit surprising given Kardashian's marital status with Humphries, and Kardashian was already on the defensive about her potential "unethical" actions in her marriage to Humphries. As a result, West positioned Kardashian within a complex and potentially negative gender discourse in relation to maternity. And, equally important, the term *baby mama*, whether raced or not, has potentially lingering negative and patriarchal connotations of a woman who is a gold digging, emotionally starved, and shady woman who had a baby out of spite or to keep a man. Given that Kardashian was already situated within a discourse of fame that positioned her as an over-the-top and excessive reality star and the fact that she was married to another man and in the midst of divorce proceedings that were challenging her authenticity via her potentially "unethical" or "shady" actions, it would be difficult for the negative connotations associated with baby mama to not "stick" in relation to Kardashian.

Additionally, when this is coupled with Middleton already situated within a discourse of fame that positioned her as a real-life princess who had a "real-life-soon-to-be-king" as a husband and who also showed that good things come to those who wait—everything a baby mama seems unable to do—it is unlikely that West's positioning of Kardashian as a baby mama did anything but further reinforce Middleton's authentic maternal position as the good post-second wave princess and future good mother in relation to Kardashian's potentially inauthentic maternal position as the bad over-the-top Reality TV star and future bad mother. Additionally, given the discourse of fame that was already shaping each woman's maternal subject position, even if Middleton had been referred to as Prince William's baby mama, given the discourse of fame that Middleton was situated within, her baby mama status would probably be the more neutral, newfound use of the term that Turner suggested, while, given the discourse of fame that Kardashian was situated within, Kardashian's baby mama status is more likely the older, negative use of the term.

As a result, while the term *baby mama* may be losing some of its racialized meanings and it seems clear that West described Kardashian in this way positively and in light of its more neutral meaning, given Kardashian's maternal position, baby mama racialized Kardashian's position. Indeed, as Tyree suggests, especially in media's use of racialized terms about African American women, baby mama racializes mothers in very specific and problematic ways. Racialization is a type of racism under white privilege that designates nonwhite people as other based on physical traits and characteristics, reinforces presupposed, stereotypical qualities of and about nonwhites, and reproduces hierarchal arrangements that further reinforces white privilege, while denying that privilege and, often, makes "whiteness" seem "neutral" or a nonracial category. And in contemporary culture, this is a form of racism that is often implied or alluded to rather than being an overt form of racism. So, for example, often, someone is racialized through "code" or language that has been racialized. Michael Tesler, argues, for example, that "inner city" is now racialized code for "black" (691). Baby mama has a history of being used as one such code; and, in using it to announce her pregnancy, whether intended or not, West racialized Kardashian and her pregnant maternal body, particularly in relation to Middleton's maternal body and announcement; both of which were done in "good taste" and via a "traditional" marriage, unlike Kardashian's.

Kardashian's Already Racialized Body

Equally important, Kardashian's body had been racialized prior to her pregnancy in problematic ways, and this racialization was further ingrained rather than challenged after she became pregnant. Kardashian's body was first racialized because of her "famous assets": in common parlance, her "big booty." As was already noted, as the *huffingtonpost.com* chart revealed but other media regularly note in their discussion of Kardashian, Kardashian's fame has come, in part, by her "sizable assets," which is code for her curvy and large "booty." Larger posteriors are often coded racially and used to preserve whiteness as the norm, especially when comparisons are made between a "slender" posterior and a "larger" posterior. In her own analysis of Jennifer Lopez's celebrity and large posterior, Helene Shugart, in fact, argues, "As noted, the large rear end has been associated with women of color and fetishized accordingly for a very long time, and notably, that has been especially true historically of black women. Although the large rear end has been and continues to be a notable standard of beauty in many black communities, arguably more consistently so than in Latino communities, it was introduced into the mainstream (white) public discourse on the body of Jennifer Lopez" ("Crossing Over" 127–128). Even so, however, the focus on nonwhite women's big booties works to preserve racial differences rather than challenge racial differences because, as Shugart also suggests in her analysis of Lopez,

> Lopez' posterior almost invariably gets a mention, and it is often the sole subject of that coverage. Indeed, perhaps the most compelling evidence that Lopez' rear end functions to preserve rather than erase ethnic difference . . . is that despite the fact that it has gotten noticeably smaller in the last ten years and is arguably not much bigger than the historically acceptable "white" female rear end it continues to be fetishized and circulated in the popular media, especially as a characteristically "Latina butt." (126)

Unmistakably, then, because much of Kardashian's fame is rooted in her often-mentioned sizable assets, even when pregnant, as with Lopez, the focus on Kardashian's assets both racializes her and preserves racial differences. And, while Middleton and Kardashian's posteriors are not explicitly compared, in the slender-pregnant comparisons, they are done implicitly when Kardashian's is mentioned while Middleton's is not. In other words, in explicit comparisons between Middleton and Kardashian, when Kardashian's large posterior is mentioned and Middleton's is not, this does not mean that the women's posterior are not being compared. Rather, because the framework of comparison was established so overtly and explicitly in the media coverage of the two women, when Kardashian's large posterior is noted explicitly, Middleton's is noted implicitly. And, as with the "Kate the Waif" versus "Kim the Whale" image that opened this chapter and the *huffingtonpost.com* chart comparison of the women's fame, the implied comparison is made exceedingly clear: Kardashian's racialized big booty is negatively compared to Middleton's racialized white, tight nonbig booty.

Moreover, as I show next, because much of the coverage of Middleton's pregnant body focuses on her "small" and "tightly toned" body in relation to Kardashian's excessive and out-of-control body, it is clear that Kardashian's booty is more than "just big"; it is an excessive or over-the-top booty in comparison to the white norm that Middleton embodies. And, again, similar to Lopez's, the axis in which Kardashian's booty turns is excess. Or, as Shugart argues,

"Clearly, excess is the axis on which the representation of Lopez' buttocks turns if only as defined relative to an established cultural (white) norm, in the context of mainstream mediated popular culture, that ordains a small, tightly toned, fairly contained female rear end" ("Crossing Over" 124–125). And, this is a rear end that is consistent only with a slender-pregnant (white) maternal body, not a racialized, curvy, and excessive pregnant body and booty.

In addition to playing into racialized gender discourses about Kardashian, the "tightly managed" versus "Hollywood blabbing" announcements continued to reinforce the contained and waiting versus excessive and over-the-top discourse and maternal subject positions at battle via the two women's pregnancies. As I reveal next, however, the pregnancy announcements also set the stage for the tightly managed, perfectly good celebrity pregnancy and future mother versus the unmanaged, excessive, awful celebrity pregnancy and bad future mother. It also set the stage for the profiles to make the case that good celebrity pregnancy must also include middle-class taste that is tied to whiteness, tightness, and the small, slender-pregnant body type that Middleton embodies perfectly, "just like a good white princess should," while suggesting that that the racialized, excessive, fat pregnant body type that Kardashian embodies is a warning, "just like any awful over-the-top Reality TV star is."

The Bump Watch: Middleton's Right Kind of Bump versus Kardashian's "Well . . . a Belly"

As soon as Middleton and Kardashian's pregnancies became public, media began what is commonly referred to as *the bump watch*. Indeed, because slender pregnancy is now the pregnant ideal and pregnant women are suppose to be slender everywhere except in the "belly," media fixate on "watching for the bump" to emerge, then, once emerged, focus obsessively on watching and analyzing how celebrity mothers "dress the bump" via the celebrities' maternity styles. This means, according to Nash, "the postmodern baby has been given new meaning in global popular culture in its representation as a 'baby bump,' a term that first appeared in a 1987 British style article in the *Guardian* (Safire, 2006)" (4). Thus, even though slender pregnancy is a relatively new cultural phenomenon with new meanings attached to the bump watch, slender pregnancy and the bump watch have a history, which is playing out in the bump watch and maternity wear coverage in the profiles of Middleton and Kardashian's pregnancies. As a result and to continue to make the case that slender-pregnant profiles are now the first stage of a new two-stage process in celebrity mom profiles, that history warrants some attention.

Brief History of Maternity Wear and "the Bump Watch"

Prior to the early 1990s, women and celebrities primarily hid their pregnancies in the public sphere, in part, because pregnancy was associated with sexuality. As a result, there was no bump to watch; it was hidden. In a review of the past 100 years of maternity wear, for example, the "What to Expect" website, in an article titled, "100 Years of Maternity Fashion," suggests, "up until the early 20th century, pregnant mothers masked their growing bumps (even while the corsets they wore accentuated their feminine curves!). Those in the upper classes even disappeared from public view entirely in a period of 'confinement'" (par. 1). Throughout the early twentieth century, "maternity wear was modest and reserved" (par. 4). Below a black and white picture of Jackie Onassis sitting on the floor, cutting something out from a newspaper for her daughter Caroline, "What To Expect" reports, by the 1960s, "Fashions in the early 1960s emulated First Lady Jackie Kennedy's effortless, elegant look—here she was photographed at home with her daughter circa 1960, pregnant with her son, John Jr. Women continued to hide their pregnancies, which was easy to do in the era's simple, geometric 'shift' dresses, boxy suit jackets with oversized buttons, and capris. Later in the decade, the hippie flair for bellbottoms, tie-dye, and flowing tunics took hold among the young-and-trendy set" (par. 9).

By the 1970s and 1980s, "despite the emergence of dare-to-bare miniskirts and leggings in the 1980s, most moms-to-be continued to dress their baby bumps modestly in 'tent-like' dresses" (par. 11). Finally, also noting the importance of Princess Diana's maternity wear, "What to Expect," writes, under a picture of Princess Diana at an official Royal ceremony when she was pregnant with William, "Princess Diana was an emulated style icon in the 1980s; during her pregnancy she opted for baggy, tent-like dresses with neck-bows and contrast collars" (par. 11). Thus, maternity wear was modest and reserved, hiding the pregnant woman's body and baby bump through the 1980s.

All of that changed, however, in the early 1990s. In 1991, movie actress Demi Moore posed naked on the cover of *Vanity Fair* when she was seven-months pregnant. Famed photographer Annie Leibovitz took the cover photo. The photo sparked controversy for both *Vanity Fair* and Moore, with some newsstands refusing to sell the issue without putting the issue in a brown paper bag reminiscent of the need to cover-up adult magazines like *Playboy*. With the cover title, "More Demi Moore," Moore is posed sideways, naked, with her right arm across her breasts as a "handbra," and her left arm cupping her pregnant belly and strategically covering her pelvic area. Reviewing the controversy, the *Los Angeles Times Online*, notes that, at the time, Moore was quoted as saying, "It did seem to give a little bit more permission to feel sexy, attractive when you're pregnant," Moore told *V* magazine, "But I really didn't expect for the response to be what it was. I was pretty shocked" ("Vanity Fair: Demi Moore Poses" par. 1). The photo and controversy were widely discussed on television, in newspaper articles, and on the radio.

The groundbreaking impact of the Moore cover photo was significant. Scholars (Earle; Hefferman, Nicholson, and Fox; Jette; Nash) mark the newfound focus on both pregnancy and the maternal body of pregnant celebrities with Moore's *Vanity Fair* cover. Or, as Nash writes, "The 1991 *Vanity Fair* cover photograph of naked and heavily-pregnant American actress Demi Moore is regarded as having reconfigured western cultural views of pregnancy" (6). Moreover, Moore's cover also began the process of "uncovering" or "undressing" the pregnant maternal body and the bump. Indeed, there was no longer a need to hide the pregnant body and instead it gave pregnant women "permission" to feel sexy and attractive, as Moore seemed to understand herself. Or, as Kristin Hefferman, Paula Nicolson, and Rebekeh Fox, writing in 2011, also suggest, "The transmogrification of maternity fashion, alongside the increased coverage of pregnant bodies in the media during the past two decades, invokes the idea that pregnancy is something women no longer need to 'cover up.' Such images have been purported via the media through a new generation of 'celebrity mums,' whose pregnancies are touted almost as a 'fashion accessory' (Fox et al. 2009; also see Longhurst 2000, 2001)" (322).

As a result, pregnancy and the pregnant maternal body became much more public, with media focusing on the pregnant body, its bump, and fashioning of that body and bump. And, as already noted in the Introduction, the slender-pregnant body is now intertwined with, as Nash puts it, "discursive cultural constructions that illustrate appropriate ('good') or inappropriate ('bad') performances of pregnancy" (6–7), while also, as I suggest, illustrating and predicting appropriate (good) or inappropriate (bad) future mothering. Moreover, I also suggest that, as the pregnant maternal body became more public, slender-pregnant profiles began to develop and work to set the first stage of acceptance, even embrace, of post-second wave split subjectivity. Thus, the media bump watch, including the "analysis" of dressing the bump, is also a watch for the appropriate good bump and good future mothering or inappropriate bad bump and bad future mothering.

The Battle of the Bumps:
Middleton's Authentic Bump versus Kardashian's Inauthentic Bump

As the opening example reveals, media pitted the two women in relation to one another in terms of "the battle of the bumps," while also asking two central questions that framed that watch: Was Middleton too thin and was Kardashian too fat? The "Kate the Waif" versus "Kim the Whale" example also conveys a key message: even though both women have a "weight problem," Middleton is happy and glowing, while Kardashian looks unhappy, which also raised the second related implicit concern: Which of the two was happier pregnant? Once showing, then, the way that each woman's bump was described revealed a significant difference between the two women in terms of the "appropriateness" of their maternal bodies, weight, and happiness and comfort with and about their pregnancies and pregnant bodies.

Almost immediately and throughout the bump watch, Middleton's bump was deemed appropriate, while Kardashian's bump was deemed inappropriate. Early in their pregnancies and bump watch, for example, in describing each woman's bump, the *huffingtonpost.com* chart revealed: Kate: "Belly looks like a mini soccer ball." Kim: "Belly just looks like . . . well, a belly" (Blickley). Moreover, later in her pregnancy, Middleton's bump was also described as a "barely visible" bump (Hill and Kent-Smith), a "small," "tidy," and/or "neat" bump (Ley). These descriptions clearly suggest that Middleton has the appropriate-size bump: a small bump framed by her slender-pregnant body, while Kardashian does not. Indeed, describing Kardashian's bump as looking "well . . . like a belly" is code to suggest that she looks like she is just carrying excess weight; she looks fat not pregnant. From the beginning of the bump watch, then, Middleton's bump was deemed an appropriate or authentic, small bump that showed that Middleton was "just pregnant," while Kardashian's bump was deemed an inappropriate or inauthentic nonbump that seemed to show that Kardashian was fat rather than pregnant in the "right" way.

A related issue for both women then was each woman's eating and pregnancy cravings in relation to their growing (or not) bump. So, for example, the *huffingtonpost.com* chart noted the cravings of both women: Kate: "Pregnancy craving is reportedly Lavender Shortbread Biscuits."; Kim: "Pregnancy cravings are Pizookies cookies, artichokes, Chinese chicken salad and French fries" (Blickley). In terms of Middleton, however, there was very little media coverage of Middleton's cravings, in part because Middleton suffered from severe morning sickness early in her pregnancy, which meant Middleton "could not keep food down" and seemed unable to eat (Clark par. 5), while much more was said about Kardashian's cravings, and, regularly Kardashian was portrayed as lacking control, constraint, and/or discipline in relation to her cravings and eating. So, for example, *In Touch Weekly*, in an article titled, "Pregnant Kim Kardashian Indulges in Cravings: Chicken and Waffles, Risotto, Decadent Desserts and More," reveals "Pregnant Kim Kardashian has let her raging cravings take over!" (par. 1). Titles also made explicit links between Kardashian's cravings and fast food. So, for example, Cyna Burton's article about Kardashian's cravings was titled, "Kim Kardashian Reveals Her Biggest Pregnancy Craving, Favorite Junk Food."

Equally interesting, coverage of Kardashian's eating was extensively detailed. The *In Touch* story just noted also reveals to readers that "*In Touch* has learned that in recent weeks, the expectant star has indulged in high-calorie, carbohydrate-heavy meals including creamy risotto, chicken and waffles, decadent desserts and more. Also reported, On March 17, she was spotted at South City Kitchen in Atlanta scarfing down greasy chicken and waffles, along with smashed bliss potatoes, collard greens, and mac and cheese. Back in Beverly Hills days later, she stopped—twice in one week—into one of her favorite Italian restaurants, Il Pastaio, for carb-heavy lunch" (Burton pars. 2–3). In addition to "indulging," letting her "raging cravings take over," and "scarfing" down "greasy" and "carb-heavy" food, in a *Mail Online.com* report, after readers are told that Kardashian had been keeping to a healthy diet, readers then learn "But it seems that Kim Kardashian has finally given into her temptations as she posted a picture of a huge burger and chips covered in melted cheese on Thursday, which came in at nearly 1000 calories. Having finally succumbed to her cravings, the star stopped by fast food restaurant In-N-Out and tucked into the fattening meal after weeks of being careful" ("Kim Kardashian Finally" pars. 1–3).

Clearly, reports about the women's cravings and Kardashian's eating begin to reveal the class-based issues tied up in these reports: Middleton's limited cravings are sophisticated and "tasteful" biscuits, while Kardashian's excessive cravings are nonsophisticated and primarily for "cheap" fast food. This means that media positioned Kardashian as having out-of-control cravings for trashy fast food, while Middleton is positioned as barely eating, but able to control her cravings for sophisticated food when she can eat. In addition to continuing to garner sympathy for Middleton and lack of sympathy for Kardashian, these craving reports also continued to position Middleton as a tasteful and sophisticated pregnant woman in relation to Kardashian as an indulgent, cheap fast-food-loving pregnant woman; and these media stories work rhetorically to support the notion that Middleton had "the right kind of bump" and maternal attitude because of her appropriate eating or lack thereof, while Kardashian had, "well . . . a belly" and the wrong kind of bump and maternal attitude because of her inability to control herself and her excessive eating.

The Weight Problem Battle: Too Thin versus Too Fat

While the media discussion of the cravings alluded to each woman's maternal body, media coverage of each woman's weight problems explicitly addressed each woman's management of their maternal body in relation to the slender-pregnant ideal, and this coverage emerged quickly in the bump watch. Media reports about the women's maternal bodies also reveal how class and control continued to be intertwined in the discussion of the two women's weight problems. Scholars (Dworkin and Wachs; Earle; Jette; Nash) have already established that managing the pregnant body, primarily through exercise and diet, is now a prerequisite for slender pregnancy today. However, until recently, the pregnant body was viewed as fragile and incongruous with physical activity. Shannon Jette, for example, argues that, until the 1980s, "pregnant women were advised by many medical professionals to avoid exercise more intense than a light stroll, because the pregnant body was viewed as fragile and incongruous with physical activity" (331). As the general fitness boom of the 1980s coincided with second wave feminism, a generation of physically active women began to have children and wished to remain fit during pregnancy. Jette also argues that questions began to arise about whether or not fitness would be safe for pregnant women and their fetuses. There was very little scientific data to answer these concerns; however, starting in 1985 and continuing through the 1990s, the medical community began to study pregnancy and exercise. Today, "while the pregnant body is still construed as 'at risk,' pregnant women are now encouraged to engage in moderate exercise. In fact, the risks of *not* engaging in physical fitness while pregnant are emphasized in contemporary North American medical discourse" (italics in orginal, Jette 332).

By the 1990s and continuing through today, the fitness industry has also capitalized on the shifting discourse of the medical community and has created a fitness industry that links pregnancy fitness both with privileged women's post-second wave empowerment but also with the newfound acceptance of women's physical strength that develops via their body work. Dworkin and Wachs, in fact, suggest that fitness during pregnancy is now linked with successful deliveries and better postpartum recovery (120). Thus, as the slender-pregnant body has become the new contemporary maternal body norm, media regularly dissect how well pregnant celebrities are managing their pregnant bodies in relation to this norm, a focus that most often begins in the bump watch and via the analysis of celebrities' weight gain or not.

In the case of Middleton and Kardashian, then, from early in the bump watch, media raised concerns that Middleton was "too thin," while for Kardashian the concern was that she was "too fat." In addition to the "Kate the Waif" versus "Kim the Whale" example, an *US Weekly* (6/24/13) story about the women, reveals, "the mums-to-be have experienced night-and-day pregnancies (Kim has been relentlessly mocked for her growing belly, Kate has been criticized for not gaining *enough* weight)" (emphasis added, Grossbart 53). These are two very different "weight" problems with very different meanings and cultural value. "Too thin" was code for worries that Middleton was suffering from pregorexia during her pregnancy. Pregorexia,[5] while not a clinical disorder, is a term used to describe a pregnant woman who is anorexic or is eating disordered. This was a key concern in media coverage of Middleton's weight problem. Examples of article titles reveal this concern: Tom Sykes of the *Royalist* wrote an article titled, "Pregorexia: Is Skinny Kate Too Thin For A Pregnant Woman?"; *Time* had an online article by Bonnie Rochman titled, "Is Kate Middleton Too Thin to Be Pregnant?" and Jeanne Adams wrote an article titled, "Is Kate Middleton Still Anorexic And Can She Put Baby Before Body Insecurities?"

Adams' article title also reveals that concerns about Middleton's weight preceded her pregnancy with her dieting for her wedding. Indeed, Middleton was even accused of "Brideorexia": again, not a clinical term but a popular culture term for women who lose weight too quickly and/or in unhealthy ways in advance of their weddings, so they are "skinny brides." After noting media celebrations of "svelte brides," Meredith Melnick reports, "the British tabloids have been making a fuss over how much Kate Middleton's 5-ft. 10-in. frame has whittled down since the 29-year-old made her first official appearance as Prince William's fiancée on Feb. 24. It does appear that Middleton has shrunk from a reported U.K. size 10 (size 6 in the U.S.) to a tiny U.K. size 6 (U.S. size 2), but whether she has developed a case of brideorexia is unclear" (par. 6). Moreover, after the wedding and before she became pregnant, speculation began that Middleton was too thin to become pregnant. Bonnie Rochman, for example, noted, "Eating disorders aside, blogs have been bursting with curiosity about whether Middleton is 'too thin to conceive' and/or 'too thin to bear an heir'" (par. 6). While being too thin is problematic in pregnancy, in the context of a slender-pregnant ideal, being thin is not problematic and, in fact, is the required ideal. Moreover, as Helen Grimillion reveals, "while anorexia is considered to be a psychiatric illness, it must be situated within new cultural expectations about ideal femininity. Anorexia's incidence increased more than 50 percent in the 1970s, at the same time that there was an increasing focus in mainstream U.S. culture on women and girls achieving autonomy, self-control, and bodily fitness through dieting and exercise" (381). Hence, given the slender-pregnant imperative and already-existing norms of ideal slender (white) femininity, Middleton's "weight problem," is less of a problem in comparison to Kardashian's.

Most media discussions about Kardashian's weight problem were similar to the following article title: "Is Kim Gaining Too Much Weight, Too Fast?" (Clark par. 10). Moreover, media speculated that Kardashian exceeded the recommended total weight gain early in her pregnancy. So, for example, even though Lisa DeFazio MS, RD had noted the different body types of the two women,[6] she too compared the two women in relation to the slender-pregnant ideal, when Sandra Clark reports that DeFazaio also suggested, "'In general, a woman at a healthy weight should only gain 25 to 35 lbs. during the entire pregnancy,' Lisa explains. 'Kim appears to have already gained 20 pounds and she still has 5 months to go! Yes, she is exercising but my advice is to put as much effort into her diet as she is with her workouts!'" (par. 6). And DeFazio suggested that Middleton's problem was the opposite. As Clark reports, "'Kate may have the opposite problem and need to see a dietitian to help her gain weight,' says Lisa. 'She may not have an appetite, but there are food combinations she can eat that are high in calories and are not overwhelming portions for her'" (par. 11). Thus, again, media reports are relatively unsympathetic toward Kardashian's maternal body, accusing her of gaining "too much, too fast" and being undisciplined in terms of her diet, even though she was adhering to the imperative to continue to work out during pregnancy, while reports about Middleton are sympathetic and, as always, imply that she has the opposite problem, "too little" food, not enough high-calorie food, and the need for smaller portions, all of which are also consistent with maintaining the slender-pregnant ideal.

Interestingly, each woman's desire to eat was also connected to their weight problem. Readers are told, "As *HollyBaby.com* previously reported, Kate has been working with a hypnotherapist to help her with extreme morning sickness and her lack of desire to eat" (Clark par. 12). While Middleton lacked the desire to eat, Kardashian had the opposite problem. So, for example, readers learned from Kardashian's mother that Kardashian was making all the wrong choices about what to eat. Clark reports that E! News, for example, reported that "Kim has been eating more! Her mom, Kris Jenner revealed her cravings to E! News, saying that her daughter was 'craving giant cookies from BJs, French fries, Chinese chicken salad and artichokes'" (par. 4). Thus, in addition to continuing to play into the "tight-lipped versus too much" battle that began in the pregnancy announcements, the concerns about the women's weight also, implicitly, explored Middleton's "lack of desire for food" and Kardashian's "excessive desire for food."

In contemporary culture where weight, food, and desire are tied up in complex ways, especially for understandings of the good disciplined and controlled slender-pregnant body, it is clear that Middleton's problem was a far better problem to have in comparison to Kardashian's problem, because Middleton's problem helped her achieve a slender-pregnant body that requires and symbolically represents control and self-mastery of food and the self. As Susan Bordo famously observed, the slender female body, including the anorexic body, symbolically represents traditional femininity and a woman's ability to conform to self-mastery, denial, and control, especially the ability to control the unruly female body; a body that is often perceived as being out of control (*Unbearable Weight* 149). And control is pivotal to slender pregnancy because, as Nash argues, "Such control takes on a new importance during pregnancy, which is a time when women's bodies are thought to be out of control" (169).

Managing out-of-control pregnant bodies is required and demands that pregnant women regain and/or find control because having a slender, firm pregnant body carries specific symbolic meanings today. As I have already noted but is important to reiterate, Nash also argues, "Having a firm, managed body for such women is a 'symbol of correct attitude,' particularly in pregnancy: 'working out' suggests that a mother cares about herself and her unborn child" (169). Moreover, Bordo also argued about slenderness in general but is also now relevant to the slender-pregnant body today, that slenderness has "deep associations with autonomy, will, discipline, conquest of desire, enhanced spirituality, purity, and transcendence of the female body" (*Unbearable Weight* 68). Thus, Middleton's weight problem and slender-pregnant body garnered sympathy and support for her weight problem, especially during her hospitalization, her lack of desire for food, and in the reports that she was having difficulty holding food down because both she and her maternal body symbolically and literally embody the slender-pregnant ideal, while also representing deep symbolic and embodied associations with will, discipline, conquest of desire, and enhanced maternal femininity. In contrast, Kardashian was "fat shamed" for her weight problem, her lack of discipline, and her inability to control her excessive eating, which also had deep symbolic and embodied associations with a lack of will, control, and discipline, and an inability to defeat her excessive desires.

KARDASHIAN'S MATERNAL BODY DEFENSE: "I'VE ONLY GAINED 20 POUNDS"

And, unlike Middleton, Kardashian needed to and did defend herself in light of what her "fat" racialized body represented symbolically: her lack of control and the wrong future maternal attitude. In fact, as noted earlier, Kardashian was relentlessly mocked for her weight gain and pregnant body. Indeed, in addition to being labeled a *whale* in relation to Middleton's *waif*, probably the cruelest example of the fat-shaming and mocking occurred when Kardashian was compared to an Orca or killer whale after she wore a dress that was black in the back and white in the front. A side-by-side picture of Kardashian in the dress and an Orca became one of the most popular memes at the time ("Kim Kardashian Vs"). As a result, *hollywoodlife. com* reported "Amid all of the reports surrounding Kim's pregnancy weight gain, the mom-to-be fired back at critics when she visited 'Live With Kelly & Michael' on March 26, and revealed she hasn't gained anywhere near 65 pounds! Kim Kardashian's weight has come under scrutiny since revealing she was pregnant with her first child, but the petite reality star revealed . . . that she isn't anywhere near 200 pounds like some reports have claimed!" ("Kim Kardashian Reveals" Stiehl pars. 1 and 2). In fact, in discussing the episode, *hollywoodlife.com* also reported that Kardashian, talking about her sister Kourtney, said, "I've gained 20 pounds, at this stage Kourtney had already gained like 30,' Kim told Michael Strahan and his guest co-host Kristin Chenoweth" (Stiehl par. 3). Finally, also implicitly denying the reports that she is craving unhealthy food, Kardashian also said, "I want to have those cravings that everyone is saying, like cheeseburgers, I really haven't had that," the reality star added. "I just want to go home and sit in bed and pig out, and I really only crave healthy food" (Stiehl par. 6).

There are many reasons why Kardashian had to defend herself. First, she was already on the defensive for her excessive maternal position. Second, when Kardashian was fat shamed, part of her shame was her divergence from normative white femininity, a femininity that Middleton embodied perfectly. And, diverging from normative femininity is especially problematic in pregnancy because, as Earle argues, "As soon as a woman diverges from normative femininity, her body becomes a target: women can either be 'fat' or 'pregnant,' with nothing 'in-between'" (6). And, this is especially the case for pregnant celebrity moms. Indeed, as pregnant actress Olivia Wild put it in describing why she chose a form-fitting gown for the 2014 Golden Globes: "You go form-fitting so people know you're pregnant. I wanted to be like, 'I'm not fat, I'm pregnant'" ("Stars, Style, Secrets!" 31). Unlike Wild, then, it is clear that Kardashian became a target because it was unclear if she was fat or pregnant, and she was the target of vicious attacks, attacks that even the media acknowledged. Third, Kardashian had to defend herself against charges of overeating, lack of control and discipline because questions about excess body weight, especially during pregnancy, raise questions about moral culpability and self-control. Again, Earle is helpful here in describing her interviewees' concerns that, if they appeared fat rather than pregnant then people would think that they were gaining weight because they lacked self-control: "The comments made above highlight the moral culpability associated with being fat and the perceived relationship between over-eating and lack of self-discipline and control" during pregnancy (247).

For all of these reasons, Kardashian had to defend herself because her maternal body suggested that she did not have the right kind of maternal attitude about both herself and her future child, especially in relation to Middleton's conforming and obviously well-managed, firm, and tight maternal body. And, it is important to note just how much Middleton conformed to the white ideal: Middleton's body represented "perfect" control, discipline, restraint, and the right kind of bump and slender-pregnant maternal attitude and future mothering. As a result, media further entrenched the battle being won by Middleton by making the case that good celebrity pregnancy must also include middle-class taste that is tied to whiteness, control, restraint, tightness, and the small, slender-pregnant body type that Middleton embodies perfectly, "just like a good princess should," while suggesting that the racialized, excessive, fat pregnant body type that Kardashian embodies requires a defense and, equally important, is a warning "just like any awful over-the-top Reality TV star is."

The Battle for Comfort and Happiness

Given all the focus and discussion on their maternal bodies, media also revealed that both women had different levels of comfort with and happiness about their pregnant body. In fact, media reports were quite different in terms of the women's comfort levels with and happiness about their pregnant bodies, themes that were also confirmed pictorially. So, for example, and again, implicitly comparing the two women, on May 22, 2013, *US Weekly Online* had the following two headlines, one for each woman: "She's Glowing! Kate Middleton Shows Off Baby Bump in Yellow Coat Dress" (Takada and Scobie); "Kim Kardashian on Pregnancy Curves: 'How the F-ck Did I Get Like This?'" (Johnson). Clearly, Middleton is "glowing" and showing off her baby bump, implicitly suggesting how content and happy she is with her slender-pregnant body. Kardashian, on the other hand, is reported as disliking her pregnant body or being shocked by her pregnant body, clearly having a hard time accepting her pregnant body, and is struggling to feel comfortable with her pregnant body.

Moreover, an *US Weekly* cover story about Kardashian's vacation in Greece with her family details Kardashian's struggle for happiness and how and why Kardashian finally found happiness and comfort with her maternal body. The cover photo for the article is of Kardashian in a brown string bikini, and the copy reads, "Kim Dares to Bare," which is followed by large yellow font and all caps, "YOU CALL THIS FAT?" In the cover story, readers learn "Bullied for her weight gain, a newly confident Kardashian celebrates her seven-month bump on a family trip to Greece" (O'Leary 59), which is accompanied with a full-page photo of Kardashian in a white string bikini. O'Leary also reports that a family friend revealed, "'Kanye showers her with love and reassurance, constantly telling her how beautiful she is,' says a family insider" (60). However, immediately following this report, under a heading titled, "Body Struggle," O'Leary also reports that "West has faced an uphill battle. Practically since he let slip news of her pregnancy in December, his love has been hounded by weight bullies" (60). Finally, O'Leary reports that Kardashian herself revealed how hard the pregnant body changes have been for her, when he reports that Kardashian said, "'It was really hard for me to accept, you know, the body changes,' Kim told US at an April 22 E! event" (60). These reports make it clear that Kardashian was not just uncomfortable with her pregnant body, she found her pregnant body distasteful and difficult to accept, which is the opposite of media reports about Middleton.

Media also reported that Kardashian only became comfortable with her pregnant body when her belly finally grew. As O'Leary reports, "Her growing belly is making her feel more comfortable with the pregnancy, a pregnancy she recently called 'painful.'. . . Three months ago, she just wanted to have the baby and be done. Now she is feeling more feminine and more maternal" ("Kim Dares" 60). As a result, O'Leary also reveals to readers that Kardashian, has a "new found appreciation for her body. In her third trimester, the mom-to-be, 32, has finally conquered the self-consciousness that plagued her first two. Fat-shamed by tabloids and internet trolls for her weight gain, the woman known for her gorgeous curves had trouble coping" (59). But, according to a source on the trip with Kardashian, now that she is "'feeling very confident in her body. . . . She had no second thoughts about wearing bikinis on the trip'" (O'Leary 60). Also reporting on Kardashian's bikini-wearing Greek vacation, *hollywoodlife.com* reports, "That bikini proves it—Kim looks amazing!" ("Kim Kardashian Showing Off," Steihl par. 8).

Moreover, in the *hollywoodlife.com* report about the *US Weekly* cover story and cover photo of Kardashian in a bikini, Christina Stiehl also notes, "Kim Kardashian has been the target of viscous fat jokes and incentive comments about her changing curves ever since she announced she was pregnant with her first child. But the proud mom-to-be took back control of her pregnant body, and showed off her fit figure in a tiny bikini. We love that Kim is taking ownership of her new curves, and is a great example of how women shouldn't be ashamed of their changing bodies!" ("Kim Kardashian Showing Off" par. 1). By suggesting that Kardashian "took back control of her pregnant body," this report makes clear that Kardashian's pregnant body had been out of control and in need of control. As such, while a positive report about Kardashian, the warning via Kardashian's maternal body is made clear: out-of-control pregnant bodies become targets for "viscous fat jokes" and fat shaming, and, ultimately, out-of-control pregnant bodies make the pregnant woman uncomfortable and unhappy until the pregnant woman takes back control of her pregnant body.

The media reports also make it unambiguous *how* a fat-shamed pregnant woman can take back control, become more comfortable with her body, and, ultimately, "prove" that comfort and new-found happiness. Indeed, as the *US Weekly* cover story revealed, a fat-shamed, weight-bullied woman must "dare to bare" the bump and prove a "new confidence" by wearing a bikini, all of which Kardashian is reported as understanding. Indeed, Kardashian was able to celebrate her seven-month bump for one reason: because her belly had popped, which is code to mean that it finally became clear that Kardashian was pregnant and not fat. Or, as O'Leary reports about Kardashian, she blogged: "'I've gotten wider—but my belly hasn't popped yet,' she blogged in March. 'So I struggle finding things that don't make me look heavy'" ("Kim Dares" O'Leary 59). Once popped, however, media reported that Kardashian had "no second thoughts" about wearing bikinis; indeed, the bikinis prove it: Kardashian now looks "great," "confident," and "happy," both with her pregnancy and her pregnant-maternal body.

That Kardashian only began to feel comfortable about her maternal body after she was visibly pregnant and not fat is typical of many contemporary women living under the slender-pregnant regime and reveals just how much contemporary women must prove that they are not fat, just pregnant. In fact, in her interviews with pregnant women, Earle reports that a significant number of participants reported feeling relieved to look pregnant and not fat. Earle also found "The data suggest that the distinction between pregnancy and 'fatness' emerges very early in pregnancy" (247), a finding that was also confirmed by Nash. And, the most important confirmation is when the bump appears so that, visually, two things are clear: first, that a woman does not have, "well . . . a belly" and instead is gaining weight due to pregnancy; and, as a result, two, that there is no doubt that a woman is pregnant rather than fat. Indeed, Earle suggests, "it is the development of this 'bump' that woman [sic] appear to particularly covet. The interview data clearly indicate a distinction between fatness and the characteristic shape of pregnancy. Many respondents were pleased to report that most of their weight gain could be attributed to this 'bump'" (249). It is clear, then, given the slender-pregnant ideal, that comfort with and happiness about a maternal body is dependent on having the "right kind" of bump and slender-pregnant body; until she looked obviously pregnant rather than fat, Kardashian was going to be uncomfortable with her maternal body. And, there is no better way to prove that you are pregnant and not fat than by wearing a bikini; or, as *hollywoodlife.com* put it, "That bikini proves it—Kim looks amazing!"

This means that from the beginning of the bump watch, because Middleton had the right kind of bump and slender-pregnant body, almost every picture of Middleton works rhetorically to convey her comfort and happiness with her pregnant body, which caused her to "glow" and "show off" or "flaunt" her body; while, also from the beginning of the bump watch, because Kardashian did not have the right kind of bump and slender-pregnant body, almost every picture of Kardashian before the bikini-wearing Greek vacation, works rhetorically to convey Kardashian's discomfort and unhappiness with her pregnant body, which caused Kardashian to experience her pregnancy as "painful" and to be unhappy about her pregnancy. And, equally important, the Kardashian coverage also conveys the basic message and a warning that no pregnant women can be happy and comfortable until she takes back control of her unruly, out-of-control body.

Pregnant Fashion Icon versus the Pregnancy Fashion Disaster

In addition to winning the battle between maternal body comparisons and comparisons that were quite vicious in terms of Kardashian, Middleton also won the maternity-wear battle, which was also mean-spirited. Given the intertwined connection between the pregnant body and maternity wear, after both women were showing, media obsessively dissected each woman's maternity wear choices, almost always in comparison but sometimes individually. And, in almost every case, especially early in her pregnancy before her bump emerged, Kardashian was diagnosed as a "fashion disaster," or as having regular "wardrobe malfunctions." So, for example, a *Hollywood Life* video posted at YouTube, is titled, "Kim Kardashian Baby Bump Wardrobe Malfunction Vs. Kate Middleton." Or, in another example, a *Mail Online.com* article by Emily Hunt and Emily Kent-Smith was titled, "It's Kate vs Kim . . . The bump off! One's an English duchess. The other is Hollywood royalty. And when it comes to maternity wear, they really ARE oceans apart" (capitalization in original). Accompanying the story are various side-by-side photos of both women in similar outfits—either by style or color—and the following assessment, "Here we look at how Kim so badly lost out to Kate in the battle of the bumps" (par. 7).

Moreover, when explicitly compared in the video titled, "Kim Kardashian, Kate Middleton Redefine Maternity Wear," which is embedded in a *huffingtonpost.com* article, Alicia Menendez and Rebecca Adams discuss and analyze Middleton's and Kardashian's maternity styles (Blickley). As soon as the video begins, Menendez says, "Kate Middleton took her royal baby bump to a wedding this weekend." Then, Menendez opines, "She looked stunning as usual." In discussing Middleton's maternity style, Adams responds, "She really is. She looked so stunning at the wedding. She went completely classic, pill box hat, coat. She is wearing classic icon pieces that she has worn in the past." Then, Menendez moves on to Kardashian in the following way: "A less stylish attempt at dressing her bump, Kim Kardashian arrived in Paris for fashion week in a slightly bizarre monochromatic look. . . . It seemed a strange choice. Rebecca: please rationalize that decision for me." Adams responds: "I don't even know what to say; it goes against every cardinal rule of dressing a baby bump. . . . I don't think Kim is going the demure route in pregnancy." Menendez: "Do you blame Kanye?" Rebecca responds: "It's hard not to . . . ah no, they have his and her styles."

In another article titled, "Kim Kardashian Flashes Thong: See-Through Wardrobe Malfunction," by Katrina Mitzeliotis, readers learn that "While the short, flared hemline of her frock managed to stay put the fabric seemed sheer in the bright spring sunlight, putting her tiny thong on full display! I'm shocked the cautious reality star wouldn't have covered up to prevent this embarrassing mishap" (par. 1). In another video titled, "Kim Kardashian Baby Bump Wardrobe Malfunction Vs. Kate Middleton," Chloe Melas, who is talking to her co-host Bonnie Fuller, says of Kardashian's maternity style, "She has just not mastered this at all." Later, after also noting the "thong incident," Melas opines "You think she would know everything that could be a wardrobe malfunction." Meanwhile, in yet another Bonnie Fuller and Chole Melas video, titled, "Kim Kardashian vs. Kate Middleton Pregnant Fashion Style," the two women discuss Middleton and Kardashian's styles when Kardashian is six-months pregnant. Melas begins by complimenting Kardashian for "finally looking comfortable while pregnant," which seems to be code for "now that Kardashian looks pregnant rather than fat, she is more comfortable with her body."

After complimenting Kardashian, however, Melas continues with the "too-tight" theme connected to Kardashian's maternity style. As she puts it, "She's been wearing some very tight outfits recently." Then, Fuller responds, "She also wore that very strange looking, Game of Thrones–type dress to go get yogurt the day before and her bust was just hanging out of it; it looked like she had a blanket on." Melas states later, "We know that she is experimenting with all these outfits." Fuller then replies, "She should take a hint from Kate Middleton. Kate Middleton has looked so chic, so stylish, every single time she has stepped out. And, she is doing it by wearing very pretty, body skimming, not tight coats." Melas replies, "Look, she looks so conservative, Kate, and Kim definitely likes to show off her assets a little bit more. . . . Look, Kate is so perfect in every way and I really think Kim and Kate should share pregnancy wardrobe tips." Fuller responds, "Look, I think that all Kim has to do is look at the picture of Kate and she can see what she [Middleton] is doing right. . . It has a lot to do with length; the coats are three-quarter length." Melas interjects, "and slimming," Fuller responds, "yes." Again, in the comparisons, it is clear that Middleton is not just the "winner," she is the "perfect" winner who has classic and tasteful maternity style and whose body-skimming style is "just right" in terms of showing Middleton's attractiveness and slender-pregnant body. So much so, in fact, that Middleton should be Kardashian's role model, because Kardashian is not just an inappropriately showing-off-her-assets loser partnered with a man who possibly has his own style issues that may be impacting her negatively (as he did when he blabbed about her pregnancy), she is a malfunctioning loser who ought to be able to see what she is doing wrong by just looking at Middleton's appropriate, conservative, sophisticated, chic maternity style.

Meanwhile, in the *US Weekly* story titled, "Battle of the Bumps," after previously noting that Kardashian is "America's reigning reality queen" (52), Grossbart's article, in a section titled, "Who's the real Princess?," which is accompanied by six pictures—three of both women—announces that "Both shell out for style, but only one can wear a crown" (54). There are three competition categories, accompanied by side-by-side pictures of the two women: "prints," "black and white," and "icy pastels" (Grossbart 54 and 55). Again, in each of the three pictures of Middleton, she is smiling, looking happy, and at ease; while in each of her three pictures, Kardashian is not smiling, including having her mouth drawn tightly in two of the three pictures, and she is looking straight ahead and unhappy. Underneath each picture is the supposed cost of each dress. Again, as with the wedding, Middleton's maternity outfits actually total more—$4,656—than Kardashian's, which cost $4,174, but it is clear pictorially and by the story that only one of the women can be the "real" princess and one is happier and making better maternity-style choices. Thus, again, even though both women may be considered "royalty"—Kardashian American and Middleton British—only one can be a "real" royal and "wear the crown," while also smiling and being at ease: Middleton.

Middleton: The New Jackie O

Individual cover stories about each woman also continue to work rhetorically to entrench the narrative that Middleton is the comfortable, happy, slender, disciplined fashion icon versus Kardashian as the mostly unhappy, uncomfortable maternity fashion disaster. When each woman was seven-months pregnant, they were both featured in profiles that further reinforced these narratives. *People*, for example, did a feature of Middleton, titled, "Kate's Baby Bump Diary!" with the additional subtitles, "Tons *of* Dazzling Photos!" and "Plus Her 10 Best Maternity Looks" (italics in original Zuckerman et al.). The cover photo is of Middleton, posed sideways, smiling broadly, and wearing a white dress with navy blue, large polka dots, a blue blazer, and Middleton is holding a black clutch purse under her pregnancy bump. In the cover story, the entire feature focuses on Middleton's "Top 10 Secrets" and lessons she can teach other pregnant women. In fact, Suzanne Zuckerman, Simon Perry, Monique Jessen, and Philip Boucher report, "Kate's Style Diary Her Top 10 Secrets! From hairstyles to hemlines, all about her tricks for looking great while dressing for two" (62). Again, framing her maternal position with her "princess" status, rule one is titled, "Fit for a Princess," and notes that Middleton also has to "face the challenge of accommodating her new body shape" (62). In doing so, rule two is, "Keep it Classic: Say hello to the new Jackie O" (63). Then, quoting British Maternity expert, Rosie Pope, Zuckerman et al. reveal to readers, "Kate reminds me of Jackie Onassis when she was pregnant. She's happy to show some leg with that 1960s vibe, but in general she covers up" (63).

Another theme of the feature is that Middleton has every right to "flaunt" her pregnant body because she has earned it through fitness and her "remarkable" ability to dress her "figure perfectly." As rule seven, puts it, "Maximize Your *Assets*" (italics in the text 65). Also including a picture of Middleton from the previous month, Zuckerman et al. write, "Six months pregnant, Kate pulled off this non-maternity floral Erdem frock (left) and thigh-grazing coat by Goat (above) while showing off her toned claves. 'She's got great legs,' Alexander says. The fitness enthusiast, who enjoys yoga, has every reason to flaunt the results. 'Kate does a remarkable job of dressing herself in silhouettes that flatter her figure perfectly,' Pennie says" (65).

Finally, rule eight, "Pregnant in Heels," which is accompanied by a picture titled "Still in Stilettos!" and shows Middleton in stiletto boots, a field hockey stick, and a blue-and-green plaid coat dress. Zuckerman et al. report, "That she fences with Prince William . . . shoots hoops in a Scottish arena and dusts off her field hockey skills at her former prep school (above)—often in 4-in. heels—is impressive. That she does so with a baby on board seems superhuman. But spiky shoes, it seems, are the spice of a royal life" (66). In addition to suggesting that Middleton has the "approved" (and not-racialized) right kind of assets to show off or flaunt—Middleton's toned calves and legs—media also positioned Middleton as having, "superhuman, perfect" style. And, this style is also "award-winning" maternity style. As Kelby McNally reports in another feature about Middleton: "SHE'S received countless amounts of awards for her maternity style since announcing her pregnancy in December, and it seems as though Kate Middleton's pregnancy glow is still working for her" (capitalization in original par. 1). This profile was even titled, "The Duchess of Cambridge claims top spot in favorite pregnant celebrity hairstyle poll" and concludes, "Pregnancy really seems to suit her. Her skin and hair look amazing and she's got her maternity wardrobe just right." (par. 6)

Finally, unlike Kardashian, whose maternal body responded immediately to being pregnant, Rebecca Adams notes, "Now that Kate Middleton *is finally showing*, we're pleased to report that she's dressing her baby bump in some lovely fashions" (emphasis added par. 1). Also discussing the same picture of Middleton at six-months pregnant that was noted in the *People* story, probably because it was the first time Middleton did not cover her bump in a coat, Adams continues, "At six months pregnant, Duchess Kate (we know that's not her real title, but it sounds cute) chose a printed Erdem frock for her visit to Willows Primary School in Manchester. The square neckline and three-quarter sleeves are *the prim and proper staple* we've come to expect from the 31-year-old, but the funky floral pattern was a nice change of pace. Not to mention this is the first time that we've seen the sizable bump without a cute coat shrouding it" (emphasis added par. 2). In these individual profiles of Middleton, the messages are clear: pregnancy suits her—her slender-pregnant body even allows her to still wear a nonmaternity dress—she is happy, comfortable, and she is the perfect maternity fashion icon with good taste, restraint, and class; in short, Middleton is the new Jackie O.

The reference to Jackie O is particularly significant given that the Kennedy family has long been considered "American Royalty," especially in relation to John Kennedy and Jacqueline (Jackie) Kennedy. And, even after she married Aristotle Onassis in 1968 and became Jackie Kennedy Onassis or "Jackie O," she was often still considered American royalty. By suggesting that Middleton was the new Jackie O, media were "arguing" that Middleton also had the same "effortless style and elegance" that Jackie O had had when she was pregnant with Caroline (a picture of which the "What to Expect" website included). As a result, when media positioned Middleton in this way in relation to the Kardashian family generally and Kim Kardashian specifically, who had earned "sometime satirical analogies to American versions of celebrity as royalty," media were implicitly reinforcing the argument that "celebrity as royalty" was fake, while also suggesting that Middleton was more like "American Royalty" than the American Kardashian. This confirms, again, that Kardashian's "celebrity as royalty" is inauthentic, even tasteless and fake, suggesting that only certain types of former ordinary women can be "authentic royalty," with the authentic maternal body and attitude.

Kardashian: The Squeezed-In Fashion Disaster

While individual media profiles portray Middleton as the perfect Jackie O, the individual profiles of Kardashian continue to work rhetorically to reinforce the theme that Kardashian is a pregnant fashion disaster who makes bad choices, as evidenced in her "wardrobe malfunctions." Interestingly, however, another critique that was often linked with Kardashian's unfortunate choices was Kardashian "squeezing" into "tight" clothes, an issue noted earlier. In another example, in a *hollywoodlife.com* video titled, "Kim Kardashian Baby Bump Fashion Disaster," Fuller and Melas again discuss Kardashian's maternity wear choices and style. Fuller begins, "So, it's another day and it's another outfit Kim Kardashian has squeezed herself into. I don't understand it. I don't think there is anything wrong with wearing, tight body-conscious clothing when you are pregnant, but Kim just looks so uncomfortable. These are very structured . . ." Melas responds, "I agree. She has the money to buy any type of outfit she wants and I don't know why she is squeezing into these outfits day after day." Fuller then concurs and suggests that Kardashian could be wearing more skimming maternity wear, if she just chose the right kind, which is followed by Melas saying, "She's so pretty. . . . She could look so much happier and comfy." In addition to reinforcing the idea that Kardashian is unhappy and uncomfortable and that looking attractive, even sexy, is now acceptable as long as the pregnant woman does so appropriately in body-skimming rather than squeezed-into maternity wear, this individual coverage also suggests that having money does not mean you have good taste—some things are priceless—an issue that also emerged in the wedding coverage of the two women and, again, something that media report Middleton seems to understand but Kardashian does not.

The idea that Kardashian continued to squeeze herself into maternity wear was even an issue in terms of her shoes. So, for example, a *Mail Online.com* report by Iona Kirby and Jade Watkins about Kardashian's footwear choices was titled, "Suffering for style! Heavily pregnant Kim Kardashian squeezes her swollen feet into perspex stilettos." This story is accompanied by several pictures of Kardashian's swollen feet and shoes. In one picture, of black "caged Givenchy heels,"—shoes with crisscrossing straps—the reader sees a picture of Kardashian's swollen feet, a picture that Kardashian was said to have tweeted, with her left foot in the shoe and appearing to bulge out of the straps, while her right foot is shoeless, swollen, and the crisscrossing pattern is embedded in her foot. Another photo that accompanies the story is of Kardashian in the "Perspex stilettos," which are stilettos that have a nude-color strap around the ankle, a clear Perspex cover over the foot, and are open-toed. Under the picture is the following commentary: "Suffering for style: Kim Kardashian squeezed her swollen feet into a pair of perspex stilettos as she ran errands and filmed her reality show in Los Angeles on Thursday" (par. 3). In short, this profile suggests that, even though she is pregnant, Kardashian is still trying to squeeze into—and suffering for it—her prepregnant priority: her Reality TV star life.

Kirby and Watkins also report of these shoes, "The 32-year-old's feet were so swollen that she barely managed to squeeze them into the footwear. Puffy, her ankles were also clearly suffering, even appearing severely pinched in the stylish shoes" (pars. 5 and 6). Finally, in the next paragraph, they also report "But Kim was keen to power on, strutting around while wearing another item of clothing that was very tight" (par. 7). This focus on her shoes and Kardashian's persistence in squeezing into her maternity style also reveals further Kardashian's excess, while also revealing Kardashian's inability to "give up" her prepregnancy life: she is so swollen in pregnancy that she has to squeeze into everything, including her shoes, and this is causing much suffering, but Kardashian is still "powering on" and trying to maintain her prepregnant Reality TV star life. And, again, even in the shoe battle, Kardashian loses: Middleton wears the perfect stiletto shoes to highlight her right-kind-of assets, while, again, Kardashian chooses shoes she "barely managed to squeeze into," which only highlight how swollen Kardashian is, her bad choices, her seeming unwillingness to let go of her prepregnancy life, and her inappropriate, even malfunctioning, maternity style. Thus, even though there were some media reports later in the women's pregnancies that pronounced Kardashian as finally confident and happy, these individual profiles continue to shape Kardashian's maternal position and maternity wear as pregnancy disasters and Kardashian as an unhappy, suffering pregnant woman who continues to squeeze herself into her prepregnancy-entrepreneur life and tasteless, odd, even strange, maternity wear, even though she can afford to do so differently.

The obsessive media focus on the women's maternity wear, shoes included, in both the individual profiles and comparisons reveal much about the connection between "dressing the bump" of the maternal body and perceptions about maternal attitude and future mothering. For Middleton, the profiles work rhetorically to suggest that her maternity wear is "appropriately" form-fitting and slimming, classic, sophisticated, and attractive but also still prim and proper, which means that Middleton's body and maternity style suggest that she has the right maternal attitude and, as a result, she is making all the right choices that "withstand the test of time," that withstand the cultural changes at the intersection of the post-second wave and neoliberal turns. On the other hand, for Kardashian, the profiles work rhetorically to suggest that her maternity wear is "inappropriately" a disaster, trendy, malfunctioning, too tight, and excessive, which means that Kardashian's body and maternity style suggest that she has the wrong maternal attitude and, as a result, she is making all the wrong choices that "do not withstand the test of time," that cannot withstand cultural changes at the epicenter of contemporary motherhood.

Middleton Prepping versus Kardashian Vacationing

A final key theme emerged in the Middleton-versus-Kardashian pregnancy battle that put the "finishing touches" on these slender-pregnant profiles making the case that Middleton embodied the perfect maternal position to emulate, while Kardashian embodied the maternal position that was an admonitory warning about maternal excess. And this discussion also served as code for media assessing Middleton as appropriately having "made the turn" to making her future mothering her priority above all else, while assessing Kardashian as inappropriately having not made the turn to making her future mothering her priority above all else. These assessments of the two women emerged late in their pregnancies when media began to focus on how the women were preparing for the birth of their babies; and, in this battle, the primary theme was that Middleton was prepping for her impending motherhood, even "nesting," while Kardashian was traveling, vacationing, and being "uprooted" and possibly irresponsible via her travels.

The *US Weekly* titled, "Countdown to Baby," for example, reported stories about how each woman was preparing for their impending births (O'Leary and Scobie). However, the cover photo features Middleton. Middleton is facing forward, smilingly broadly, holding a bouquet of flowers and wearing a green and white box coat and a brown hat. Near Middleton's right shoulder is a smaller picture of her standing sideways in a tangerine-color dress and coat of the same color but a darker shade of tangerine. The copy reads, "New bump photos." Below the smaller picture, we read, "Ditching the baby nurse, choosing a name, shopping for the nursery—inside Kate's preparations." In a column to the right, there are three smaller photos and story titles: a picture of Jennifer Aniston and Justin Theroux, "Wedding on Hold"; below that, a side-by-side picture of Reality TV stars and teen moms Farrah Abrahm and Jennelle Evans, "What Went Wrong. Teen Mom Monsters," and below that, a picture of Kardashian in a red, form-fitting, sleeveless dress; she is posed sideways and holding a camera. Below the picture, is the following title: "Beach Bump Photos: Kim's Greek Babymoon."

Visually and through the titles, the cover makes several arguments: first, unlike Kardashian, Middleton is prepping and preparing for the impending birth. Second, as is the pattern, Middleton is front and center and the featured happy and at ease celebrity mom; she is the real, even exemplar, pregnant celebrity mom, which is further confirmed by the length of the Middleton story in comparison to the Kardashian story inside the magazine: the Middleton story is five pages long, while the Kardashian story is a paragraph. Third, by placing Kardashian below but still in relation to reality teen mom stars, "teen mom monsters," Kardashian continues to be linked to her Reality TV roots and the discourse of fame that suggests that she too might be an awful ordinary mother like the teen mom reality stars.

Furthermore, inside the magazine, the ongoing theme that Kardashian's Reality TV star status is problematic in relation to her impending motherhood is also reconfirmed. In addition to being the featured celebrity pictorially on the cover, inside the issue, the cover story about Middleton is first and much longer, while the very short

Greek-vacation story about Kardashian comes after the Middleton story. Immediately following the Kardashian story is the teen mom story, which is titled, "Porn, drugs and plenty of denial: Inside the tragic downfall of Farrah Abraham and Jenelle Evans" (Abrahamson 72). The focus of the profiles is on how awful each teen mother is, and that both are still looking for fame and thrive "on the attention" they get in the media, including bad publicity (Abrahamson 72). Moreover, under the heading, "Hunger for Fame," Abrahamson reports, "Farrah wasn't happy with her waning fame. She thought a sex tape would increase her fame, like it did for Kim Kardashian" (Abrahamson 75). In other words, this story "re-reminds" readers about the "awful ordinary people" featured on Reality TV—those awful people "who make entrepreneurial bids for media exposure"— and explicitly links the awful celebrity teen mom Abraham to Kardashian. As a result, when *US Weekly* positions Kardashian in relation to the teen monster moms and then explicitly links Kardashian to Abraham and the discourse of fame associated both with Kardashian's rise to fame and her fame as a Reality TV star, the magazine is making the case implicitly and not so subtly for "guilt by association": the magazine suggests that Kardashian might be more like the teen monsters than like Middleton.

"Making the Turn" to Intensive Mothering: Middleton's Embrace versus Kardashian's Inability

That Kardashian is a celebrity and future mother of "a different caliber" in comparison to how Middleton is preparing for motherhood was also made clear in other media reports. In the "Count Down to Baby!" *US Weekly*, for example, readers learn the following about Middleton: "With Just two months left until the royal arrival, William and Kate are prepping the nursery, choosing a birth plan and picking names" (O'Leary and Scobie 62). In another cover story about Middleton, under a heading titled, "Kate Nests," readers learn that Middleton and Prince William are "spending as much time together as possible in Kate's final month, with Kate lightening her workload to only three outstanding engagements" (Grossbart 53). In popular parlance, *nesting* is commonly thought to be the time when pregnant women stay at home more, preparing, and getting ready for their child. When pregnant women are nesting, women are viewed as doing the very things that Middleton and William are described as doing: preparing the nursery, choosing a birth plan, and so on. Equally important, nesting late in pregnancy is also a way for a future mother to signal that she is prioritizing mothering above all else, especially for a first-time mother who has to shift from her unencumbered prepregnancy life to her new life as a mother. As such, nesting is the period when a pregnant woman embodies fully her maternal status and her nesting activities reveal that her priority is her future baby and impending motherhood, regardless of any other responsibilities.

In addition to her nesting at home, when she is out, Middleton is shown in the *US Weekly* feature also preparing for the impending birth. In one picture, Middleton is shown shopping with her mother for a portable crib, a "Moses basket," and readers also learn that the two women shopped for "baby buggies and car seats" (O'Leary and Scobie 65, 66). Moreover, in the first paragraph of the *US Weekly* feature, readers learn that Middleton spent the "afternoon at Naomi House Children's Hospice," and that "'Kate really engages with children. She's a natural. She's going to be a great mum.' Graham Buland of Hospice Charity Each Tells *US*" (O'Leary and Scobie 63). O'Leary and Scobie also report that Middleton is "fascinated by the life growing inside her and is full of questions . . . [and] devours parenting books as fast as Amazon can deliver them" (O'Leary and Scobie 62). In other words, as one heading in the article put it, Middleton's focus is almost exclusively on "Getting Ready" for the impending birth by preparing, nesting, and reading as much as she can, and, when out, she is either engaging in more preparations or spending time with children (O'Leary and Scobie 62). Thus, in addition to devoting time with children, Middleton continues to "get ready" for becoming a mother, while also being "fascinated" by her future child and is beginning to rely on "experts" to answer all of her parenting questions.

These media reports, then, suggest that Middleton has made the turn to embracing the new momism, the intensive mothering ideology. As noted in the Introduction, the intensive mothering ideology rests on three core set of beliefs and values: the insistence that no woman is complete until she has children; that women are the best caregivers of children; and that good mothers must devote their entire physical, emotional, and psychological beings to their children all day, every day. These three core beliefs also require mothers to develop professional-level skills, such as therapist, pediatrician, consumer products safety instructor, and teacher, in order to meet and treat the needs of children. Finally, the new momism also defines women first and foremost in relation to their children and encourages women to believe that mothering is the most important job for women, regardless of any success a woman might have had prior to motherhood. The late-in-pregnancy profiles of Middleton clearly suggest that Middleton has embraced these tenets as she nests, shops with her mother, is a "natural" with children, and in her commitment to reading as many books as possible to enhance her ability to develop the necessary professional-level skills required of a new mother. In short, she is a real future celebrity mom who has embraced the new momism.

Unlike Middleton, the same "Count Down to Baby!" *US Weekly* reports that Kardashian is on a Greek vacation with her family rather than nesting, instead of making the turn toward intensive mothering. In fact, Eric Anderson reports, "Every Kardashian under the sun was, well, under the sun when the family hit Greece" (70). Then, Anderson writes, "Opa! The Kardashian-Jenner clan (13 of them!) headed to Greece for a week of horseback riding, jet-skiing, and cruising the Mediterranean" (70). And, pictures of the clan doing so make up the rest of the story, including a picture of all thirteen in a large speed boat being filmed for the family's reality show, "Keeping up with the Kardashians" (Anderson 70). Clearly, this feature about Kardashian places Kardashian's Reality TV roots front and center, reminds readers about the over-the-top size of the family—13 of them!—and only notes that Kardashian is vacationing, maybe even working, given the filming of the vacation. Thus, unlike Middleton who is nesting, this media report suggested that Kardashian is not signaling that she is prioritizing mothering above all else nor is she embracing her impending future mothering; in fact, she might still be on the job as a Reality TV star, which means that the vacation might be fake and scripted.

The "YOU CALL THIS FAT?" *US Weekly* cover story about the Greek vacation and Kardashian's bikini-wearing, however, is an eight-page story and reveals much more detail about how Kardashian is managing her third trimester, while also further entrenching the theme that she has not yet embraced intensive mothering.

Under a heading titled, "Kim Kicks Back" and after noting that Kardashian's sisters are letting Kardashian relax, Grossbart also reports of Kardashian, "For workaholic Kim, that's a tall order" (56). Then, Grossbart notes, that Kardashian has "slashed her schedule in half," and the "reality star is also logging plenty of hours surfing mommy blogs. 'She reads up on how to prepare for life as a new mother,' says a source. 'She's terrified she won't know what to do!'" (56). Moreover, unlike Middleton who is shown with William, Kardashian is shown alone or surrounded by pictures of her family. Readers also learn "While not on the trip, Kim and Kanye are in constant contact by phone calls and texting. Kanye is her biggest cheerleader" (Grossbart 61). Grossbart then continues, "Other expectant parents may scoff at Kim and West's system, but the workaholics want to grind away at their projects before taking time off to enjoy their new family" (61). In short, while William and Middleton are "prepping the nursery, choosing a birth plan and picking names," *together*, and Middleton is already a natural with kids, Kardashian is alone, "grinding away" at work, "vacationing" (possibly skill working) with her large family, is not a natural with kids and, in fact, is terrified of her impending motherhood. Thus, while Kardashian is reported as consulting the experts also, her turn to doing so is out of fear rather than because she is a natural who is fascinated with the life inside of her and wants to develop the professional-level skills required of devoted good mothers.

Although there are some reports, like the above, that suggest Kardashian was cutting back on travel, there was still much discussion about whether she traveled too much throughout her pregnancy but especially during her last trimester. So, while readers learn that Middleton was cancelling engagements and limiting her travel as part of her preparation for the impending birth, media also discussed the fact that Kardashian might be traveling too much. So, for example, *huffingtonpost.com* "battle chart" notes: Kate: "Limits her traveling and royal engagements." Kim: "Travels to Miami, Paris, Los Angeles, NYC, back to Paris, back to L.A., heads to Rio de Janeiro, and then goes to London." Moreover, an *omg*! article about Kardashian was titled, "Kim Kardashian's Pregnant World Travels— Is It OK to Be Flying in Her Third Trimester?" (Gornstein). The article goes on to reveal that as long as the pregnancy has been "normal" and "risk-free," then it is acceptable to travel on flights that are no longer than five to six hours. The article closes, however, with an interview with Dr. Keith Eddleman, while also noting his expertise as director of obstetrics in the Department of Obstetrics, Gynecology and Reproductive Science at the Mount Sinai Medical Center in New York: "But many doctors frown on traveling in a third trimester simply because 'it separates you from your care provider'" (quoted in Gornstein par. 12). The doctor's—the "expert's"—warning is implied: although it is technically safe to travel, it is risky, possibly irresponsible, and doctors frown on the travel because it takes the pregnant woman away from her doctor. In short, it is safer to limit travel—to not travel back and forth from L.A. to Europe—to be at home and close to the doctor. Thus, the media concern about Kardashian's traveling too much, even late in her pregnancy, makes it clear that this is another way that she has not made her impending motherhood her priority and, instead, is powering on, grinding away, and continuing to squeeze into her unencumbered life, even though her birth is impending, while also engaging in risky, possibly irresponsible behavior; all of which suggests that Kardashian has not yet made mothering, children, and a commitment to following the advice of experts her priorities above all else, as Middleton has late in her pregnancy. And, as a result, only one conclusion can be drawn about Kardashian: she has yet to "make the turn" to embracing the new momism, which means she will be an awful ordinary bad future mother.

Conclusion

From the beginning of the obsessive media coverage of Middleton and Kardashian's pregnancies, the slender-pregnant celebrity mom profiles represented Middleton as the contained and disciplined maternal subject who also had effortless style and ease in her "Jackie-O-like-royal" pregnancy: from her tight-lipped and reluctant pregnancy announcement, disciplined (or not) eating, controlled and disciplined weight management, happy glow, lack of travel (and royal engagements), tasteful, attractive but still prim and proper "perfect" maternity wear, even her appropriately tasteful asset-revealing shoes, and appropriate impending nesting preparations. As a result, for Middleton pregnancy was just a small bump in the road in her waif-like maternal body and to her new identity as a future inten-sive mother, an identity that she embraced fully. In short, Middleton made all the right choices and managed both herself and pregnant maternal body perfectly. From the beginning, media represented Kardashian as an out of control, excessive, and racialized "other" maternal subject who also had an uncomfortable, unhappy "Real-ity-TV-star-like" pregnancy: from her Hollywood-style pregnancy announcement, excessive and cheap eating, uncontrolled and undis-ciplined weight management, fashion-disaster, even malfunctioning, maternity style, mostly unhappy and uncomfortable scowls, exces-sive, even possibly irresponsible, travel, and inability to stop work-ing, which also meant that Kardashian continued to try to squeeze into her prepregnancy life, including, even, her shoes. As a result, for Kardashian pregnancy was an "excessively large and possibly insur-mountable bump in the road" in her "whale-like" maternal body and to her new identity as a mother, an identity that she was unable to embrace fully. In short, Kardashian made all the wrong choices and mostly managed herself and her pregnant maternal body badly, even irresponsibly.

Consequently, in every battle or skirmish media reported between the two future first-time mothers, Middleton won. As such, the profiles also positioned Kardashian as an "admonitory warn-ing" about the consequences of awful ordinary future mothering done wrong, while also revealing *how* a bad excessive and over-the-top Reality TV star future mother makes all the wrong, tasteless, inappropriate, problematic, and bad choices in her body manage-ment, maternity wear, and lack of preparation for her impending motherhood. Middleton, on the other hand, was positioned as the exemplary ordinary future good mother who did everything right, while also revealing *how* a perfect post-second wave neoliberal good mother makes all the right, tasteful, appropriate, exemplary good choices in her body management, maternity wear, and appropriate preparation for her impending motherhood.

Moreover, as media reports positioned Middleton as the perfect winner and Kardashian as the scary loser, media also explored the boundaries between the real and scripted, the authentic and inau-thentic, classiness and trashiness and quality and nonquality of post-second wave neoliberal motherhood and intensified intensive future mothering today. In so doing, Middleton came out on the winning side of these battles also. As the analysis earlier shows, Kardashian's maternal body and subject position were positioned by media to represent anxiety and ambivalence about a racialized, excessive, inauthentic, possibly scripted, often trashy and tasteless, bad future motherhood that her pregnancy embodied and enacted as Kardashian made all the wrong and mostly tasteless or Hollywood-style choices throughout her pregnancy.

This means then that, unlike Middleton who is judged as a perfect ordinary future mother who has legitimately been made special because of her good choices, willingness to wait, body management, and appropriate turn to embracing an intensive mothering maternal subject position that reveals that she, indeed, will be a good future mother, Kardashian is judged as an awful ordinary future mother who is not special and is, in fact, a warning about impulsive excess, bad weight and body management, and an inability to make the turn to embracing an intensive mothering maternal subject position, all of which reveal that Kardashian, in fact, will be a bad future mother. Consequently, each woman's maternal body, style, and pregnancy combine to make the case for why, when making post-second wave neoliberal maternal choices, the better, more appropriate, authentic, tasteful, valuable, and real position is the post-second wave neoliberal princess with the perfect intensive maternal subject position and slender-pregnant, even waif-like, maternal body.

Accepting, Even Embracing, Post-Second Wave Split Subjectivity

In exploring how media positioned Middleton and Kardashhian in a battle in relation to one another, one of the central questions also addressed in this chapter has been: Why were these two pregnant celebrity women covered so obsessively and together at the expense of other pregnant celebrities? As I have tried to show, this was the case, in part, because the two women represented two ends of the post-second wave neoliberal gender continuum: a perfect post-second wave real-life princess and a post-second wave neoliberal excessive Reality TV star, which also allowed media to reflect and negotiate broader gender, race, cultural, class, and family values intertwined with the post-second wave and neoliberal turns. As I have also tried to show, then, the battle between these two women is also a morality

tale for all first-time mothers who are also post-second wave neoliberal women who came of age within the post-second wave and
neoliberal turns: women who took advantage of post-second wave
gains and who also must learn to mother in a world that, as Peggy
Orenstein puts it, is "half-changed," where women are still primarily
responsible for childrearing, childcare, and privatized solutions for
both family-life management and any work-life struggles, regardless
of how their unencumbered relationships worked prior to becoming mothers and regardless of whether they continue to work in the
public sphere after becoming a mother. Thus, the slender-pregnant
profiles of the Middleton-Kardashian battle also work to train and
discipline post-second wave neoliberal future mothers to live within
this half-changed gender world and to accept, even embrace, their
maternal responsibilities, including mostly unchanged gender-based
assumptions still embedded in the private sphere (including, clearly,
that post-second wave beneficiaries still want to be princesses with
"fairy-tale weddings").

To put it another way, as I argued in the Introduction, once a
post-second wave neoliberal woman becomes a mother, she has a
split subject position or subjectivity: her life is split between much
gender equity in the public sphere that unencumbered privileged
men and women experience and ongoing gender-based and privatized inequity in the private sphere due to her role as primary caregiver of children and for family life. Consequently, when a post-second wave woman becomes a mother, especially a first-time mother,
she also must make the turn from gender-equitable expectations as
an unencumbered post-second wave woman to embracing an intensified intensive mothering position and ideology that not only hold
her responsible for all of family life but also ask her to embrace her
maternal role intensively. As such, I suggest that the slender-pregnant celebrity mom profiles analyzed here *are now the first step* in
that training: by focusing on the maternal body as the symbol and
embodiment of future mothering, slender-pregnant profiles construct the maternal body as the "weapon of choice" in making the
case that the measure of a good future mother is tied to *how* she
manages her pregnant maternal body—how she manages her weight
gain, her maternity style, her comfort and happiness with her pregnant body, and how she prepares for her impending birth—and, as I

show in the next chapter, these profiles are also the first step toward encouraging good body management to train for a third shift of body work postpartum.

The media focus on who has the best pregnancy between Middleton and Kardashian, then, is also a question about which of the two women made the best turn to her future intensive maternal position; who is going to be the best future post-second wave neoliberal intensive mother who has also accepted, even embraced, her future post-second wave split subjectivity? While media tried to answer that question and often did so by noting "how different" these two women were, as I have tried to show in this chapter, it is Middleton and Kardashian's similarity as former ordinary post-second wave beneficiaries first then their different positions on the post-second wave gender continuum second that is what makes these two celebrities so important in crystallizing the slender-pregnant profiles. Indeed, because they were both ordinary post-second wave beneficiaries who then became famous, they are easier for readers of the profiles to identify with in many ways.

Even more important, however, is the fact that they were both pregnant for the first time, unlike Busy Philipps or Jessica Simpson, for example. As such, both Middleton and Kardashian needed to make the turn from unencumbered post-second wave beneficiaries to post-second wave neoliberal mothers. As such, obsessively covering how their pregnancies unfolded allowed the media to craft a morality tale about *how and what* the perfect post-second neoliberal mother *should do* in making the turn toward intensive mothering demands and a future split subjectivity via Middleton, while also crafting a warning about *how and what* should not be done and why powering on in unencumberedness is problematic with the morality tale being that this kind of maternal position is fake, often scripted, excessive, and an over-the-top inauthentic post-second wave neoliberal mothering that will be met with excessive, even over-the-top, shaming and criticism.

In short, the obsessive focus on Middleton and Kardashian's battle also provided media the opportunity to crystallize a response to a core tension that undergirds post-second wave neoliberal mothering today. That core tension is the belief that women should enjoy the gains for equality and independence fought for and won by second wave feminisms, but not at the expense of their obligations at home in the private sphere once they become mothers; obligations that have intensified as the family unit in general and motherhood in particular have become the primary neoliberal institution for privatizing costs and social responsibility for all social ails—from work-life struggles to crime to disease and even economic depression. Thus, slender-pregnant profiles need to lay the groundwork to train post-second wave beneficiaries to become post-second wave neoliberal mothers mothering at these conflicting and contradictory crosscurrents, while also encouraging mothers to reconcile the core tension in ways that allow them to embrace rather than reject their split subjectivity.

Moreover, it is important to note that this training is especially important for first-time mothers because becoming a mother for the first time is the crucial moment when a post-second wave beneficiary must also make the turn to embracing the intensive mothering ideology—the new momism—and neoliberal privatization of all social ills, but most especially family and work-life struggles. Thus, while the structure of celebrity mom profiles have changed to accommodate the post-second wave and neoliberal turns, the importance of the profiles have not, and slender-pregnant profiles, along with the postpartum profiles I analyze in the next chapter, continue to be the most influential media form to sell the new momism and its core principles, while also working, today, to train, discipline, and *prepare* mothers to embrace the new momism *prior to becoming a mother*.

I also argue, then, that this case study suggests that slender-pregnant celebrity mom profiles have also changed to add a "preparatory" focus on the maternal body in slender-pregnant profiles to train mothers to accept, even embrace, the post-second wave split subjectivity that will emerge postpartum and undergirds the post-second wave crisis in femininity. The analysis here reveals that this is the case because, if a post-second wave split subjectivity emerges after a woman becomes a mother, gives birth, then, how a woman manages her pregnancy reveals much about how well positioned she will be to manage both her post-second wave split subjectivity and the future post-second wave crisis in motherhood. In other words, if a good post-second wave neoliberal mother is devoted and embraces the notion that maternity is still her responsibility, she must begin to prepare for that responsibility, not in a pre-second wave way, that is, as if maternity is her destiny, but instead in a post-second wave way, that is, as if mothering is her post-second wave neoliberal *maternal choice*. And, slender-pregnant profiles are now the first step in preparing mothers to become good post-second wave neoliberal mothers who make good maternal choices postpartum.

Consequently, by pitting these two women in a battle, media were also able to reflect on and negotiate gender issues at the crosscurrents of our neoliberal and post-second wave context and begin to train pregnant women to accept, even embrace, individualized and privatized solutions, specifically how and what should happen when unencumbered post-second wave women have to reconcile how their gender equity in the public sphere does not match ongoing inequitable gender roles in the private sphere, once a woman becomes a mother. I suggest, then, that, when media positioned Middleton as the perfect future mother while also positioning Kardashian as the warning about what happens to a pregnant woman who is unable to keep herself and her maternal body under control and who is also struggling to make the turn to devoting herself to prioritizing her future mothering above all else, media also positioned Kardashian's excess as the excess of "too much" unencumbered gender equity in the public sphere—she is powering on, grinding on, going it alone, and trying to squeeze into her unencumbered life, still.

Whereas in a neoliberal context one might think that continuing to power on as an entrepreneur is a good thing, it is not for women in the context of maternity because women must still embrace their responsibility as the primary parent. Kardashian, then, is also a warning about too much or excessive gender equality in the context of maternity. The moral of the Kardashian warning, then, is this: if a post-second wave beneficiary continues to power on, or grind away at work, then, she will fail to embrace her ongoing gender responsibilities once the children arrive; in short, to be colloquial, late pregnancy is "where the rubber meets the road," and this is beginning of when, as Crittenden would put it, "the egalitarian office party is over." Because celebrity mom profiles have always been, and remain today, the most influential media form to sell the new momism and a new mother must be trained to accept and embrace ongoing gender-based inequity in the private sphere, the slender-pregnant profiles have crystallized via Middleton and Kardashian to reveal *how* and *what* must be done during pregnancy to do so, while also providing a warning about what happens if a pregnant woman fails to do so by powering on or grinding away in the public sphere: she will be shamed and ridiculed.

Moreover, as the analysis of Kardashian also reveals, when a pregnant woman fails to make the turn to embracing her new maternal position, she will be subject to attack, while her maternal body, if it does not adhere to the slender-pregnant norm, will be "the target of viscous fat jokes and incentive comments." The viciousness of the attacks against Kardashian and her maternal body reveal, in fact, just how ferociously a racialized nonslender pregnant woman will be attacked, both morally and via fat shaming, when she and her maternal body are unable to make the "necessary" turn toward slender pregnancy, good maternal body management, good future mothering, and accepting the post-second wave split subjectivity. This suggests, then, that media also focused on these two women in particular and at the expensive of other pregnant celebrity moms because they are extremes to pull all women toward the reconciliation Middleton and her maternal body represent and away from the failed reconciliation Kardashian and her maternal body represent.

Consequently, even though contemporary women might not be famous nor able to look like or have the resources that Middleton and Kardashian do, by situating these two celebrities in a comparative battle, these slender-pregnant profiles push women to be more like Middleton and her appropriate, authentic, tasteful, effortless and comfortable reconciliation between post-second wave gains in the public sphere and inequitable and ongoing gender inequity in the private sphere as she prepares to become a mother. At the same time, these slender-pregnant profiles also push women away from, while also warning them about, Kardashian's inappropriate, inauthentic, often tasteless and problematic inability to reconcile post-second wave gains in the public sphere and ongoing inequitable responsibilities in the private sphere and her inability to make the turn toward her impending intensive mothering position.

As such, these slender-pregnant profiles prepare pregnant women, especially first-time mothers, to accept, even embrace, their split subjectivity and to make the turn to embracing the new momism, while also encouraging good maternal body management to prepare mothers to engage in postpartum body work. As a result, as I show in the next chapter, these slender-pregnant profiles are also the first preparatory step to prepare postpartum women to accept and engage in the post-baby body work that is now necessary both to energize and solve their second-shift responsibilities and struggle to have it all. Thus, I now turn to analyzing how step two works rhetorically to train postpartum women to engage in the now-required third shift of postpartum body work to solve the post-second wave crisis in femininity and to erase the difference maternity continues to make in women's lives today.

3

Step Two—Being Bikini-Ready Moms

Postpartum Celebrity Mom Profiles

The proof, after all, is in the bikini.
—"My Body is Back" Kevin O'Leary, 56

Have the Baby, Keep the Body (And make it [the postpregnant body] better).
—Australian Women's Health Bump

Bye, bye baby bumps! Hello, hot bodies.
—"Celeb Bodies After Baby" Stacie Anthony and
Molly McGonigle, image 1

While both Kate Middleton and Kim Kardashian were both due in mid-July, Kardashian delivered her baby five weeks early due to preeclampsia, all of which was covered on her reality TV show "Keeping up with the Kardashians." Middleton, on the other hand, carried to term and gave birth in mid-July. As with all celebrity mom births, media focused on the first sighting of both women post-partum in what is now commonly referred to as a *post-baby reveal* or *post-baby debut*. Initially, media did not have long to wait with Middleton: a day after giving birth, she appeared on the steps of the hospital with her son and William. Her appearance garnered much media attention, in part, because of Middleton's appearance: she wore a blue dress that featured an empire waist and a white polka-dot print; the empire waist revealed her postpartum "bump," what media sometime call the *mummy tummy*. Middleton's willingness to appear so quickly postpartum, while looking so happy and at ease, even though she had a mummy tummy, was lauded by many. So, for example, *hollywoodlife.com* ran a story titled, "Kate Middleton: Glowing Beauty As New Mom Leaves Hospital" (Baez). Rebbeca English at the *Mail Online.com* wrote an article titled, "So proud to show off her mummy tummy: Mothers hail Kate's decision not to hide her post-baby bump." English also informed readers that:

> But for the mothers watching around the world as the Duchess of Cambridge walked out on to the steps of the Lindo Wing yesterday, the real delight was her "mummy tummy." That neat bump was the only thing which gave away the fact Kate had given birth to an 8lb 6oz boy just a day earlier. And the glowing duchess clearly felt no need to hide it, a decision praised immediately by mothers' groups. Netmums founder Siobhan Freegard said the duchess had dispelled the "myth that all mothers should be perfect post-partum." "In a couple of minutes on the steps of the Lindo Wing Kate has done more for new mums' self-esteem than any other role model," she said. "Sadly, too many celebrities often have ultra-fast tummy tucks or strap themselves down to emerge in tiny size six jeans, leaving everyone else feeling inadequate. Kate shows what a real mum looks like—and natural is beautiful." (pars. 3–8)

Although her first appearance did seem to challenge the need to appear quickly slender postpartum, it is significant that, even in this report, English noted that her mummy tummy was the only indication that Middleton had just given birth; unstated was the fact that, because she had had a "perfect" slender pregnancy, the only remaining evidence was the lingering postpartum bump or mummy tummy.

Even more important, however, was what happened when she was three-months postpartum. Middleton had a public appearance at a charity event. In a story titled, "Kate Middleton Flashes Flat Stomach 3 Months After Baby!" and noting, "Yeah, we're starting to think Kate Middleton never had a baby in there!" a *toofab.com* article continues, "The Duchess of Cambridge flashed her ridiculously flat stomach while playing volleyball today during a public appearance at Sportaid Athlete Workshop in London" (pars. 1 and 2). Implicitly recognizing and lauding her slender pregnancy, the *toofab* report continues, "To be fair, unlike some stars, Kate didn't really gain any additional weight while she was pregnant—and the day after she gave birth, she *almost* looked exactly like she did before she got knocked up!" (italics in original par. 5). The short report closes by pitting Middleton's quickly slender body against other celebrities with a photo feature embedded in the article titled, "Post-Baby Bods—Before & After!" "Not everybody has it as easy as the Duchess—check out the gallery above to see more pregnancy Before & Afters" ("Kate Middleton Flashes" par. 6). Thus, while Middleton's mummy tummy might have briefly challenged the norms for a post-baby reveal, given her slender pregnancy and the fact that she quickly adhered to a quickly slender norm, as I show, with the exception of her first appearance, Middleton's postpartum body also became a "perfect" quickly slender postpartum maternal body.

Unlike Middleton and unsurprisingly given the fat shaming she endured and the fact that she delivered early due to preeclampsia, Kardashian disappeared from the public eye initially postpartum. An August 2014 *US Weekly* cover titled, "Tortured by her Body," had the subtitle "WHY KIM'S HIDING," which was then followed with this sentence: "She's lost 30lbs in 2 months—but the new mom won't leave her house until she gets her bikini body back" (O'Leary). Other media reported that she was seen occasionally, while still noting how unusual it was for Kardashian to be out of the public eye. As Justin Ravitz, for example, reports "Kim Kardashian's post-baby evolution continues. Over three months after the premature birth of daughter North West, the suddenly scarce reality star, 32, made another rare, low-key outing in Los Angeles on Wednesday, Sept. 18. Heading into City Hall with her assistant, the first-time mom kept things supremely casual in a loose gray t-shirt, an open denim button-down and baggy grey combat pants. Deflecting flashing cameras with sunglasses, Kardashian [is] still sporting blonde hair and wore little-to-no makeup" (par. 1.) However, at four-months postpartum, Kardashian's post-baby "come back," began. Kardashian posted a selfie of her postpartum body. A *Yahoo! Celebrity* article titled, "Warning: dangerous curves ahead!" reports, "Four months after giving birth,

Kim Kardashian is feeling confident enough to show off her post-baby body, and the only way we can describe it is bootylicious" (pars. 1–2). Next, readers learn, "The new mom snapped a mirror selfie—one of her favorite pastimes before getting pregnant with daughter North West—in which she is wearing a very revealing white bathing suit. Not only does the sexy shot show sideboob, but it also puts the blonde's famous backside on full display" (par. 3).

At five-months postpartum, Kardashian revealed her postpartum bikini body in a December 2014 *US Weekly* cover titled, "MY BODY IS BACK!" Below that, also in yellow, was the following: "No gimmicks, no surgery!" Then, in black, "Kim slams the fat bullies and gets her sweet revenge." In the cover photo, Kardashian is wearing a white, string bikini, and facing the camera directly and smiling. This is accompanied by smaller picture of her in same white string bikini, and she is facing sideways. Below it is the subtitle, "Exclusive New Photos!" On the first page of the cover story are two pictures: one is a small before photo in June of Kardashian largely pregnant in a gray, snake-skin-like bikini, while the second, after and larger photo also features her in the white bikini. Also titled, "My Body's Back!" readers learn in the first paragraph, "How sweet it is! Kim Kardashian debuts her bikini body five months after welcoming daughter North—and it's better than ever" (O'Leary 53). Equally important, the June 2, 2014, *People* magazine cover story, "Most Talked about Bodies of 2014," had a picture of Kardashian in the white string bikini and declared it one of the "Body Moments of the Year" (119).

Despite the fact that media had relentlessly compared Kardashian and Middleton in relation to one another and vilified Kardashian as a warning about an excessive, racialized pregnant maternal body while positioning Middleton as the perfect slender-pregnant celebrity mom, postpartum images and media coverage of the two women are consistent with media coverage of celebrity moms postpartum and confirm the connection between the preparatory slender-pregnant profiles with the postpartum profiles: the entire focus postpartum is the debut of the quickly slender, even bikini-ready, postpartum maternal body, which both Middleton and Kardashian swiftly conformed to postpartum. In fact, today media are saturated with postpregnant celebrity mom profiles and images: magazine covers and articles, gossip websites, and even on television.

In all of these media formats, pictures abound of postpregnant celebrity moms looking slender and fit shortly after giving birth and highlight celebrity moms' quickly slender, even bikini-ready, bodies.

In addition to Kardashian's postpartum bikini reveal, for example, the *OK* magazine cover story, already noted in the Introduction, also features celebrity Kendra Wilkinson-Baskett in a blue bikini holding her eight-week-old son, Hank (Bass). In keeping with the extremely fast weight loss and return to the slender body, the *MSN Wonder Wall* reveals of Holly Madison, "Just three months after giving birth, Holly debuted her svelte post-baby bod in Las Vegas— and, no that taut tummy is no illusion" (Anthony and McGonigle image 16). Moreover, in another example, the *omg!* website declares, "Jennifer Garner Debuts Post-Baby Body!" Describing her after the birth of her second child, in a picture of Garner with her three-year-old daughter, Violet, readers also learn, "That was fast! Jennifer Garner showed off her slim post-baby body on Tuesday—just two weeks after giving birth to Seraphina" ("Jennifer Garner" par. 1). While neither Garner nor Nicole Richie were in bikinis, *omg!* also profiled Richie's fast return to a slender body after the birth of her second child: "One week after welcoming son Sparrow, Nicole Richie is back to her svelte self. Wearing a flowy maxi dress, the mother of two, 27, debuted her post-baby body Wednesday while running errands in Los Angeles with daughter Harlow, 20 months" ("Nicole Richie" par. 1).

In this chapter, I analyze quickly slender celebrity mom profiles like the examples just noted. Whereas in the last chapter I argued that the slender-pregnant maternal body reveals the right kind of future mothering and the necessary turn to accepting, even embracing, the post-second wave split subjectivity and an even more intensive new momism, in this chapter, in continuing to explore *how* celebrity mom profiles work today, I contend that the right kind of postpartum maternal body now reveals the right kind of post-second wave crisis management for contemporary mothers.[1] Moreover, I also contend that understanding *how* the quickly slender, even bikini-ready, body works rhetorically adds important insights into both how celebrity mom profiles and the new momism are continuing to develop and shape the contemporary rhetorical situation of motherhood, while also providing more-specific solutions to contemporary mothers about how to manage the contemporary crisis in

femininity through a third shift of body work and ideological messages embedded in those practices.

As a result, I also suggest that postpartum celebrity mom profiles continue to negotiate broader gender, race, class, and family anxieties related to contemporary mothers' ability to have it all
at the crosscurrents of the post-second wave and neoliberal turns.
Indeed, as I noted in the Introduction, both the new momism and
early celebrity mom profiles assume that contemporary mothers are
also second-wave beneficiaries who are free to make any maternal
choice that they want, regardless of whether any particular woman is
a feminist or not. Nonetheless, as the new momism has become even
more intensive, conversations about how difficult it remains to have
it all continue to emerge. Indeed, as I also noted in chapter 1, Anne-
Marie Slaughter's *Atlantic Monthly* cover article, "Why Women
Still Can't Have It All" and Edruado Porter's June 12, 2012, *New
York Times* article, "Motherhood Still a Cause for Pay Inequity," and
the various responses to both, for example, reveal that women are
still finding it difficult to have it all, and that it may be, in fact, that
women still cannot have it all. Given that celebrity mom profiles
have been the most important media vehicle for promoting and reinforcing the new momism—that relationship has not changed and
instead has only become more entangled—as the second iteration of
celebrity mom profiles emerge, these profiles must respond both to
the intensification of the new momism and this larger conversation.

In doing so, I contend and the analysis that follows shows, in
fact, that postpartum celebrity mom profiles have developed a new
response to the broader cultural anxieties about "juggling it all": an
even more entrenched post-second wave neoliberal understanding
of maternal choice fueled by an energizing third shift of body work
within the context of the neotraditional family. Thus, my larger
argument in this chapter is that the quickly slender, even bikini-
ready, maternal body promoted in postpartum profiles also works as
a rhetorical device to strategically manage the post-second wave crisis in femininity in ways that draw on post-second wave neoliberal
empowerment to reestablish mothering, beauty, and body work as
the most important components of maternal femininity, while also
mobilizing a third shift of body work as the individualized, privatized, and now more-specific energizing solution to manage the
post-second wave crisis within neotraditional family configurations,

which supports and justifies the ongoing gender-based division of household labor and functions ideologically and at the body level to erase the difference maternity continues to make in women's lives. This means, then, that I also argue that postpartum celebrity mom profiles continue the trajectory begun in the slender-pregnant profiles of making the maternal body *the primary solution and postfeminist management tool*—the "weapon of choice"—for managing the difficulties of contemporary motherhood at the crosscurrents of the post-second wave and neoliberal turns. To put it another way: I suggest that postpartum celebrity mom profiles are the second step in the process of offering privatized and individualized maternal body solutions for managing the post-second wave crisis in femininity. Consequently, in this chapter, I evaluate the new postpregnant quickly slender, even bikini-ready, body as a rhetorical phenomenon within the broader context of and cultural anxieties associated with the profiles, the intensified new momism and the post-second wave crisis in femininity.

Quickly Slender Body Analysis: "Bye, Bye Baby Bumps! Hello, Hot Bodies."

Although having a fit body is not new to postpartum celebrity mom profiles nor is the job requirement for celebrity women to have fit and slender bodies to be considered viable female celebrities, what *is new* is the more pronounced focus on the postpartum body of the celebrity mom in post-baby reveals, the new imperative for a quickly slender, even bikini-ready, body, and the fact that both celebrity mothering and children are secondary and/or completely ignored now in the profiles. Understanding just how important, in fact, the postpartum maternal body has become in celebrity mom profiles is hard to overstate. As the website *Popeater* puts it: "There is no question about it—celebrity baby stories sell. But recently post-baby body reveals have become such a big magazine staple, they'll stop at nothing to scoop the story" (James par. 2).[2] Moreover, as McRobbie ("Yummy Mummies") writes, while also reminding readers that celebrity moms have the means to buy childcare to train with a personal trainer, "In recent months the svelte figure of the high-income yummy mummy who can squeeze into size six jeans a couple of weeks after giving birth, with the help of a personal trainer, has become a favourite front-cover image in the celebrity weeklies" (par. 1).

In order to continue to address the how question—How does the quickly slender body work rhetorically?—I unpack the themes that have emerged in quickly slender, even bikini ready, postpartum celebrity mom profiles[3]: "bouncing back: faster and better," "the before-and-after format," "the third shift of body work," "debuting the new, even better postpartum body to be a 'sexy' mom," and "not denying women's reproductive capacity: rather, erasing any signs of pregnancy and maternity." I argue that these themes reveal that, in addition to continuing to refine and intensify intensive mothering standards and expectations, the shift to the quickly slender body shows that body work is becoming a new core and required fourth tenet of the new momism. As such, the new momism now suggests that the solution to mothers' post-second wave crisis in femininity is to engage in more and faster body work to erase any visible signs of maternity on the postpartum body, while also entangling the neo-liberal solution of body work with a hegemonic neotraditional family formation that also denies the difference maternity continues to make in women's lives today.

Bouncing Back: Faster and Better

As the body of the celebrity is becoming the focal point of postpartum celebrity mom profiles, having "just" a fit body is no longer the norm; instead, celebrity moms need to "bounce back" more quickly to a new, even better body. Feminist scholars primarily in sociology (Cunningham; Dworkin and Wachs; Jette; Pitts-Taylor) have established that bouncing back after pregnancy is central to pregnancy advice in women's fitness magazines. Indeed, in their work on pregnancy fitness advice, Dworkin and Wachs argue, "Regaining control of the unruly pregnant form is normalized in the pursuit of an openly stated central goal: to return to one's former size" (115). As the last chapter revealed, the primary preparatory route toward that goal is slender pregnancy and good pregnant body management. Previously, however, bouncing back was primarily tied to women "recovering" their prepregnant body. Moreover, rather than profiling new celebrity moms months or even several years after they give birth and surrounded by pastels and suffused in white light,[4] as they were done previously, celebrity moms are now quickly "debuting" new, better postpartum bodies, often in bikinis and sans their children. In other words, rather than *only recover* their prepregnant body, the new quickly slender profiles suggest that celebrity moms need both to *bounce back faster* and, second, *even better* than before. Thus, simply recovering is no longer the openly stated goal and instead a new, improved, and better body is the goal.

In addition to the Kardashian postpartum bikini cover photo and story titled, "MY BODY IS BACK!" that suggests that her postpartum body is "better than ever," another recent example of quickly slender and improved bikini-ready celebrity moms is a *Harpersbizaar.com* article, written by Christine Lennon and titled, "BETTER BODY AFTER BABY," with a subtitle sentence, "Legions of alpha moms are emerging from their post-pregnancy figure slimmer and trimmer than ever." In the first paragraph, readers learn, "Who hasn't seen the pictures? The snaps of Miranda Kerr's infinite legs gliding through the airport with baby Flynn perched on one hip, J. Lo sleek and six-packed in a Lanvin bikini after the birth of her twins and Jessica Alba with her sinewy arms toting her daughters to the park: They're proof that women can come out of the postpartum fog as Mom 2.0, a leaner, faster, stronger version of their prepregnancy selves" (par. 1). To prove further this point, on the second page, three side-by-side pictures of celebrities at pools, two of whom are in bikinis, are embedded at the end of the article.

Moreover, earlier in the article, even though Lennon later acknowledges that it might not be as easy as model Arizona Muse suggests, she does quote her when Muse says, "'I think my body was better after I had a child, actually,' Muse said in an interview. 'I remember my mom saying that after you have a baby you get really thin. You're breast-feeding and you're busy and you're tired'" (par. 3). In yet another example, just shy of one-month postpartum, media reports emerged about singer Beyonce postpartum. In one such media report, which is accompanied by a picture of a slender-looking Beyonce in a red, form-fitting dress with vertical ruching pleats and a plunging neckline, the reader learns "The Queen B is back, and she's better than ever. On Monday night, Beyonce stepped out in public for the first time since the birth of Blue Ivy Carter on Jan. 7" (Giantis par. 1).

After the birth of her second child, in another example, a five-months postpartum Jessica Simpson was featured on the cover of *OK! USA* magazine. The cover photo has a before-and-after format. The larger photo shows Simpson in a black form-fitting dress, with her hand resting on either side of her waist, which highlights her small waistline. To her left is a smaller image of her slightly slumped over, in black workout clothes, and to right of the image is, "Before 195 lbs" with a white arrow pointing to the cover photo. Between the two pictures is the following: "70lb weight loss!" Finally, in large yellow lettering and all caps, "HOW I GOT MY BODY BACK!" Inside the story, also titled, "How I Got MY BODY BACK!," opens with another before-and-after photo. Above the before picture, the copy reads, "Having one pregnancy under her belt 'made Jessica's approach to her weight loss much more effective,' an insider tells OK!" (Beetman 4). The article also reveals to readers, "With her spectacular post-baby weight loss, Jessica Simpson is happier and healthier than ever" (Beetman 5). Thus, not only is Simpson's body better postpartum, she has become a better person: she is happier and healthier.

In keeping with the new imperative to bounce back more quickly and achieving an even better body after pregnancy, an *US* cover story also reveals, "Stars' Flat Abs Secrets, Get Thin Fast, How They Get their Best Bikini Body after Baby" (Grossbart). The cover story features celebrity moms Gwen Stefani after her second pregnancy, Jennifer Lopez, Ashlee Simpson-Wentz, Heidi Klum, Britney Spears, and Christina Aguilera after her first pregnancy. The cover, however, features Spears and Stefani in two pieces, while Alba and Aguilera are shown in short, form-fitting minidresses in the lower middle of the cover. Inside, the story is titled, "How Stars Get Thin, Woa, baby! Learn how these sexy moms achieved their best bodies ever" (Grossbart 44). Inside, in describing her new postpartum body, Aguilera says of her postpartum body, "I'm tighter and stronger" and she has "gotten even tauter with a low-sugar diet and 90 minute toning sessions five days a week" (Grossbart 47). Thus, the quickly slender profiles also now reveal that postpartum celebrity moms' bodies are even better, sometimes even stronger, postpartum.

Children as Props or Secondary

Also continuing the theme of being healthy and fit, postpartum pro-files also suggest that readers should admire or applaud celebrity moms' better, more improved bodies—their "Mom 2.0" bodies. In a *huffingtonpost.com* article titled, "Celebrity Bikini Bodies After Baby: Stars Looking Fit, Healthy And Fab Post Kids," for example, read-ers learn, "Kristin Cavallari showed off her perfect post-baby bikini body in Mexico this week, just eight months after giving birth to her baby boy Camden. Similarly, Molly Sims flaunted a perfect figure in Cabo last week, only nine months after son Brooks was born" (par. 1). Readers also learn, "And though the issue of baby weight and los-ing the pounds after delivery is a touchy and private matter, we can't help but admire these in-the-spotlight moms for their killer phy-siques. Whether stripping down to their swimsuits merely months after their babies were born or a few years later, these ladies deserve all the applause for keeping themselves in such great shape" (par. 2). In the twenty-three images that are also embedded in the arti-cle, only three pictures show celebrities with their children and all of these are with the celebrities walking on the beach with or holding their child; the other twenty photos show the celebrity mom alone and in a bikini or a revealing one-piece bathing suit. In these images, yet again, there is no discussion of celebrities' mothering, and when children do appear, they are also only secondary images or "props" in the focus on celebrities' postpartum bodies.

Yet another example of children as props or secondary is the 2010 *OK Weekly* cover story and photo of Kendra Wilkinson-Bas-kett,[5] which features her holding son, Hank, in the crook of her left arm. The title of the cover is, "My Body after Baby," which is fol-lowed by "How I Lost 25 lbs in 8 Weeks" and "My Easy Diet Fit-ness Secrets Will Work For You, Too!" On page one of the cover story, which is flanked by two pictures of Kendra in her bikini, one of her alone and another picture of holding, Hank, the title reads, "How Kendra got her body back" (Bass 32). This is juxtaposed with a picture in the lower right corner of a pregnant Kendra, with the description, "A very pregnant Kendra enjoys her baby shower—and a giant jar of pickles—in LA" (Bass 32). After being asked if getting back to the gym was tough, her response is, "I actually did a better job working and working up a sweat than I did before the baby!" (Bass 35). Thus, this profile only uses Hank as a prop and focuses entirely on Wilkinson-Baskett's body bounce back and her even better body work and postpartum body.

More Pregnancies = Even Better Postpartum Bodies

Moreover, even though many women believe that each pregnancy takes more time to recover from and that each pregnancy does more "damage" to the postpartum body, this is not the case in postpartum profiles. Indeed, quickly slender celebrity mom profiles suggest that one of the benefits of subsequent pregnancies is that celebrities become even better at recovering fast and have even better bodies with each subsequent pregnancy. In the *OK USA* cover story about Simpson, for example, readers learn "'Jessica's weight-loss journey was a total breeze this time around,' a close family pal tells OK!. Adds an insider, 'she has her diet under control, she knows her recipes, learns not to overindulge when she's out and she has downloaded the Weight Watchers app on her phone. It really has made things so easy'" (Beetman 4). In yet another example, in describing actress Sarah Rafferty, Donna on the USA Network hit *Suits*, Lennon reports that Rafferty was three-weeks postpartum when she was booked for the first photo shoot of the show's second season. Lennon then reveals to readers that Rafferty said, "'I was literally sitting on a bag of ice when I got the call about the shoot,' she says. Nine weeks after her second daughter was born, she was back on camera looking sleek. 'I was smarter about food the second time,' says Rafferty, who did Pilates, light weights, and cardio up until three weeks before her delivery. She got the okay to exercise two weeks after. 'My doctor said, 'If your boobs can handle it, do it.'" (pars. 9 and 10). The Simpson profile also reveals that Simpson's second pregnancy, "finally made her weight struggle a thing of the past" (Beetman 6). The profile is accompanied with a sidebar column on the right side of the first page of the profile that is titled, "She's Struggled for Years!" Underneath this title are five images of Simpson throughout her career, two of which are images from both her pregnancies. Beside these two pictures, under a title, "Pregnancy Looks," readers learn "Jessica seemed enormously uncomfortable while pregnant with her daughter Maxwell in the spring of 2012.

The second pregnancy, with Ace, went easier" (Beetman 5). Thus, according to postpartum profiles, more than one pregnancy, in fact, makes a celebrity mom better at recovering her quickly slender postpartum body, while also making her even better at pregnancy and dieting postpartum.

The preceding examples also reveal the concurrent imperative for a better, more improved body and postpartum fitness regime; and this imperative requires intense training and work to fulfill. As Wilkinson-Baskett suggests, for example, being postpartum makes celebrity moms even better and more intense at fitness. Indeed, celebrity moms seem to train their bodies *even more* intensely after giving birth. This means that, if good slender-pregnancy management requires a disciplined, controlled diet and pregnancy fitness, then postpartum profiles require even more intense management and body work. In fact, when asked what her workout routine is like, Wilkinson-Baskett reports, "I do 45 minutes of hardcore training and weightlifting, and then I get into my fat-burning zone. I'm really motivated to just do as many reps as I can until I feel a burn—and then I try to do a few more. After that, it's just some treadmill to burn calories. I just go until I'm tired" (Bass 35). Whereas in the *OK USA* profile of Simpson, readers learn, "Jessica is kind of a machine when she wants to be. It's all about repetition of things like planks, Supermans, skater lunges and modified push ups. . . . A huge thing that Jessica makes sure to do is that even on her 'rest days' from working out and training she makes sure she's moving 10,000 steps a day" (Beetman 5). This reporting is accompanied with two small, side-by-side photos that Simpson posted on Instagram that "prove" that all this training works. Readers learn, "Jessica Instagrammed a photo from her WW [Weight Watchers] campaign (left) and shared a bikini pic from her Jessica Simpson Collection shoot (right)" (Beetman 5).

The fact that postpartum body work is now a central, featured component of the quickly slender, even bikini-ready, celebrity mom profiles suggests that the bikini-ready body is also deeply tied to the post-1980s fitness boom, which also incorporates the post-second wave idea of women's empowerment and strength. The convergence of these two cultural changes has had a profound impact on the understanding of both the pregnant and postpartum body and plays a central role in how the quickly slender, even bikini-ready, body works rhetorically to simultaneously acknowledge and refute second wave feminism. As noted in the last chapter, in terms of the pregnant body, until recently, the pregnant body was viewed as fragile and incongruous with physical activity. Jette argues that, until the 1980s, "pregnant women were advised by many medical professionals to avoid exercise more intense than a light stroll, because the pregnant body was viewed as fragile and incongruous with physical activity" (331). As the general fitness boom of the 1980s coincided with second wave feminism, a generation of physically active women began to have children and wished to remain fit during pregnancy. Today, then, "while the pregnant body is still construed as 'at risk,' pregnant women are now encouraged to engage in moderate exercise. In fact, the risks of *not* engaging in physical fitness while pregnant are emphasized in contemporary North American medical discourse" (italics in original, Jette 332).

By the 1990s and continuing through today, then, the fitness industry has capitalized on the shifting discourse of the medical community and has created a fitness industry that links pregnancy fitness both with privileged women's post-second wave empowerment and with the newfound acceptance of women's physical strength that develops via their body work. Dworkin and Wachs, in fact, suggested that fitness during pregnancy is now linked with successful deliveries and better postpartum recovery (120). Here, then, I extend Jette and Dworkin and Wachs' work by suggesting that bouncing back faster and better is now so entrenched in postpartum profiles that both notions are also starting to appear in pregnancy fitness advice. So, for example, issue one of Australian magazine, *Women's Health BUMP*, had a cover story, "HAVE THE BABY KEEP THE BODY (AND MAKE IT BETTER!)."[6] In another example, *FitPregnancy* has a 2014 cover story, titled, "The secret to getting your body back fast" (Hanson). Equally important and related, the analysis in the last chapter also revealed that an additional risk that now must be managed to prepare for motherhood is the "risk" of a "fat" pregnancy. Moreover, the analysis also revealed what happens to a woman like Kardashian who fails to keep her body risk-free and within slender-pregnant norms: she will be viciously fat shamed. Thus, as the new quickly slender, even bikini-ready, body becomes the new body norm within postpartum celebrity mom profiles, the profiles draw on both slender-pregnant profile requirements, while also simultaneously intensifying the bounce-back norm and utilizing women's post-second wave empowerment and strength *in the service of* demanding that moms quickly create new, even better postpartum bodies.

The Before-and-After Format

In addition to integrating the convergence of second wave feminist ideas and fitness discourse within postpartum celebrity mom profiles and the new momism, a second key rhetorical element of the quickly slender profiles is the before-and-after format; a format that was used in both the Jessica Simpson and Kim Kardshian cover stories. In another example, a March 2014 *people.com* photo feature, for example, has fifteen before-and-after photos of celebrity moms and was titled, "Body After Baby: Star Moms Who Bounced Right Back," with the subtitle, "Go figure! See how quickly Kate Winslet, Halle Berry, Jessica Simpson and more returned to their fab physiques." In this feature, for each celebrity covered, readers see two side-by-side pictures: one before picture of the celebrity clearly late in the pregnancy and largely pregnant, and the second after picture of the quickly slender celebrity. In each of the quickly slender photos, in the lower right corner at the bottom of the photo, is a green circle with white letters that reveals how many weeks "post-baby" the celebrity is in the photo.

The first celebrity featured is Kate Winslett. In each of the two photos, she is wearing a long, scarlet or red, formal dress. In the second "after" photo, "14 Weeks Post-Baby!" she wears a form-fitting dress that highlights her slender postpartum body. This is accompanied with the following text to the right of the images: "she was completely stunning three months after welcoming son Bear in a scarlet SAFiYAA dress at the Hollywood premiere of *Divergent* on March 18" (image 1). The second celebrity is Halle Berry after her second pregnancy. In her before photo, she wears a gray, long sundress, with a gray, sleeveless summer sweater on top of the dress. In the after picture, she is shown "16 Weeks Post-baby!" wearing a short, body skimming, sleeveless "little" black dress. The copy to the right reads, "Did the actress really give birth to son Maceo-Robert less than four months ago at age 47? Seeing is believing: Her *caliente* body was back to its legendary form" (italics in original image 2).

In 2009, *usmagazine.com* also had a before-and-after feature webpage devoted to celebrity moms who have had twins. Titled "Body After Twins!," on page one, actress Rebecca Romijn, for example, is shown both pregnant and one month after having twins. In the before picture, Romijn is largely pregnant and shown in a sleeveless, light green sun dress. In the after image, she wears a form-fitting long, green top with form-fitting blue yoga pants. To the right of the after picture, readers learns, "A month after welcoming twins, the Ugly Betty star—who said she was 'a beached whale' near the end of her pregnancy—showed off her fit body while on a walk in Calabasas, California, on Jan. 29" ("Body after Twins" image 2). Celebrity moms Jennifer Lopez, Julia Roberts, and Marcia Cross are also shown, among others. All are looking slender and fit within a month to three months at the latest after giving birth to their twins. The use of the before-after-format also permeates other celebrity mom profiles. The *US Weekly* (Grossbart) cover story about celebrities' flat stomachs, for example, also employs this format. Each of the stars featured are shown in a before-and-after format: both in the late stages of pregnancy in a smaller picture, then, with their slender post-baby body; Stefani and Spears are in bikinis, while the other celebrity moms are shown in body-hugging minidresses in their after photos. Thus, at the most basic level, the before-and-after format works rhetorically to juxtapose the late-in-pregnancy and largely pregnant body in relation to the quickly slender postpartum body.

In yet another more recent example, as noted in the introduction of this chapter, in the December 2013 Middleton story about her ridiculously flat stomach three-months postpartum, the article has an embedded link to "Post Baby Bods—Before & After" ("Kate Middleton Flashes" *toofab*). Rather than "labeling" the before-and-after photos with commentary, this gallery of pictures is labeled by dates with very little other commentary, which makes the "quickness" of the recovery the central issue in the profile. So, for example, in a before picture of Halle Barry, she is shown late in her pregnancy in a long, sleeveless, blue-and-white horizontal sundress late in pregnancy, and she is posed sideways, which accentuates the largeness of her pregnant belly. In her four-months postpartum after picture, she is facing the camera from the front, smiling, and is shown in a short, body-skimming black, sleeveless dress. Underneath the pictures is the following: "Halle Berry on September 23, 2013, and on January 29, 2014—4 months after her son Maceo Robert Martinez was born" (picture 3). In an even faster postpartum picture in a bikini, Reality TV star Kim Zolciak, pregnant with twins, is shown in a before picture at seven months pregnant wearing a black-and-white bra-and-underwear set. Her after picture is a one-week postpartum selfie, and she wears a tight, body-skimming sleeveless top, with a plunging neck line, which highlights her large breasts, and she wears black, body-skimming pants. The copy reads, "Kim Zolciak in October, 2013, and on December 4, 2013—one week after her twins Kaia Rose and Kane Ren were born" (picture 5). Clearly, the pictures and dates make the case that quickly slender postpartum bodies are the new and most important norm for celebrity moms.

Decoding how this before-and-after format works rhetorically is complicated because of the variety of meanings conveyed both within the images themselves and the cultural meanings of the slender body for women. Indeed, as Bordo ("Reading") argues, deconstructing body images is a "complex business" due to the intersection of race, class, and ethnic differences (469). Bordo also suggests that the slender-feminine body "admits of many variants and has multiple and often mutually 'deconstructing' meanings. To give just one example, an examination of the photographs and copy of current fashion advertisements suggests that today's boyish body ideals, as in the 1920s, symbolize a new freedom, a casting off of the encumbrance of domestic, reproductive femininity" (469). However, when the muscular and bulky masculine body is viewed *in relation* to the slender female body, because of the oppositionality of the images, different meanings are suggested. As Bordo argues, "in these gender/oppositional poses, the degree to which slenderness carries connotations of fragility, defenselessness, and lack of power over against a decisive male occupation of social space is dramatically represented" (470).

In the same way, then, when the before and after images are read *in relation* to one another and *in relation* to the slender-pregnant profiles that precede them, very specific meanings emerge. The before-and-after format works rhetorically to frame the largely pregnant or late-in-pregnancy body as a bad body, even if it is a late-stage slender-pregnant body, while the quickly slender body is a good body. In fact, the before-and-after format also suggests several

bad versus good meanings: worse versus better; gross versus pleasurable, out of control versus controlled and disciplined; all themes
also deeply embedded in media comparisons between Middleton
and Kardashian's pregnant bodies. This juxtaposition of the late-
in-pregnancy maternal body and quickly slender postpartum body,
then, also reinforces the idea that even the slender late-in-pregnancy
body is "gross," still repulsive, and must immediately and intensively
be worked on postpartum. The before-and-after rhetorical strategy
also continues to communicate that the pregnant body is an out-of-
control and unruly body that needs to be feared, managed, and put
through fitness training during the pregnancy but most especially
and intensively postpartum to become a good, controlled, and disciplined postpartum body.

The before-and-after format also works rhetorically to heighten
mothers' body anxiety about the changes that occur to women's bodies when pregnant and the cultural anxiety about pregnant bodies
being out of control and unruly. Dworkin and Wachs, for example,
report that postpartum women confess that they view postpartum
bodies "as sinful, out of control, shameful, or as evidence of a lax
body that must be quickly corrected" and controlled (117). Although
she is not postpartum, a recent interview with celebrity fitness expert
Gillian Michaels, again, reveals just how much body anxiety women
now have about the maternal body—both pregnant and postpartum—making women "fat" or "damaged" in a *Women's Health* interview. While the larger story was about her prominence as a fitness
expert, near the end of the article, Michaels reveals that she hopes to
have children someday.[7] She says, 'I'm going to adopt.' One of the
reasons: Gillian admits to having an aversion to pregnancy, the result
of being an overweight kid. 'I can't handle doing that to my body,'
she explains" (Allyssa Lee 45). In the context of the media messages
about fat pregnant bodies and the vicious fat shaming that results, as
the analysis of Kardashian's maternal body revealed, then, Michaels
is smart in that she understands what happens to damaged or problematic maternal bodies, either when pregnant or postpartum.

In addition to revealing her personal history, Michaels' quote
also reveals how contemporary women's maternal bodies have been
redefined. Women's maternal bodies, for example, have been redefined from the traditional religious view of women's bodies as birthing centers to women's bodies as first and foremost sex objects.[8]

And, in fact, women's bodies as sex objects is at the root of Michaels' worry: she "isn't doing that to her" body because she isn't going to "ruin" or "wreck" her body. At the root of this worry, then, is Michaels' and contemporary women's concern about how pregnancy fundamentally challenges the contemporary slender, sexy ideal for women's bodies. Rather than assuage this worry, the before-and-after format works to heighten body anxiety by visually juxtaposing a largely gross pregnant image with a quickly slender pleasurable and sexy postpartum body.

Managing the "Fat" of Pregnancy

Equally important, these images are often accompanied with fast weight loss advice, which often focuses on the lingering bulge or fat on a postpartum body. Given the slender-pregnant ideal, this means there is an obsessive focus on the postpartum belly or mummy tummy, as media did in the coverage of Middleton as she left the hospital after giving birth. In an article titled, "Kate Middleton and Other Celebs Feel the Pressure to Lose the 'Mummy Tummy' Fast," which reveals the importance of celebrities eliminating the mummy tummy fast, Aida Ekberg informs readers, "Kate Middleton isn't the only celeb who is feeling the pressure to bounce back after giving birth. *US Weekly* reports that Kim Kardashian will debut her post-pregnancy bod on Kris Jenner's talk show, but it doesn't sound like the new mom is ready to rock a bikini just yet" (par. 1). In addition to confirming the ongoing comparisons between Middleton and Kardashian and the newfound connection between the postpartum body and bikinis, Ekberg also confirms that, given the slender-pregnant pressure to be pregnant in belly only, then, the mummy tummy should be the only lingering evidence of pregnancy; and it must be eliminated as quickly as possible.

Postpartum profiles provide advice about how to lose the lingering mummy tummy quickly. The *US Weekly* cover story about various celebrity moms' quickly slender bodies, for example, is followed by "10 Foods That Fight Fat" ("How Stars" Grossbart 48). Next, readers learn: "These healthy bites—some of Hollywood's faves—curb cravings and help any pudge finally budge" (48). Or, alternatively, celebrity moms promote particular diets that they suggest help them lose postpartum weight fast. As already noted, for example, Jessica

Simpson used Weight Watchers to help her lose "over 70lbs!" In another example, in her postpartum bikini debut, readers learn that Kardashian, "got to work as soon as she received the all-clear from her doctor. 'I've been doing the Atkins diet,' she told *US* of the meal plan heavy on lean proteins and healthy fats like nuts and avocado. 'But, of course, I have my cheat days'" ("My Body" O'Leary 54).

In another example, a 2010 *OK! Weekly* featured a cover story about Reality TV star and sister of Kim Kardashian, Kourtney Khardasian[9] one month after giving birth. Although Kourtney Khardasian was not in a bikini nor promoting a specific diet brand, the focus of the story was on the quick weight loss her sisters, Kim and Khloe, were helping her with in hopes of getting Kourtney quickly bikini ready. Immediately below the *OK!* title is a pink box that reads, "Kourtney's Body After Baby Exclusive." To the right of that box is Kourtney in a lavender dress and holding her son. The cover also has the following blurb, "How Kim and Khloe are helping me lose the baby weight FAST." Inside was a feature "Lose 10 pounds in 10 days," which gave specific diet advice for losing weight fast (Glines 34). Finally, the text reports that Kim and Khloe are helping Kourtney Get a "bikini body fast" (Glines 34). All these profiles make it exceedingly clear that even a slender-pregnant body must eliminate the bulge or "eruption" of the pregnancy; the mummy tummy must be quickly recontained, even erased.

When these profiles make the bulge or the eruption of the pregnancy the primary focal point of quickly slender postpartum body work, the connection between slender-pregnant profiles and postpartum profiles is exceedingly clear. Slender-pregnant profiles focus on managing and containing the fat of the pregnant body so that only the bump of pregnancy is acceptable and evident, while everything else on the body remains slender. In fact, as noted in the previous chapter, Dworkin and Wachs argued that fit pregnancy advice focuses on containing the unruly pregnant body, particularly the stomach. They also argued that fit pregnancy magazine articles explain how pregnant women can counteract the bulge of their growing belly by focusing on keeping their arms and legs fit. As they noted, "articles explain 'no matter how big your belly gets, nicely toned arms and legs will help you feel beautiful'" (114). Jette also argued that, in "Fit for Two" monthly columns in *Oxygen* magazine, "a common theme emerges: The models all have toned bodies showing little evidence of weight gain other than the growing fetus" (345). If pregnant women adhere to this pregnancy advice, then, they can maintain the slender-pregnant ideal, as Middleton did, which makes the "logical"[10] focus of postpartum body work on the recontainment of the stomach.

Slender pregnancy with small bumps and small pregnancies are easier to recontain, even erase, because the bulge of pregnancy is less difficult to quickly eliminate in the bounce back to an even better postpartum body. This means then that a central aim of slender-pregnant profiles is also *to prepare* pregnant women for the postpartum body work that will be required of them and that is promoted in the postpartum profiles. In fact, there is no better way to prepare for a quick bounce back, even an erasure of the bump, then, by making sure to maintain a small bump, as Middleton did and Kardashian was unable to do. Celebrity moms' postpartum reports analyzed here make it clear that they understand this connection well. A recent interview, however, with movie actress Megan Fox also confirms this connection. In a report about her quickly slender maternal body, Ekberg tells readers that Fox reportedly "told Access Hollywood about how she lost her pregnancy weight: 'My baby was kind of small and my pregnancy was small—I walked out of the hospital kind of like this'"[11](Ekberg par. 7). Thus, adhering to slender-pregnancy norms helps postpartum women *prepare for* the quick recontainment of the only "acceptable" lingering evidence of the pregnancy: the small mummy tummy.

Clearly, the before-and-after format in tandem with dieting advice that focuses on eliminating the fat of pregnancy work visually and rhetorically to reinforce the need for immediate postpartum body work as a means to an end to regain control of the "unruly" pregnant body, primarily the bulging stomach area. The bikini then becomes the ideal vehicle for highlighting a new mom's quick recontainment and erasure of the fat of pregnancy, the out-of-control bulge, because the focal point of any bikini is the woman's stomach. Indeed, the bikini is a perfect way to display a woman's stomach, because highlighting the stomach is the primary difference between the bikini and other kinds of bathing suits. By focusing more generally on the postpartum body and specifically on the fat or bulge of pregnancy, then, these new profiles only heighten the body anxiety women are taught when pregnant, while creating even more exacting standards for a quick, even better, bounce back. According to the quickly slender profiles, the primary means for getting bikini ready is by taking control of the postpartum body: both by disciplined diets and controlled and intense body work.

The Disciplined and Controlled Postpartum Body

And, take control of their bodies is exactly what celebrity moms do. That discipline and rigorous body control are pivotal to the quickly slender body is evident, for example, in the advice found in the *US Weekly* cover story, "How Stars Get Thin." Indeed, the profiles reveal that postpregnant bodies require much work, restrictions, and regulation.[12] The magazine reports that a friend of Stefani's, for example, reports, "It's all about her diet . . . a low-carb plan: eggs and toast for breakfast, salad with chicken for lunch, salmon and veggies for dinner and a protein bar or turkey slices for a snack" (Grossbart 44). Lopez also has a "disciplined diet," "a menu packed with veggies, turkey and rice also helped the star drop 50 pregnancy pounds" (Grossbart 45). Moreover, in a profile titled, "Jennifer Lopez Shows Off Bikini Bod," *omg!* reports that Lopez also admits that dropping the baby weight takes a lot of work. As she put it: "I thought it was gonna drop off easily because I had been in shape my whole life, but it wasn't," she told *Entertainment Tonight* in June 2010. She continued, "I gained about 50 pounds with my twins, and the first 30 dropped off like that, and I was like 'Ha, this is going to be easy.' That last 20—that took a while" (par. 5).

The postpartum bikini reveal of Kardashian also reveals Kardashian's discipline. Immediately after Kardashian reported "cheating" on her Atkins Diet, O'Leary reveals, "She's being humble. In reality, Kim brought Jedi-level discipline to her efforts. 'She wakes up and does more than 100 squats every single morning,' marvels the confidant. 'Even now, when she can wear the things she did before her pregnancy, she still wants to tone her body'" ("My Body" 54). After giving birth the second time, in a *people.com* article about an upcoming issue that has a story about Laila Ali, titled, "Laila Ali: How I got my Bikini Body Back," readers learn that "'I'm naturally a big girl,' Ali explains. 'I have to work to be fit. I love running. I run three times a week and I do strength training and weights. And sometimes I throw a little spinning in there'" (Lewis par. 6). Lewis reports, however, "Apart from her time in the gym, Ali watches what she eats by sticking to lean proteins and vegetables most of the time" (par. 7). In yet another example, Beyonce was also featured in the same June 2, 2014, *People* magazine article "Most Talked about Bodies 2014" as Kardashian, and Beyonce is quoted as saying, "I was 195 lbs when I gave birth. I lost 65 lbs. I worked crazily to get my body back. I wanted to show that you can have a child and you can work hard and you can get your body back" (72).

Moreover, in the *US Weekly* cover story, "How Stars Get Thin," readers learn, Brittany Spears "loves to flaunt her toned tummy in a parade of itty-bitty bikinis" (Grossbart 47). A friend also reports that Spears feels more confident now, and that Spears also keeps a "clean diet of salads with chicken or shrimp, soups, and fruit. And, says an insider, 'she doesn't eat dessert'" (47). Meanwhile, Klum "eats a bread-free diet and everything apart from carbs!" (46). Simpson-Weitz and Aguilera both admit that dieting is a struggle, but they both stay slim with diet and exercise (46–47). Simpson-Weitz "stays slim by dancing in Broadway's Chicago and working with her trainer Mike Alexander and restricts calories to 1,500 a day most days" (46). Finally, readers also learn, even though Aguilera admits to loving her mom's Southern cooking, she "decided to cut out white carbs and refined sugars" (47).

In yet another before-and-after post-baby body feature titled, "Celebrity Post-Baby Bods," a 2013 *Yahoo! Celebrity* features 12 different celebrities: Jenna Dewan-Tatum, Kristin Bell, Holly Madison, Amber Rose, Molly Sims, to name a few. Reality TV star "Snooki" of Jersey Shore Fame is also featured. While she is shown one-year postpartum, her before picture is late in her first pregnancy and she wears a short, form-fitting, blue sundress and white sweater, which highlights her large belly late in pregnancy. In the after picture, she wears a white, "bustie-like" top and a form-fitting black leather skirt. Beside her picture, readers learn, that she has lost 50 pounds postpartum. They also learn, "She posted the following message on Instagram: 'To all my pregnant ladies, IT IS possible to get your body back and better than ever after having a baby! All you need is motivation to workout & eat healthy! Anything is possible.' The secret to her success? The 25 year-old works out with a trainer five days a week, eats more protein, and (believe it or not) she's cut out alcohol" (image 7). Obviously, all these profiles suggest that the quickly slender postpartum body requires disciplined and controlled dieting (even no alcohol for a Reality TV star who had been famous for her drunken escapades prior to pregnancy) and body work, even "Jedi-like" discipline, especially for a formerly fat pregnant celebrity mom.

Further Reinforcing the White Slender Body Ideal

While these profiles overwhelming feature white celebrity moms, when nonwhite celebrities are featured, their rigorous postpartum workouts and quick bounce are also featured. Additionally, the nonwhite celebrities are always featured in relation to their ability to reconfirm the white slender ideal. As has already been noted, for example, African American actress Halle Berry has been frequently covered by media after the birth of both of her children. In yet another example, two months after giving birth the first time, *Celebrity Parents.com* also reported about Berry that "People magazine recently published a copy of her strict workout regime and diet. How does circuit training 60 minutes a day, five days a week sound to you? Don't forget a diet consisting of lean protein, lots of water, vegetables and complex carbohydrates, which I'm guessing is well below the average American's 2,000-calorie a day consumption" ("Body After Baby" par. 2). And Beyonce was described by media as "debuting" her quickly slender body one-month postpartum, while Kim Kardashian provided proof of her return to a "more acceptable" slender ideal in her postpartum bikini reveal. Thus, even when nonwhite celebrities are featured, they are featured as conforming and in relation to the white slender ideal, as is also the case with slender-pregnant profiles.

Interestingly, a relatively new magazine, *Juicy*, explores the lives of celebrities of color, primarily African American celebrities. In its second edition, the magazine had a story titled, "Mommies With Great Snapback!"(Gipson 50–51). While it did not feature the quickly slender issues as prominently, this story also employed the before-and-after format and focused almost entirely on the celebrity moms' successful "snap back," which is also synonymous with "bounce back." It is important to note that one significant difference in this story was the acknowledgement that losing baby weight is difficult. As the subheading put it: "Losing Baby Weight After Childbirth is Damn Difficult, But It's Not Impossible. *Juicy* Takes a

Look at Celebs Who've Dropped The Pregnancy Pounds Successfully" (50–51). Consequently, even though there was some acknowl-
edgment of the actual difficulty of losing postpartum weight, *Juicy*
also follows the quickly slender imperative to lose that weight, uses
a before-and-after format, and encourages snapping back. Thus,
quickly slender profiles reveal that postpartum bodies require enormous amounts of body work and discipline from *all* celebrity moms,
while also reinforcing the white slender body ideal.

A clear imperative of the quickly slender celebrity mom profiles, then, is that postpartum, post-second wave neoliberal motherhood requires an enormous amount of dedicated body work and
controlled and disciplined dieting for all celebrities. Equally important, the quickly slender, even bikini-ready, body is now held up, as
the analysis also showed, as improving celebrity moms' postpartum
bodies and making them even better women and mothers. As the
quickly slender, even bikini-ready, body becomes a more prominent
feature of celebrity mom profiles—as the new momism continues to
be refined in response to changing cultural imperatives by incorporating this postpartum body work within the new momism—then,
both celebrity mom profiles and the new momism are integrating,
what sociologists (Dworkin and Wachs; Jette) describe as *a third
shift of body work*.

The Third Shift of Body Work

By their own reports, celebrity moms are revealing that quickly slender celebrity moms are now responsible for a third shift of body
work in addition to the second shift of family life. Arlie Hochschild, in *The Second Shift*, was the first feminist scholar to argue
that women's second shift as primary caregivers and managers of
both children and the private sphere indicated a "stalled revolution"
in women's lives as second-wave beneficiaries. Indeed, Hochschild
argued that, as women gained more and more access to educational
and professional institutions, there was very little change in women's
roles as primary caregivers of children. Consequently, she argued,
many American women had two shifts as second-wave beneficiaries: the first shift as workers and/or professionals and the second
shift of household management, labor, and childcare. More recently,
sociologists (Dworkin and Wachs; Jette) have begun to argue that

contemporary women are now expected to engage in a third shift
of body work and management when pregnant to regain their femininity. Jette, for example, in describing Dworkin and Wach's early
work on fit pregnancy and postpartum body work, argued "Indeed,
the authors point to the way in which the magazine positions new
mothers as responsible for an additional third shift of body work in
order to get rid of baby fat and regain their femininity" (337). In
other words, because the body work and body management in fit
pregnancy are done to regain postpartum slender femininity, body
work is a prerequisite for the maternal body today—both pregnant
and postpartum.

In the context of celebrity mom profiles, I contend that this now
means that slender pregnancy requires good maternal body management so that a postpartum woman is fully prepared to regain, even
improve, the normative slender feminine body ideal postpartum.
As a result, as I argued in the last chapter, slender-pregnant profiles
work to train and discipline pregnant women for good pregnancy
body management *to prepare* women, especially first-time mothers, to accept, even embrace, both their split subjectivity and intensive mothering norms, while *also preparing* women to accept, even
embrace, a third shift of postpartum body work as crucial to postpartum maternal femininity. Thus, the quickly slender, even bikini-
ready, profiles analyzed here reveal that this imperative is also now
becoming entrenched in postpartum celebrity mom profiles.

Ironically, much of the third shift ideology, like the new
momism, also integrates second wave feminist rhetoric and ideas.
Indeed, in their work on fit pregnancy advice, for example, Dworkin and Wachs suggest that much of that advice "strategically draws
on a feminist stance to help women 'get their body back' but paradoxically reinscribes women to the domestic and privatized realm
of bodily and household maintenance to do so" (119). Equally trou-
bling, then, rather than address the struggle mothers have juggling
childcare and paid labor, fit pregnancy magazines and now postpartum celebrity mom profiles are noticeably silent on mothers' second
shift responsibilities. Instead, according to Dworkin and Wachs, fit
pregnancy advice emphasizes "how a third shift of fitness is necessary to allow for the successful completion of the second shift of
household labor and childcare" (120). In short, I argue that postpartum celebrity mom profiles now also suggest that a third shift

of body work *will energize* the second shift of household labor and childcare.

In fact, in describing the cultural construction of feminine fitness in the context of neoliberal healthism, Gremillion also argues, quoting Robert Crawford, "since the mid-1970s in the United States, fitness has become a dominant icon of bodily health and individual productivity. Eating well and working out are now seen as markers of success, and health is a do-it-yourself en-deavor, encoding a work ethic. As Robert Crawford (1985) writes, 'The ethic of health must be like the ethic of work. The Protestant world view extends to the body; it invades the domain of leisure' (67)" (398). This new ethic of health, however, is also being used to energize and cultivate work. As Gremillion continues, "But Crawford notes that fitness is not only imagined as an expression of self-control; it also encodes 'release.' Exercise, in particular, revitalizes, reduces stress; working out 'works out' tension. In turn, exercise is said to energize work" (398). In other words, workplaces, especially via "Wellness at Work"[13] programs, promote fitness and health as a means to an end to manage workplace stress and to energize workers, so that they become both more contented and productive at work.

In the same way that the neoliberal ethic of health and wellness-at-work programs work to energize workers and ultimately make them more productive at work, I argue that postpartum celebrity mom profiles have integrated a third shift of body work to energize mothers' second shift responsibilities and to make them even more productive at their second shift responsibilities. In short, rather than challenge the second shift, celebrity mom profiles now integrate second wave feminist ideas in the service of promoting a third shift of body work as something essential mothers can and should do as a means to train for success in the second shift of household labor and childcare. The analysis in this and the last chapter reveals that this is done first via good body management in slender-pregnant profiles, then, second, explicitly in postpartum celebrity mom profiles.

As a result, as the third shift becomes central to the focus on the maternal bodies of celebrities in contemporary postpartum profiles, women's responsibility for the second shift of household labor not only becomes more entrenched, *the more-specific solution* offered to manage women's difficulty having it all is a third shift of intense and rigorous but also energizing body work. This also means that women's post-second wave split subjectivity is also further reinforced via postpartum celebrity mom profiles, while also reinforcing privatized and individual solutions for any difficulty a mother experiences juggling or managing her first and second shift responsibilities. In short, postpartum celebrity mom profiles now work to argue that "contented" intensive mothers must manage their own stress, learn to live with that stress, and must rely on their own initiative via energizing body work to manage better the stress of having it all, while also becoming more productive at their first and second shift responsibilities.

This "argument" about the third shift energizing the second shift, then, is similar to the ways that exercise is said to energize work in the public sphere. In short, today a third shift of body work is seen as essential to energize postfeminist success: both at home and in the public sphere—success as both women and mothers. Moreover, the third shift is also a postfeminist neoliberal ideology because it employs feminist rhetoric about women's strength and empowerment in the service of reinforcing ongoing feminine beauty ideals and maternal responsibilities in the private sphere. Or, as Nash puts it about the pregnant body but is also now the case for the postpartum body: in a post-second wave context, "a disciplined and objectified pregnant body is equated with freedom or liberation for middle-class women, or what may be considered as a *post-feminist* construction" (italics in original 169).

One of the reasons, then, why the third shift is especially dangerous is because, while it may seem like gender ideologies have changed in families in the private sphere, many have not and a seemingly progressive-but-not exercise regime is being added to women's work in the private sphere. Indeed, even though some previous gender priorities have shifted—maternity is no longer women's exclusive destiny, for example—women's basic beauty and maternal responsibilities have not changed and, in fact, have intensified. In addition to acknowledging women's ongoing domestic responsibilities, Gremillion also describes this shifting and contradictory gender landscape when she suggests, "Women may still perform the majority of domestic labor in the United States, but 'the joy of cooking' has moved from the kitchen to the exercise room (and has supposedly liberated women in the process)" (402). Thus, while many gender-based assumptions and roles have changed in the public sphere for unencumbered women, in the private sphere, little has changed at the same time that a new regime of body work and exacting maternal body standards have been added to and have intensified "women's work" in the private sphere.

"Debuting" the New, Even Better Postpartum Body to be a "Sexy" Mom

As well as promoting a third shift of body work to enhance second shift responsibilities, the quickly slender profiles also reveal that postpartum celebrity moms are training to debut an even better and sexy postpartum body. Indeed, the first sightings of celebrity moms' new, better bodies are often described in the following ways: "showing off": "Kendra Shows off her new body"; "flaunting her body": "Gosslin flaunts her bikini body"; "unveiling": "Nicole Richie unveils her post-baby body." In yet another and more recent March 2014 example, an *abcnews.go.com* report titled, "Celebs Flaunt Their Amazing Transformations," opens with Kate Winslett three-months postpartum, with the subtitle, "Kate Winslet Reveals Her Slim Post-Baby Body" (image 1). In the same report, readers also learn, "Wow! Ivanka Trump Flaunts Her Post-Baby Body" at five-months postpartum (image 2). Finally, at three-months postpartum, readers are told "Halle Berry Debuts Her (Amazing!) Post-Baby Body!" (image 4). As with the Berry example, however, the most often used descriptor is *debut*. Thus, the quickly slender body profiles feature the language of *debut*, suggesting yet again that celebrity moms are unveiling an even better postpartum body: "Beyonce Makes her Post-Blue Debut!" (Giantis); "Emily Blunt Debuts Slender Post-Baby Body One Month After Daughter Hazel's Birth" (Esther Lee); "Thandi Newton Debuts Stunning Post-Baby Body Five Weeks After Giving Birth" (Webber).

Etymelogically, a debut is to make a first public appearance on television, stage, and/or in a film. A debut, then, is something new, not a return or a comeback. Debut is also linked to the idea of debutantes and is deeply embedded within the notion that the most important life goals for a woman are marriage and a family. Indeed, traditionally a debutante was a young woman who was formally introduced into society when she was ready to marry. Consequently, at a debutante ball, she was formally debuted or unveiled to acceptable and eligible young men. While today debutantes and debutante balls are not as strongly linked to marriage and instead primarily introduce young women to society, debutante balls continue to debut or display young women, often on the arm of her father who is presenting her to her young male escort who walks her away from the stage. So, although the debut is no longer as focused on marriage, it is still an unveiling of a young woman by and for men.

By framing the first sightings of celebrity moms postpartum as the debut of their quickly slender bodies, the quickly slender profiles work rhetorically to focus on the unveiling of a new, even better body and woman for men. This is yet another way that celebrity mom profiles integrate another unquestioned gender assumption: like slender-pregnant profiles that continue to reinforce the idea that all post-second wave women still wish for "fairy-tale weddings," postpartum profiles reinforce the notion that all women still want to unveil or debut their bodies and selves for men. Just as important, the debut of the new, better body also clearly communicates—via her postpartum maternal body—that the celebrity mom has "it all" under control; she is a "real" post-second wave neoliberal mother who manages to juggle it all—her post-second wave crisis in femininity—well and through *her own personal strength and body work*. As a result, the language of debut is yet another key rhetorical device in the quickly slender profiles that works to make it clear that the new goal of the postpartum body is no longer just recovery but instead creating a new, even better sexy body that symbolically communicates post-second wave women's strength and personal ability to do it all, have it all under control quickly and even better than before giving birth.

Coupled with this new imperative, then, is the requirement to become a new "sexy mom" with a sexy postpartum body. As noted earlier, the *US Weekly* cover story of celebrity moms also links the "best bodies" of moms with being sexy moms: "How Stars Get Thin, Whoa, baby! Learn how these sexy moms achieved their best bodies ever" (Grossbart 44). In yet another example, an *Us* magazine online story declares "Hot mama: Kate Gosselin flaunted her bikini bod while vacationing with her eight kids (and bodyguard Steve Neild) at Bald Head Island, NC, Sunday" ("Kate Gosselin Flaunts" par. 1). A 2014 *InTouch Weekly* online story about Black Eyed Peas singer Fergie one-month postpartum had the title, "Hot Mama Alert! Fergie Flaunts Post-Pregnancy Figure: See 4 More Recent Impressive

Bodies After Baby!" (Sitzer). Yet another profile in *Us* magazine online also had a picture and short story about Jennifer Lopez. The feature, "Jennifer Lopez Shows off Bikini Bod" was also accompanied by the phrase: "Hot mama" ("Jennifer Lopez" *US* par. 1). Moreover, the profile continues: "Jennifer Lopez, who turned 40 July 24, showed off her bikini body while sunbathing on a yacht in Capri Monday." Thus, in addition to debuting a new, even better body, the debut also reveals celebrity moms' emergence into a particular kind of femininity: their entry into sexy femininity as sexy moms for men.

If "Extreme" Moms Can Be Sexy, So Can You

That being a postpartum sexy mom is essential to quickly slender celebrity mom profiles is also revealed by a 2010 cover story of an "extreme" mom: Nadya Suleman, commonly known as the "Octomom." *Star* magazine had a cover story that featured Suleman in a red bikini and described her as a "sexy mom." Also keeping with both the imperatives for a new, improved body and gaining control of the body, the title of the cover declared, "My new Bikini Body! How I Did It! No Nips, no tucks, no lip, Nadya's secrets to flat abs & erasing stretch marks" (Cronin 52). The before-and-after format is also part of the copy. In fact, the first two pages of the cover story have full-page pictures of Suleman in a black polka dot bikini with green piping on the bikini top and waist of the bottoms. On the bottom right corner of page one, however, are two small, side-by-side pictures of Suleman largely pregnant. One of these pictures is a side shot of Suleman's extremely large pregnant stomach, which is also covered with so many stretch marks that the center of her stomach is purple. The second of these smaller pictures is a front shot of Suleman, which also reveals an abnormally large stomach covered in purple stretch marks.

Although this cover story appeared one year later, it is especially impressive because Suleman was bikini ready even after birthing eight children. Even more striking is the recovery of her largely "grotesque" stomach: there are no visible stretch marks and her stomach is now fit and flat. The only evidence of her pregnancy is her belly button, which appears slightly elongated. The copy surrounding these four images reads, "The stretch marks that once crisscrossed her belly are almost invisible, thanks to Nadya's hard work. But,

she had some help. 'I use creams with growth hormone to stimu-
late collagen production. And vitamin C! That's my secret. I put it
on my face too" (Cronin 53). A featured quote above her head in
the full-body shot reads, "People think I had surgery. No way!" (53).
Between the two large pictures, again, now in green, "My new bikini
body! How I did it. One year and 150 lbs. later, Nadya Suleman tells
Star how Octomom became one hot mama" (52). Clearly echoing
the notion that women are strong and in control, Suleman's advice
to other women is, "A lot of women say there's no time—you have
to make the time. . . . It takes discipline, but it makes me feel good
about myself that I have the strength to do it [workout]—emotional,
physical and psychological strength" (54).

One of the most interesting features of the Suleman cover is that
even the "most extremely" pregnant woman—in terms of number
of children she was carrying, the fact that she already had six other
children, and because she was unmarried and used artificial insemi-
nation—is featured in exactly the same way as the normal celebrity
moms. Even though Suleman, as is Kate Gosslin (mother of a set of
twins and sextuplets), is an extreme celebrity mom, her story conveys the same message: postpartum bodies, even extremely pregnant
postpartum bodies, also can be better than before, sexy postpartum,
and shown off in a bikini. Implicitly, then, the octomom profile also
suggests that normally pregnant women have no excuse. If the octomom and Kate Gosslin can become bikini-ready and sexy, then, all
mothers must also do so.

Another term, "yummy mummy" also suggests how important
it now is for moms also to be sexy postpartum. In her work on fit
pregnancy advice, Jette argues that "'yummy mummy' discourse permeates fit pregnancy advice and that celebrity moms are the quintes-
sential yummy mummys" (345). Also noting that pregnant women
are taught to fear weight gain and to view the pregnant body as "out
of control," Jette also contends that images in fit pregnancy magazines suggest to the reader "what the body of a fit mother can (and
even should) look like and that she, too, can be a 'yummy mummy'
if only she has the discipline to work out" (346). Clearly, then, the
quickly slender body is also tied to the larger cultural trend of now
seeing moms as sexy and/or "hot mamas" that began with the Demi
Moore 1991 *Vanity Fair* cover photo when she was pregnant. Indeed,
as I noted in the last chapter, the *Vanity Fair* cover is regarded by

scholars (Earle; Hefferman, Nicholson, and Fox; Jette; Nash) as having reconfigured Western cultural views of pregnancy by making pregnancy public, fashionable, and attractive. Postpartum celebrity mom profiles have added the final piece to the reconfiguration by adding sexiness postpartum as the logical conclusion for mothers.

Indeed, contemporary culture reveals an important shift from viewing mothers as matronly to sexy. Today, for example, a common moniker for a sexy mom is "MILF."[14] In a posting in *urbadictionary.com* for MILF, several postings declare that a MILF is a woman whose body "hasn't been wrecked by giving birth" (entry 17). Clearly, then, the bikini-ready body suggests a very specific kind of sexiness for mothers: sexy moms are sexy because their "bodies have not been wrecked by pregnancy." In fact, these are sexy or hot mothers because they have even better postpartum slender bodies that have quickly and completely erased the one currently "acceptable" visual marker of slender pregnancy: the stomach. In other words, because slender-pregnant profiles are the first step in encouraging pregnant women to be pregnant in belly only, and quickly slender, even bikini-ready profiles encourage mothers to engage in a third shift of rigorous and intense body work to erase the bulge or fat of pregnancy, postpartum women quickly erase the one acceptable sign of pregnancy, so they can remain sexy women, regardless of their maternal status.

Moreover, expecting women to remain sexy, both when pregnant and postpartum, is so strongly tied to the now-public and no-longer-in-hiding maternal body that the logic of the maternal body today is the following: first, if pregnant women adhere to the slender-pregnant ideal, then, they can remain sexy because they are "only" pregnant in one place: their bump. To put it another way, as Cunningham suggests of sexy pregnant moms Kelly Preston and Cindy Crawford, these celebrities "aren't sexy because they are pregnant, but rather because they are pregnant in a particular way—*slender everywhere else except their* bellies" (italics in original 444). Consequently and as a result, second, it naturally follows that expecting and demanding that postpartum women quickly return to an even better and sexy slender ideal should be easy because only the lingering fat will remain and can be quickly erased.

Intriguingly, then, the continued drive for women to prioritize sexiness as central to femininity continues, even within our post-second wave neoliberal context, and now is also central for mothers. In other words, even though women are now being raised to believe that they can "be anything," they also simultaneously continue to be taught that being sexy is still central to success as women. As Joan Brumberg puts it, describing contemporary female college students, "On one hand, their parents and teachers told them that being female was no bar to accomplishment. Yet girls of their generation learned from a very early age that the power of their gender was tied to what they looked like—and how 'sexy' they were—rather than to character or achievement" (195). That sexiness is now part of maternity, then, is also not so surprising given the conflicting gender imperatives girls and then as unencumbered women are taught as post-second wave beneficiaries at the conflicting crosscurrents of our contemporary era. If young women are raised to believe that they can be anything they want to be but that they must also be sexy, it makes sense that they would continue to believe this as mothers. When this is coupled with the newfound importance of the sexy maternal body—both during pregnancy and postpartum—it is not at all surprising that remaining sexy throughout the maternal process is now expected and demanded of women. Thus, the quickly slender celebrity mom profiles now promote and reinforce the idea that empowered sexy young and unencumbered women also need to be empowered, sexy moms postpartum.

It is crucial to point out, however, the fact that when the quickly slender, even bikini-ready, body profiles suggest women can and should now be sexy moms, this imperative is not really about mothers finally moving away from matronly nonsexuality or perceptions of being asexual to a maternal sexuality *as mothers*. Rather, quickly slender profiles support a very specific, prepregnancy sexiness that reentrenches unencumbered sexiness, the unencumbered, nonmaternal body, and they do so for a reason. Indeed, Cunningham also argues of postpartum yummy mummys, "Similarly, bodies that come back after pregnancy aren't sexy because they are now the bodies of mothers, but because they are bodies which have returned to their pre-pregnant measurements—measurements which can still command the male gaze and still land the contract" (444). Because they have erased the one acceptable visible sign of pregnancy—the bump—the postpartum fat, and because the quickly slender profiles now demand more than just the bounce back and instead require an even better postpartum body, the sexiness promoted within these profiles is even more exacting, even more demanding of postpartum mothers and requires postpartum women to still command the male gaze. Thus, yet again, as the quickly slender, even bikini-ready, postpartum maternal body becomes more and more entrenched as the primary focus of celebrity mom profiles, even more exacting postpartum body standards of sexiness are reinforced for women, while yet another unquestioned gender assumption is also embedded: all women *must always* command the male gaze regardless of maternity and any maternal responsibilities.

The Bikini: The Perfect Symbol of and for Both Women's Empowerment and Ongoing Objectification

At the heart of the quickly slender, even-bikini ready, body profiles then are two conflicting messages for post-second wave neoliberal beneficiaries: being female is no "bar" to accomplishing whatever you want *and* make sure that you engage in the necessary body work to remain sexy postpartum women who can still command the male gaze. The bikini is the perfect symbol for these conflicting messages. Symbolically, the bikini has had a complex and conflicting gendered history. To summarize that history briefly: the bikini has been viewed as both a symbol of emancipation for or oppression of women. While the bikini itself is more than "1,700 years old, according to mosaics dating from 300 AD at the Villa Romanan del Casale in Sicily, . . . it took off as a fashion item in the late 1950s" (Wescott pars. 6–7). In an article about the sixtieth anniversary of the modern bikini, the BBC also reports that, when it was introduced in America in the 1950s, the bikini was considered too risqué for women and was symbolic of indecent sexuality, primarily because it "exposed the navel and that was frowned upon" (Westcott par. 18).

During the sexual revolution of the 1960s, however, the bikini gained acceptance in America and "made its own contribution to the changing relationship between men and women" (Westcott par. 21). In fact, French fashion historian Olivier Saillard argues that the "emancipation of swimwear has always been linked to the emancipation of women" (quoted in Westcott par. 23). Moreover, while the bikini was less popular in the 1980s, today it is a mainstay of the swimwear market. Finally, Brumberg, in her work specifically about college-age women's body work and their desire to wear bikinis, reports that her female college students insist they "regard the ability to display their bodies as signs of women's liberation, a mark of progress, and a basic American right" (xxii).

The BBC also reports, however, that "Teenagers and young women are said to be the major buyers, but women over 30 make up an increasing share [of buyers]" (Wescott par. 26). In fact, the BBC suggests that the newfound popularity of the bikini for over-thirty women is directly linked to the post-1980s health and fitness movement. As Westcott puts it: "Some argue that the key to the bikini's re-found popularity is the ageing baby boomers who signed up to the fitness-obsessed culture" (par. 28). Moreover, the BBC interviewed Kathy Peiss, a professor of women's history at the University of Massachusetts. According to Peiss, the baby boomer group is 'inculcated with the idea that they won't ever grow up'" (quoted in Westcott par. 28). In short, over-thirty mothers—having grown up in an era of women's empowerment and as neoliberal fitness-focused unencumbered women—no longer believe that they need to be "matronly" once they become mothers and instead believe they can and should remain sexy bikini-wearing moms. In this way, being a bikini-wearing postpartum mom symbolizes women's empowerment and strength.

At the same time, however, the bikini is also a viewed as a symbol of the oppressive beauty myth and exacting body standards that lead young girls and women to body disorders and, sometimes, even self-inflicted pain. Also describing young female college students, for example, Brumberg suggests that young women now wear the most "minimalist" bikinis possible. To do so, however, they must employ various painful body practices, primarily hot waxing, in order to remove hair from the bikini-line area. Brumberg goes on to report that her female college students justify this procedure because they report that wearing a bikini makes them feel confident, even though they acknowledge that wearing minimalist bikinis may also objectify them. Although she does not use the language of post-second wave femininity, Brumberg does note, "These young women were bright enough to gain admission to an Ivy League university, and they enjoyed educational opportunities unknown to earlier generations. But they also felt a need to strictly police their bodies" (xxii–xxiii). Thus, the bikini can also be read as a problematic symbol of exacting body standards of beauty and fitness for women that continue to objectify them.

Rather than *either* being a symbol of women's empowerment *or* women's oppression, in the context of celebrity mom profiles, I contend that the bikini *always* represents conflicting contemporary gender assumptions: it is both a symbol of women's power and strength—women's post-second wave empowerment—and how women continue to be held to exacting and even more intensive and oppressive beauty and fitness standards in relation to the maternal body and body work. Consequently, today the bikini is the ideal symbol of and for post-second wave neoliberal motherhood at the crosscurrents of the neoliberal and post-second wave turns. Indeed, there is no better symbol for contemporary privileged women's postpartum body and "proof" for their return to an even more exacting sexy femininity. To be sure, as the analysis of Kardashian showed, she "proved" that she finally had her out-of-control pregnant body under control on her bikini-wearing Greek vacation and in her five months postpartum bikini reveal; both of which were heavily covered by media. And, those media reports all confirmed that Kardashian was finally happy and comfortable with her maternal body because she was *a bikini-ready mom*. Or, as *hollywoodlife.com* put it specifically about her pregnant bikini body but is also true of her postpartum body reveal: "That bikini proves it—Kim looks amazing!" ("Kim Kardashian Showing Off," Steihl par. 8).

In the same way that the bikini allowed Kardashian to prove her adherence to *both* slender-pregnant and postpartum norms, then, I contend that the quickly slender, even bikini-ready, body profiles also use the bikini as the ideal proof for celebrities' adherence to the conflicting gender assumptions and body requirements of contemporary motherhood. To put it another way: the conflicting gender ideologies and symbolism associated with the bikini makes it the perfect symbol of and proof for women's post-second wave split subjectivity, the demanding and exacting standards of postpartum sexiness that require a third shift of body work, and the embrace of the new momism. Thus, the quickly slender, even-bikini ready, postpartum body has also become a symbol for and embodiment of a successful embrace of the more-intensive new momism, "appropriate" post-second wave crisis management, postpartum women's ability to more quickly recover an even better, seemingly unencumbered form that continues to make them appear more similar than different from men, while they also prove that they remain sexy by being bikini-wearing or form-fitting-clothes-wearing sexy moms postpartum.

Not Denying Women's Reproductive Capacity; Rather, Erasing Any Signs of Pregnancy and Maternity

The quickly slender celebrity mom profiles might appear to be denying women's reproductive capacity as a solution to manage the post-second wave split subjectivity and the post-second wave crisis in femininity. Instead of denial, the analysis here and in the previous chapter suggest something different: both the slender-pregnant and new quickly slender body imperatives are about one never knowing that a woman was pregnant rather than denying women's reproductive capacity. The most obvious example of this appears in an *US Weekly* report. In it, the magazine reports of Lopez, for example, "*One would never know* the 5-foot-6 Lopez gave birth to twins. . . . in 2008" (italics added, "How Stars" Grossbart 45). In a similar vein, the postpartum bikini-ready body—that was also a slender-pregnant body, pregnant in belly only—is a body where "one would never know" that the celebrity had been pregnant. This, however, is neither a denial of pregnancy nor motherhood; instead, it is simply an erasure of a quickly forgotten pregnancy—a pregnancy that was just a "small bump in the road" of a post-second wave woman's life—as postpartum women quickly erase the visible signs of pregnancy and return to an even better postpartum body/form.

A parallel exists between the quickly slender body and mothers who have plastic surgery postpartum. In her analysis of gender and plastic surgery, Victoria Pitts-Taylor argues that postpartum women have plastic surgery not as a means to deny reproduction or motherhood but instead to recover sexy femininity. Pitts-Taylor reports the following mother's postsurgery response to her plastic surgery: "Stephanie says, 'I don't feel like I look like a mom anymore!'" (46). Pitts-Taylor goes on to suggest, "Of course, Stephanie isn't really abandoning her role as a mother, but she is delighted to abandon what she sees as the unglamorous body and face of a typical mom" (46). Or, to put it another, Stephanie is a mother who does not want her body to appear "wrecked by pregnancy" and instead wants to look like she has an unencumbered, even better, sexy postpartum body.

Moreover, a *Today Show* report, titled, "Mom, Would you Erase the Signs of Pregnancy? More and More Women are Turning to Post-childbirth Surgery," also does not deny motherhood and instead focuses on the return to an attractive postpartum body by erasing the visible signs of pregnancy postpartum. The *Today Show* continues, "*Nothing compares to the joy of motherhood, but the havoc you go through to get your body back in shape can bring tears to your eyes. That's why more mom's are turning to combined surgical procedures, also called a mommy makeover, to get back their pre-pregnancy body*" (italicized in original, Tarkin par. 1). Also noting women's split subjectivity implicitly, *Today* tells readers: "Others point out that many mothers today are not just 'mothers' they have professional and personal lives outside the home and don't want to look like the stereotypical mother" (Tarkin par. 10). Thus, the solution offered first by the slender-pregnant body, then second by the quickly slender, even bikini-ready, body is not to deny motherhood but rather *to erase the physical evidence of it* so that women can return to an even better and energized form, return to their unencumbered equality in the public sphere, while simultaneously continuing to be primarily responsible for childcare and family life in the private sphere.

At our present moment, then, I suggest that the new quickly slender, even-bikini ready, body, is not a denial of motherhood[15] but is a denial of women's pregnancy and, more significantly, women's "encumberedness." In other words, the quickly slender postpartum body denies the difference maternity—family responsibility and the reproductive body—creates for mothers postpartum and demands that mothers bounce back even more quickly and with even more energy to their unencumbered similarity with men. Or, as Cunningham puts it in terms of relationship between the postpartum body and bouncing back, "In today's world, women are expected to produce bodies which move 'fluidly' between what they have fought so hard to achieve, a place in both the home and work. And what is more fluid than a body that slips in and out of reproduction without any 'visible' aftermaths—a body which seems to regulate movement between the domestic sphere and the workplace with cellulite-free ease" (450).

One significant consequence of the quickly slender, even-bikini ready, body is that the size and shape of the maternal body—both slender pregnant and quickly slender, even bikini ready, postpartum—are now key symbols, if not "the" symbol, of the state of the unencumbered self of the postpartum women. Bordo's ("Reading") early work on the slender body, as I noted in the previous chapter, reveals "increasingly, the size and shape of the body has come to operate as a marker of personal, internal order (or disorder)—as a symbol for the state of the soul" (474). A central imperative for post-second wave beneficiaries who become mothers, then, is to "reorder" the postpartum body as the symbol of the unencumbered public-sphere feminine body, regardless of maternal and second-shift responsibilities. Indeed, Bordo also suggests that because women are no longer exclusively trained to channel their energies and desires into the home, husband, and family, today, "it is required of that energy, loose in the public world, to be stripped of its psychic resonances with maternal power, and normalized according to the professional 'male' standards of the public arena" (482). Finally, Bordo concludes that women and their bodies will pay the greatest symbolic and material toll to meet body standards. As a result, "power works also 'from below,' as women associate slenderness and self-management via the experience of newfound freedom (from domestic destiny) and empowerment in the public arena" (485). Thus, I contend that the postpartum slenderness that results from the third shift of body work now also allows mothers to embody their post-second wave similarity with men, while also erasing the signs of their ongoing domestic responsibilities.

As a consequence, within the context of women's post-second wave crisis in femininity, I am suggesting that the quickly slender, even bikini-ready, body, like the symbolism of the bikini, is now the weapon of choice to: manage encumbered female success in both the public and private spheres; quickly erase pregnancy's "small bump in the road" for post-second wave beneficiaries; reestablish and energize the ongoing division of labor for family life and childrearing in the private sphere, while simultaneously denying mothers' primary responsibility for childrearing once children arrive, and erase the difference maternity does, in fact, continue to make in women's lives today. In other words, first, the slender-pregnant, then, second, the quickly slender body also now represent both women's freedom from our previous domestic destiny—we are no longer destined exclusively to channel our energy and desires into home, husband, and family—and the contradictory fact that *we have not been freed from domestic duties and responsibilities* for children, home, and family; facts that need to be quickly erased postpartum in order to maintain the illusion of postfeminist neoliberal equality. Or, as Beyonce might put it in terms of the contemporary postfeminist illusion that celebrity mom profiles reinforce and promote: "You can have your child, and you can still have fun, and still be sexy, and still have dreams, and still live for yourself" ("Beyonce Reveals," quoted in Schutte par. 6).

Conclusions

Like the slender-pregnant maternal body, the quickly slender, even bikini-ready, maternal body is the key rhetorical element in postpartum celebrity mom profiles to reinforce and further entrench the intensified and hegemonic ideology of good mothering today. The analysis in this chapter also reveals that the new momism no longer only encourages guilt and failure but also now a *new fourth core principle and requirement* for a third shift of body work as the now more-specific solution to women's second-shift responsibilities, as the energizing solution to mothers' post-second wave crisis in femininity, and as a means to an end for women to return to their similarity with men (unencumbered or not) in the public sphere, while also returning to sexy femininity. The third shift of body work also works so that the quickly slender and maintained postpartum body literally and symbolically erases the visible sign of encumberedness from a public woman's body and, as a result, reconstructs an unencumbered body that communicates a symbolic statement about how quickly postpartum women can and should return to their public, sexy (even better) unencumbered self and supposed equality with men in the public sphere. By entrenching the third shift postpartum, the shift to a quickly slender, even bikini-ready, body also now "solves" the problem of inequality that still exists between encumbered men and women by reinforcing and perpetuating women's primary responsibilities in the private sphere, childrearing, and household labor, *while also and simultaneously* acknowledging women's freedom from a domestic destiny.

Ironically, then, a new postfeminist "super-supermom" is emerging such that doing it all now means doing work, family, and childcare, while adding a third shift of body work as a means to an end to: energize and accomplish the second shift, deny women's ongoing responsibility for that shift, and maintain the facade of women's unencumbered equality in the public sphere. Moreover, as a result, by maintaining this facade, this super-supermom also allows heterosexual fathers to also express support for and believe in women's equality, while also giving those fathers permission to support women's primary caregiving as women's maternal choice rather than as ongoing gender oppression. As such, the analysis also reveals that postpartum celebrity mom profiles further entrench contemporary women's post-second wave split subjectivity, while also revealing the preparatory connection between slender-pregnant and bikini-ready celebrity mom profiles. If the slender-pregnant profiles cultivate the acceptance, even embrace, of postpartum split subjectivity, then postpartum celebrity mom profiles further entrench that split subjectivity by erasing all visible signs of it from the postpartum maternal body.

Moreover, by promoting a third shift of body work as the route both to becoming sexy postpartum bikini-ready moms and to energize mothers' second shift responsibilities, bikini-ready celebrity mom profiles now make the maternal body *the post-second wave neoliberal management tool* for individualized and privatized solutions to work-life struggles and the post-second wave crisis in femininity. In fact, as the analysis reveals, the quickly slender, even bikini-ready, body also works rhetorically to resolve the post-second wave crisis in femininity by further reinforcing and entrenching neotraditional family configurations, while also making this family type appear to be new and progressive, even supportive of mothers "choosing" to be the primary parent. Indeed, neotraditional families appear to be new and even progressive because many contemporary, privileged heterosexual families have both an educated and professional mother and father who continue to work professionally after the birth of children. This family configuration continues to be problematic, however, because the basic foundation of pre-second wave family roles and responsibilities still hold once children arrive: mothers continue to be primary caregivers of children in this new family type, even when they maintain their professional life. Consequently, neotraditional families can be easily read as progressive, even empowered families, while simultaneously continuing to reinforce contemporary women's ongoing domestic responsibilities. Neotraditional family configurations also work to deny the real difference maternity makes in post-second wave mothers' lives by encouraging body work as the specific energizing, individual, and privatized solution to manage second shift responsibilities and to adhere to the various remaining, intertwined, and unquestioned gender assumptions that undergird the post-second wave crisis in femininity: women still want a fairy-tale wedding; being a mother is still the most important role for women, regardless of any other success that they might have in the public sphere; women must always command the male gaze, and women are responsible for family-life management and childrearing.

Even though I analyzed slender-pregnant and quickly slender celebrity mom profiles separately, because I believe that celebrity mom profiles encourage a two-step process to encourage mothers to accept and embrace their post-second wave split subjectivity and the more-intensive new momism, ultimately, as I have argued, slender-pregnant and bikini-ready profiles work together to do so. As such, in the next chapter, I detail the seven new rules that have emerged in this iteration of celebrity mom profiles.

4

Consequences, Rules, and Conclusions about Bikini-Ready Moms

Who hasn't seen the pictures? The snaps of Miranda Kerr's infinite legs gliding through the airport with baby Flynn perched on one hip, J. Lo sleek and six-packed in a Lanvin bikini after the birth of her twins and Jessica Alba with her sinewy arms toting her daughters to the park: They're proof that women can come out of the postpartum fog as Mom 2.0, a leaner, faster, stronger version of their pre-pregnancy selves.
—Christine Lennon, par. 1

I learned quickly that the gains for women in the past decades have not meant a similar gain for mothers.
—Miriam Peskowitz, 66

Individually, chapter 2 and chapter 3 addressed the "how" question of this book: *How* are celebrity mom profiles now integrating the slender-pregnant and quickly slender, even bikini-ready, maternal body as the central feature of the new celebrity mom profiles, while also continuing to refine, reinforce, and romanticize the new momism in ways that also offer postfeminist neoliberal solutions to the post-second wave crisis in femininity? Combining the analysis in both chapters allows me to now answer the three other overarching and related questions of the book: How do the new profiles work rhetorically to reshape and refine the new momism? What are the consequences of this reshaping and refining for how we understand contemporary motherhood and the post-second wave crisis in femininity? What are the key features and new rules of celebrity mom profiles?

The Redesign of and Consequences
for the Now More-Intensive New Momism

There is no doubt that there is a mutually reinforcing relationship between the new momism and celebrity mom profiles: the new profiles are reshaping and refining how the new momism works rhetorically—works to persuade mothers—to accept, even embrace the more-demanding core principles of this "good" mothering ideology. In fact, in chapter 2 the analysis revealed that slender-pregnant celebrity mom profiles *are now the first step* in persuading post-second wave woman to embrace their split subjectivity and an even-more intensive mothering position and ideology. By focusing on the maternal body as the symbol and embodiment of future mothering, slender-pregnant profiles do so by making the maternal body the "weapon of choice" in making the "argument" that the measure of a good future mother is tied to *how* she manages her pregnant maternal body—how she manages her weight gain, her maternity style, her comfort and happiness with her pregnant body, and how she prepares for her impending birth. In chapter 3, the analysis revealed that postpartum celebrity mom images and profiles *are now the second step* in persuading post-second wave woman to embrace further their split subjectivity and the new momism ideology that both now require a third shift of body work. The second stage of the process, then, happens via postpartum profiles, which occur much earlier than they did in the first iteration of profiles, and these profiles now train mothers to buy into a third shift of body work as the specific means to an end to manage and energize them as they enact the core principles of the new momism, while also enjoying their post-second wave status in the public sphere. In short, as the analysis also suggests, the second step requires mothers to accept and embrace the new fourth principle of the new momism—a third shift of body work—as a now-necessary core requirement of good mothering, so that mothers can still meet their first and second shift responsibilities with stress-free ease and contentment.

Moreover, and as a result of this two-step process, the analysis showed that celebrity images and profiles also work to erase the difference that maternity makes in women's lives today and to persuade mothers that they can now move in and out of pregnancy—as if it is just a "small bump" in the road in their unencumbered gender equality in the public sphere—and childrearing with little trouble or difficulty and without losing their newfound gender equity with men in the workplace and public sphere. And, finally, I also revealed that celebrity mom images and profiles work rhetorically to persuade mothers that their ongoing primary responsibility for childrearing and family-life management is still "normal"; and, if mothers are having difficulty managing these responsibilities, then, rather than being the weapon of choice among women, the maternal body is also a new weapon of choice in the profiles to persuade mothers that the maternal body and working on that body are the privatized solution and management tool to handle their difficulties and energize their ability both to "have it all" and "do it all" within neotraditional family structures.

This means, then, when combined, the analysis chapters also reveal that celebrity mom profiles that make the maternal body the central focus have changed in important ways, with accompanying important consequences for how the new momism is being redesigned and reinforced via the profiles. The first consequence is that celebrity mom profiles now encourage a new post-second wave neoliberal "super-supermom" such that doing it all now means doing work, family, and childcare, while adding a third shift of body work as the more-specific means to an end: to energize and accomplish the second shift, deny women's ongoing responsibility for that shift, and maintain the facade of women's unencumbered equality in the public sphere. As such, the analysis also reveals that postpartum celebrity mom profiles further entrench the post-second wave split subjectivity, while also revealing that a new preparatory connection exists between slender-pregnant and bikini-ready celebrity mom profiles. Indeed and yet another consequence is, if the slender-pregnant profiles cultivate the acceptance, even embrace, of postpartum split subjectivity, especially for first-time mothers, then, I maintain, that postpartum celebrity mom profiles further entrench that split subjectivity by erasing all visible signs of it from the postpartum maternal body. Moreover, by promoting a third shift of body work

as the route both to becoming sexy postpartum bikini-ready moms
and to energize mothers' second-shift responsibilities, postpartum
celebrity mom profiles now make the maternal body the post-second
wave neoliberal management tool for individualized and privatized
solutions to *work-life struggles and the post-second wave crisis in femininity.* As a result, another consequence is that the third shift of
body work has become a new and core fourth principle and value of
the contemporary intensified new momism and within the celebrity mom profiles that support that newly intensified and hegemonic
mothering ideology.

These consequences and resulting refinements of the new
momism are also tied to the seven rules that are crystallizing this
new iteration of celebrity mom profiles. In fact, when the analysis
of slender-pregnant and quickly slender, even bikini ready, celebrity mom profiles are viewed together, then a new set of seven rules[1]
emerge with some rules further entrenching and intensifying beauty
ideals and body work, and with some new rules tied exclusively to
the maternal body. Moreover, as the analysis revealed, because the
profiles now make the maternal body the primary focus, as I argue
next, rather than the previous set of rules that made mothering and
children primary, the new rules make the maternal body primary and
each of the seven rules is, in one way or another, tied to the maternal
body. I also maintain, however, that this does not mean that children and good mothering no longer matter in the new momism and
celebrity mom profiles as they are being reshaped; both children and
good mothering clearly do still matter and, in fact, the core goal of
the third shift of body work is *to make women better at managing
their second-shift responsibilities,* to make them better and even more
devoted to their children.

As result, being a good intensive mother still matters and
remains the ultimate goal; the difference now between the first and
second iteration of celebrity mom profiles is a matter of focus and
degree in relation to that ultimate goal. Clearly, in terms of focus,
as has been established, the primary focus is now on the maternal
body. To put it slightly differently: celebrity mom profiles continue
to assume that a mother should be a good intensive mother; that
has not changed. What has changed is the focus on the maternal
body as both the new primary symbol for and embodiment of good
and bad future and postpartum mothering and as the privatized and

more-specific solution to any work-life struggles. In terms of degree, mothers must be even-more intensive mothers—it is what good post-second wave neoliberal mothers do in the private sphere—and more intensive in their body management and body work by adhering to the new fourth core principle and values associated with a third shift of body work. This means that the logic of the new core fourth principle is as follows: if a mother engages in a third shift of body work, then she will be *an even better woman and mother*, while also erasing the difference maternity makes. Thus, while the first iteration of celebrity mom profiles also reinforced the idea that it was women's responsibility to manage any work-life struggle themselves in the private sphere, the new iteration of celebrity mom profiles has been refined such that they now offer a more-specific solution—maternal body management and body work—as the exact means to an end of managing the difficulty mothers have juggling it all as post-second wave neoliberal mothers, as they remain good, even-more devoted mothers.

As I detail the seven rules of celebrity mom profiles next, I also show that three rules are connected to slender-pregnant profiles, while four rules are connected to the postpartum body; although, all seven, ultimately, work together to persuade good intensive mothers that a third shift of body work in neotraditional family configurations is the best solution to managing the post-second wave crisis in femininity, while also energizing them so that they can be even more intensive good mothers. This means that although some of the focus of the old rules that Douglas and Michaels first revealed are still embedded in the focus on the maternal body, other components of the old rules have disappeared or are now secondary. So, for example, as I show, the feminine beauty imperatives that Douglas and Michaels detailed in Rules 1, 2, and 3 in the first iteration of profiles—Rule #1: "The mom is gorgeous, in clear control of her destiny, and her husband loves her even more once she becomes pregnant and the baby is born" (126); Rule #2: "They are radiantly happy when they are with their kids" (128), and Rule #3: "They always look and feel fabulous—better than ever—while pregnant, because they are nutrition experts and eat exactly what they should and have the discipline to exercise regularly" (128)—have intensified, while both husbands and children have mostly disappeared or are "secondary" or only "props" to highlight a celebrity mom's maternal body:

as is the case, for example, in the Wilkinson-Baskett bikini cover or when celebrity moms are shown at the beach in their bikinis with their children in tow.

Moreover, this also means that Rule 4—"Whatever your schedule, whatever institutional constraints you confront that keep you away from or less involved with your kids, it must be clear that they are your number-one priority, no matter what" (130) to Rule 6—"The celebrity mom is fun-loving, eager to jump up and play with the kids at a moment's notice" (132) and Rule 7—"Rule number seven of the celebrity profile insists that truly good, devoted mothering requires lavishing as many material goods on your kids as possible" (132)—of the first iteration are also no longer featured rules and have moved to the background in terms of the focus of the profiles; although, they continue to be presumed within the first three core tenets of the new momism that have intensified but not changed: "the insistence that no woman is truly complete or fulfilled unless she has kids, that women remain the best primary caretakers of children, and that to be a remotely decent mother, a woman has to devote her entire physical, psychological, emotional, and intellectual being, 24/7, to her children" (Douglas and Michaels 4). In short, the old rules connected to beauty ideals and body management have been intensified in the new profile structure, while husbands are gone—they rarely appear and are rarely mentioned—and children have become secondary or props to the focus on the maternal body; even though children are still important to good mothering and deserving of both enormous amounts of attention and material goods.

New Rules for Celebrity Mom Profiles

Rule #1: The maternal body is now the most important symbol for and embodiment of "good" and "bad" (future) mothering: first, via the slender-pregnant body and, second, via the quickly slender, even bikini-ready postpartum body. Because the maternal body has become central to the kind of maternal identity promoted, reinforced, and detailed in the new celebrity mom profiles, the maternal body has also become both the symbol of and *the management tool* for the mediated "body panic"—the broader anxiety and cultural tensions at the crosscurrents of the post-second wave and neoliberal turns—related to good and bad (future) motherhood. In fact, the analysis in chapter 2 showed that Rule 1 crystallized as the slender-pregnant profiles addressed anxiety and nervousness about the boundaries for future mothers in relation to issues of class, gender, taste, and authenticity, and the acceptance, even embrace, of both a future post-second wave split subjectivity and the new momism, while the analysis in chapter 3 revealed that postpartum profiles addressed the broader struggle and anxieties associated with post-second wave neoliberal women trying to have it all by enjoying their post-second wave gains and similarity with unencumbered men in the public sphere, while also meeting their obligations at home and the second-shift responsibilities associated with childrearing, childcare, and family-life management.

More specifically, chapter 2 demonstrated that the obsessive media focus on the women's maternity wear, shoes included, in both the individual profiles and comparisons revealed much about the connection between "dressing the bump" of the maternal body and perceptions about maternal attitude and future mothering. In fact, Rule 1 was also crystallized as slender-pregnant profiles also responded to the gender, class-based, cultural, and family values anxieties that were displayed in the "battle" between Middleton and Kardashian's celebrity pregnancies and future motherhood, where the battle reflected on and responded to broader cultural anxiety and nervousness about the blurring of boundaries between the "real" and "scripted," the "authentic" and "inauthentic," "classiness" and "trashiness," and "quality" and "nonquality" of post-second wave neoliberal motherhood today. As the analysis also showed, Kardashian represented the anxiety and ambivalence about excessive, inauthentic, and bad future motherhood that her pregnant body embodied as Kardashian made all the wrong choices in body management, maternity wear, and her failure to prepare appropriately for the impending birth of her child—she was a "warning" about the consequences of "awful ordinary" future mothering done wrong—while Middleton represented the tightly managed, authentic, and "exemplary ordinary" good future motherhood that her pregnancy embodied as she made all the right, good choices in body management, maternity wear, and in her prepping well for her impending birth. Thus, the slender-pregnant profiles of these two women also negotiated the boundaries between ordinary and special future mothering, between awful ordinary post-second wave neoliberal future motherhood and exemplary ordinary post-second wave neoliberal future motherhood.

The analysis also demonstrated that Kardashian's maternal body and subject position were positioned by media to represent anxiety and ambivalence about a racialized, excessive, inauthentic, possibly scripted, often trashy and tasteless, bad future motherhood that her pregnancy embodied and enacted as Kardashian made all the wrong and mostly tasteless or "Hollywood-style" choices throughout her pregnancy. This means then that, unlike Middleton who was judged as a perfect ordinary future mother who had legitimately been made special because of her good choices, willingness to wait, body management, and appropriate "turn" to embracing an intensive mothering maternal subject position that revealed that she, indeed, would be a good future mother, Kardashian was judged as an awful ordinary future mother who was not special and was, in fact, a warning about impulsive excess, bad weight and body management, and an inability to make the turn to embracing an intensive mothering maternal subject position; all of which revealed that Kardashian, in fact, would be a bad future mother. Consequently, each woman's maternal body, style, and pregnancy combined to make the case for why, when making post-second wave neoliberal maternal choices, the better, more appropriate, authentic, tasteful, valuable, and real position is the post-second wave neoliberal princess with the perfect intensive maternal subject position and slender-pregnant, even waif-like, maternal body.

In terms of postpartum profiles, chapter 3 demonstrated that the obsessive media focus on celebrity mothers' quick "bounce back" to even better, sexier bikini-ready postpartum bodies also revealed much about the connection between the bikini-ready maternal body and perceptions about mothers' ability to "have it all under control": to be energized, even better mothers, women, and post-second wave beneficiaries, as mothers also negotiate the anxieties and difficulties of having and doing it all—first, second, and now third-shift responsibilities. A clear imperative of the profiles, then, as the analysis demonstrated, is that postpartum, post-second wave neoliberal motherhood requires a "super-fit," even better, hot and sexy postpartum maternal body that requires even-more intensive and dedicated body work and controlled and disciplined dieting for all mothers. Equally important, the quickly slender, even bikini-ready, body is now held up as improving celebrity moms' postpartum bodies and making them even better women and mothers. In fact, as I also argued, celebrity mom profiles have integrated a third shift of body work to improve mothers' postpartum bodies and to energize their second-shift responsibilities, to make them even more productive at their second-shift responsibilities, and to erase any lingering evidence of reproduction on the postpartum body.

Indeed, postpartum profiles do so by integrating second wave feminist ideas about women's post-second wave choices, strength, and empowerment in the service of promoting a third shift of body work as something essential mothers can and should do as a means to manage any stress or anxiety associated with having it all, to train for success in the second shift of household labor and childcare and to erase the difference maternity continues to make in mothers' lives. This means that, as cultural anxieties and difficulties contemporary mothers face doing it all emerge in public conversations, postpartum profiles suggest that a quickly slender, even bikini-ready, postpartum maternal body is a symbol for and embodiment of a mother's ability to have it all under control, and to be an even better, more energized good mother and good woman who can still command the male gaze and move in and out of her first and second shift responsibilities with "cellulite-free ease." Thus, postpartum profiles also negotiate the anxieties and difficulties of having it all by offering the third shift of body work to make mothers even more productive, stress-free second-shift "workers" in the private sphere. Consequently, today, a celebrity mom's postpartum maternal body and body work combine to make the case for why, when making post-second wave neoliberal maternal choices, the better, sexier, hot, maternal body that has obviously engaged in a third shift of body work is now both a symbol for and embodiment of an even-more intensive good mother.

Rule #2: Slender pregnancy and good maternal body management are now prerequisites, so that pregnancy is just a "small bump in the road" in contemporary women's lives. Rule 2 is tied to the slender-pregnant maternal body in that slender pregnancy and good slender-pregnant body management are now prerequisites for both a quick postpartum bounce back and for a quick return to gender equity in the public sphere postpartum. Indeed, as chapter 2 showed, Rule 2 was crystallized from the beginning of the obsessive media coverage of Middleton and Kardashian's pregnancies. In fact, throughout and in various ways, the slender-pregnant celebrity mom profiles represented Middleton as the contained and disciplined maternal subject who also had effortless style and ease in her "Jackie-O-like-royal" pregnancy: from her tight-lipped and reluctant pregnancy announcement, disciplined (or not) eating, controlled and disciplined weight management, happy glow, lack of travel (and royal engagements), tasteful, attractive but still prim and proper perfect maternity wear, even her appropriately tasteful asset-revealing shoes, and appropriate impending nesting preparations. As a result, for Middleton, pregnancy was just a small bump in the road in her waif-like maternal body and to her new identity as a future intensive mother, an identity that she embraced fully.

Unlike Middleton, from the beginning and throughout, media represented Kardashian as an out-of-control, excessive, and racialized "other" maternal subject who also had an uncomfortable, unhappy "Reality-TV-star-like" pregnancy: from her Hollywood-style pregnancy announcement, excessive and "cheap" eating, uncontrolled and undisciplined weight management, fashion-disaster, even malfunctioning, maternity style, mostly unhappy and uncomfortable scowls, excessive, even possibly irresponsible, travel, and inability to stop working, which also meant that Kardashian continued to try to "squeeze" into her prepregnancy life, including, even, her shoes. As a result, for Kardashian, pregnancy was an "excessively large and possibly insurmountable bump in the road" in her "whale-like" maternal body and to her new identity as a mother, an identity that she was unable to embrace fully.

As such, the analysis also revealed, in fact, that slender pregnancy norms still privilege the slender white body as the ideal and requires the right kind of slender-pregnant bump—a "tidy," "neat," and/or small bump. And, inauthentic, bad, or not obviously pregnant maternal bodies—racialized bodies that appear "fat" rather than pregnant—will be ridiculed and fat shamed. Indeed, as the analysis in chapter 2 also revealed, the better weight "problem" to have during pregnancy is being "too thin" rather than being "too fat." And this kind of body requires good, disciplined food and desire management. When a celebrity mom fails or appears to fail at this management, she must defend herself publicly; she must "dare to bare" her pregnant body in a bikini to prove, finally, that pregnancy will just be a small bump in the road in her maternal life and to her maternal body.

Rule #3: A good future mother, especially a first-time mother, must make the "turn" to accepting, even embracing, both her split subjectivity and intensive mothering norms *prior to* becoming a mother. Rule 3 is the bridging rule in that this rule connects the initial acceptance, even embrace, of post-second wave subjectivity in the slender-pregnant profiles to the more-specific solution offered— a third shift of body work—for that split subjectivity in postpartum profiles. Indeed, as the analysis in chapter 2 showed, Rule 3 was crystallized when slender-pregnant profiles suggested that good mothers must accept, even embrace, their split subjectivity, while also making the turn to embracing their future intensive mothering by nesting and preparing. The importance of accepting, even embracing, both their post-second wave split subjectivity and the new momism prior to becoming first-time mothers, for example, were revealed in the late-in-pregnancy media coverage of Middleton and Kardashian. That Middleton was going to be a good future mother and that she had made the turn were clearly suggested when she nested and shopped with her mother to prepare for the impending birth of her son, as she revealed she was a "natural" with children, and by her commitment to reading as many books as possible to enhance her ability to develop the necessary "professional-level" skills required of a new good mother. In short, she was positioned by media as a real future celebrity mom who had accepted her future split subjectivity and embraced the core tenets of the new momism prior to delivery.

Again and always unlike Middleton, Kardashian was positioned alone, "grinding away" at work, "vacationing" (possibly skill working) with her large family, was not a natural with kids and, in fact, was described as terrified of her impending motherhood. Thus, even late in her pregnancy, the media concern about Kardashian traveling too much made it clear that this was another way that Kardashian had not made her impending motherhood her priority and, instead, she was powering on, grinding away, and continuing to squeeze into her unencumbered life, even though her birth was impending, while she also engaged in risky, possibly irresponsible behavior, all of which suggested that Kardashian had still not made mothering, children, and a commitment to following the advice of experts her priorities above all else prior to delivery, as Middleton had late in her pregnancy. And, as a result, only one conclusion could be drawn about Kardashian: she had yet to make the turn to embracing the new momism, which meant she would be an awful ordinary bad future mother.

Moreover, the late-in-pregnancy profiles also allowed media to explore *how and what should happen* when unencumbered post-second wave women have to reconcile the fact that their gender equity in the public sphere does not match ongoing inequitable gender roles in the private sphere, once a woman becomes a mother. As I argued in chapter 2, this means that when media positioned Middleton as the perfect future mother while positioning Kardashian as the warning about what happens to a pregnant woman who is unable to keep herself and her maternal body under control and who is also struggling to make the turn to devoting herself to prioritizing her future mothering above all else, media also positioned Kardashian's excess as the excess of too much unencumbered gender equity in the public sphere—she was powering on, grinding on, going it alone, and trying to squeeze into her unencumbered life, still. Kardashian, then, is also a warning about too much or excessive gender equality in the context of maternity. Consequently, the moral of the Kardashian warning is this: if a post-second wave beneficiary continues to power on or grind away at work, then she will fail to embrace both her split subjectivity and her ongoing gender responsibilities once the children arrive. Because celebrity mom profiles have always been, and remain today, the most influential media form to sell the new momism and a new mother must be trained to accept and embrace ongoing gender-based inequity in the private sphere, the slender-pregnant profiles crystallized *how* and *what* must be done during pregnancy to do so, while also providing a warning about what happens if a pregnant woman fails to do so by powering on or grinding away in the public sphere: she will be shamed, ridiculed, and, ultimately, judged a bad future mother.

In fact, as the analysis of Kardashian also revealed, when a pregnant woman fails to make the turn to embracing her new maternal position, she will be subject to attack, while her maternal body, if it does not adhere to the slender-pregnant norm, will also be "the target of viscous fat jokes and incentive comments." Moreover, the viciousness of the attacks against Kardashian and her maternal body revealed just how ferociously a racialized nonslender pregnant woman will be attacked, both morally and via fat shaming, when she and her maternal body are unable to make the "necessary" turn toward slender pregnancy, good maternal body management, good future mothering, and accepting the post-second wave split subjectivity. This suggests, as the analysis showed, that media also focused on Middleton and Kardashian in particular and at the expensive of other pregnant celebrity moms because they are extremes to pull all women toward the reconciliation and acceptance of both their future split subjectivity and intensive mothering that Middleton and her maternal body represented and embodied and away from the failed reconciliation Kardashian and her maternal body represented and embodied throughout most of her pregnancy.

NO NEW FOIBLES ALLOWED, NOW

A potentially significant issue about both the fat shaming of Kardashian and her perceived inability to make the turn toward her future split subjectivity is that both are interesting in relation to Douglas and Michaels' Rule 5—"There must be some human frailties, some family tragedies, some struggles or foibles that bring the celeb down a peg, make her seem a bit more like us and allow some of us to identify with her" (131). Given the obsessive focus on the pregnant body, initially, Kardashian's weight struggle might have been the new "difficulty" or "human frailty" that made her be a bit more like "us." In other words, as the second iteration of profiles make the maternal body the central focus and feature, it would seem plausible that the new human frailty could be in relation to the maternal body. Or, alternatively, given the recognition that having it all by doing it all is a challenge—hence the primary focus on offering a more-specific solution to these challenges via the profiles—struggling to embrace the split subjectivity might also have become a new foible for a celebrity mom.

Even so, I believe that the analysis in chapter 2 suggested otherwise. Indeed, the coverage and the analysis of Kardashian's weight problem and her failure to make the turn to accepting her future split subjectivity made it exceedingly clear that this was not the case. And, in fact, the media coverage made it unambiguous that these potential human frailties lead to vicious fat shaming and ridicule, both of which even media recognized. I believe that this is the case because, given the intensified demands and the need to engage in body work as the future solution in postpartum profiles, there is no longer any room for foibles or struggles. In other words, given that intensive mothering demands have become even more intensive and the solution to having it all resides almost exclusively in each mother's ability to engage in a third shift of body work that is predicated on at least the acceptance, sometimes embrace, of the split subjectivity and the fact that this third shift is being framed as the energizing solution to solving the problem of having it all by doing it all alone, foibles or struggles can no longer be tolerated.

Moreover, as I have also argued, celebrity mom profiles now encourage mothers to be super-supermoms. When both the super-supermom and third-shift imperatives are combined with my contention that this iteration of profiles also *work to deny the difference maternity continues to make in women's lives*, then, "allowing for" or "admitting" that any difficulty exists would mean also *acknowledging that maternity does make a difference in mothers' lives*. Thus, as the new momism and the profiles intensify the requirements of good motherhood today, there is no longer any room to admit to foibles or difficulties; instead, only energized super-supermoms or perfect princesses like Middleton whose maternal bodies make the difference maternity continues to make invisible—both through their body practices and private-sphere work—are now the only acceptable celebrity mothers. This also means, then, that Douglas and Michaels' "Rule 5," like the discussion of husbands, have almost completely disappeared in the new profiles in the focus on the maternal body and the exacting and demanding body work promoted.

Rule #4: A quickly slender, even bikini-ready, bounce back to an even better postpartum maternal body is required. Rule 4 was crystallized by the obsessive media focus on the quickly slender, even bikini-ready, postpartum debuts of celebrity moms. Without a doubt, the analysis in chapter 3 clearly showed that a quick bounce back to an even better postpartum body is required of contemporary mothers. Moreover, the before-and-after format in tandem with dieting advice that focuses on eliminating the fat of pregnancy work visually and rhetorically to reinforce the need for immediate postpartum body work as a means to an end to regain control of the "unruly" pregnant body, primarily via a new mom's quick recontainment and erasure of the fat of pregnancy, the out-of-control postpartum bulge.

By focusing more generally on the postpartum body and specifically on the fat or bulge of pregnancy, then, Rule 4 works to heighten the body anxiety women are taught when pregnant, while creating even more exacting standards for a quicker, even better, bounce back.

The analysis also demonstrated that postpartum profiles further entrench the idea that pregnancy must only be a small bump in the road in the postpartum body in the focus on quickly eliminating the lingering fat of pregnancy: the so-called mummy tummy. When slender-pregnant profiles focus on managing and containing the fat of the pregnant body so that only the bump of pregnancy is acceptable and evident, while everything else on the body remains slender, as I argued, the "logical" focus of postpartum body work is on the recontainment of that bulge or fat: the postpartum stomach. This "logic" makes sense because slender pregnancies with small bumps—small pregnancies—are easier to recontain, even erase, because the bulge of pregnancy is less difficult to eliminate quickly in the bounce back to an even better postpartum body. This also means that there is no better way to prepare for an even quicker bounce back, a "fast" erasure of the bump, then, by making sure to maintain a small bump, as Middleton did and Kardashian was unable to do. Thus, adhering to slender-pregnancy norms helps postpartum women *prepare for* the quick recontainment of the only "acceptable" lingering evidence of the pregnancy—the small mummy tummy—while also further entrenching the idea that pregnancy needs only be a small bump in the road in contemporary women's lives.

Just as important, as the analysis in chapter 3 also revealed, is that the debut of the new, better body also clearly communicates—via her postpartum maternal body—that the celebrity mom has it all under control; she is a real post-second wave neoliberal mother who manages to juggle it all—her post-second wave crisis in femininity—well and through *her own personal strength and body work*. As a result, the language of *debut* is yet another key rhetorical device in the quickly slender profiles that works to make it clear that the new goal of the postpartum body is no longer just recovery but instead creating a new, even better sexy body that symbolically communicates post-second wave women's strength and personal ability to do it all and have it all under control quickly and even better than before giving birth. Finally, the analysis in chapter 3 also showed that the debut of the postpartum body also continues to perpetuate the white slender ideal, while also encouraging mothers to bounce back to an even better form. Thus, today the quickly slender bounce-back rule now means that good mothers must become "Moms 2.0: leaner, faster, stronger versions of themselves" postpartum.

Rule #5: Hello hot, sexy moms and maternal bodies that can still command the male gaze; and, the "proof" is in the bikini. The postpartum profiles crystallized Rule 5 via the focus on postpartum women's quick bounce back to being sexy, hot moms. The analysis in chapter 3 revealed, in fact, that coupled with the imperative for a quick bounce back to an even better body is the additional requirement for mothers to become new sexy moms with sexy postpartum bodies that still command the male gaze. Moreover, expecting women to remain sexy, both when pregnant and postpartum, is so strongly tied to the now-public and no-longer-in-hiding maternal body such that the logic of the maternal body is: first, if pregnant women adhere to the slender-pregnant ideal, then, they can remain sexy because they are only pregnant in one place: their bump. Consequently and as a result, second, it "naturally" follows that expecting and demanding that postpartum women quickly return to an even better and sexy slender ideal should be easy because only the lingering fat of the postpartum bump will remain and can be quickly erased.

Moreover, as I also argued, the proof of celebrity moms' sexiness and that they can continue to command the male gaze is "in the bikini." Indeed, today, as I argued in chapter 3, the bikini is the ideal symbol of post-second wave neoliberal motherhood at the crosscurrents of the neoliberal and post-second wave turns. In fact, there is no better symbol for contemporary privileged women's postpartum body and proof for their return to an even more exacting sexy femininity. In the same way that the bikini allowed Kardashian to prove her adherence to *both* slender-pregnant and postpartum norms, I contend that the quickly slender, even bikini-ready, body profiles also use the bikini as the ideal proof for celebrities' adherence to the conflicting gender assumptions and body requirements of contemporary motherhood. Thus, the quickly slender, even-bikini ready, postpartum body has also become a symbol for and embodiment of a mother's successful embrace of intensive mothering and postpartum women's ability to more quickly recover an even better unencumbered form, while they also prove that they remain sexy by being bikini-wearing or form-fitting-clothes-wearing sexy moms postpartum.

Rule #6: A third shift of body work is now essential for postpartum body management to energize the second shift and to erase the difference maternity makes in women's lives. Rule 6 came together via the exacting and demanding standards of postpartum body work that celebrity mom profiles encourage. Indeed, as the analysis revealed, postpartum celebrity moms must bring "Jedi-level discipline" to their eating, dieting, and body work postpartum. The analysis in chapter 3 also showed that this is the case because postpartum celebrity mom profiles now require a third shift of body work to energize the second shift of household labor and childcare and as the now-specific solution to juggling it all within neotraditional families. This third shift works rhetorically, as I also argued, in the same way that the neoliberal ethic of health and wellness-at-work programs work to energize workers and ultimately make them more productive at work; in the same way, the third shift of postpartum body work energizes mothers' second-shift responsibilities and makes them even more productive at their second-shift responsibilities. Both the analysis chapters revealed that this is done, first, via good body management in slender-pregnant profiles, then, second, explicitly in postpartum celebrity mom profiles.

As a result, as the third shift becomes central to the focus on the maternal bodies of celebrities in contemporary postpartum profiles, women's responsibility for the second shift of household labor not only becomes more entrenched, the now more-specific solution offered to manage women's difficulty having it all continues to be placed on women's individual solutions: in this case, via intense and rigorous but also energizing body work. This also means that Rule 6 encourages and reinforces mothers' post-second wave split subjectivity, while also reinforcing privatized and individual solutions for any difficulty a mother experiences juggling or managing her first and second shift responsibilities. Finally, Rule 6 also plays a key role in supporting the idea that "contented" intensive mothers must rely on their own initiative via energizing body work to manage better the stress of having it all, while also becoming more productive at their first- and second-shift responsibilities.

Rule #7: The right kind of maternal body now reveals the right kind of (future) post-second-wave crisis management for contemporary mothers: a mother who enjoys post-second wave gains, but not at the expense of either her obligations at home nor tenets of the now-intensified new momism, while she also adheres to privatized solutions to any work-life struggles. Rule 7 crystallizes as a result of the combined impact of the previous six rules and the gender assumptions embedded within them. Indeed, the analysis chapters clearly showed that slender-pregnant profiles begin to train and prepare future mothers for good, future post-second wave crisis management, while postpartum profiles continue that training by offering a third shift of body work that also denies women's "encumberedness," and, as a result, denies the difference maternity—family responsibility and the reproductive body—makes for mothers postpartum. Equally important, Rule 7 also demands that mothers bounce back even more quickly and with even more energy to their unencumbered similarity with men to show that they can move in and out of reproduction without, as Cunningham puts it, any "'visible' aftermaths—a body which seems to regulate movement between the domestic sphere and the workplace with cellulite-free ease" (450). As a consequence, within the context of both women's future and realized post-second wave crisis, Rule 7 plays a key role in supporting the idea that the right kind of maternal body suggests that a mother "has it all together," that everything is under control. Thus, by doing so, Rule 7 also suggests that the maternal body—first, the slender-pregnant, then second, the quickly slender postpartum body—also now represents both women's freedom from our previous domestic destiny—we are no longer destined exclusively to channel our energy and desires into home, husband, and family and instead should enjoy post-second wave gains—but not at the expense of mothers' obligations at home, not at the expense of adhering to privatized solutions to any work-life struggles, while also being intensive mothers because *mothers have not been freed from domestic duties and responsibilities.*

There is no doubt, then, that these new profiles, especially via Rule 7, are responding to the kinds of work-life balance conversations I first noted in chapter 1. In fact, as I suggested in chapter 1, as contemporary mothers continue to struggle to do it all, key cultural conversations about this struggle have emerged. And the central question is: How can women manage to have it all? Clearly, the new celebrity mom profiles and the rules embedded in them offer a series of gender-based answers that, ultimately, lead to even more intensive mothering within neotraditional family structures. And, in the end, the postfeminist-neoliberal "equality" promoted in the profiles now means that, if the difference maternity continues to make in women's lives is quickly erased postpartum, then, contemporary good mothers should enjoy post-second wave gains, but not at the expense of their obligations at home and not at the expense of adhering to privatized solutions to any work-life struggles.

This also means that celebrity mom profiles offer a privatized solution that allows both professional structures and men to express, *simultaneously*, support for women's newfound equality in the public sphere, without having to change in meaningful ways, especially in the private sphere. Thus, as culture recognizes the changing post-second wave neoliberal conversations that are emerging—that having it all raises challenges (and is, in fact, really difficult) for post-second wave neoliberal mothers—the solution offered via this new iteration of celebrity mom profiles and the seven rules embedded in them provide an answer and set of rules that ultimately suggest that mothers can and should enjoy their status as second wave beneficiaries, while continuing to place the onus of responsibility for childrearing and family-life management on mothers' shoulders, alone and at home in the private sphere.

Theoretical Conclusions

Because much of this book has been theoretical and academic, I close this chapter by addressing some theoretical conclusions and issues that emerged as a result my analysis and findings. In doing so, I also offer some insights about future research on and about "mediated" motherhood. However, because I believe the profiles are so pervasive and exacting and, as a result, none of us—academics included—are immune from them or the messages the profiles promote and reinforce, in the next chapter, I close the book by proposing five strategies of resistance to the profiles and the ideological messages embedded in those profiles and images. I do so to offer some less-theoretical and more-practical suggestions to resisting contemporary celebrity mom profiles and as specific ways, as Douglas and Michaels' first suggested and I believe is even more important today, to "talk back" to the profiles and the ideological messages embedded within them.

Motherhood and Neotraditional Families
as "New/Old" Hegemonic Barriers

At the ideological level, clearly, when combined the analysis chapters suggest that celebrity mom profiles are thoroughly ensconced in supporting a hegemonic neotraditional family configuration that ultimately works as a form of gendered social control to keep mothers in their place, alone in the private sphere, while also appearing to recognize and "support" privileged women's unencumbered strides and successes in the public sphere. As such, this hegemonic family configuration continues to reinforce and normalize mothers' roles as caregivers, while appearing to be a new, even good post-second wave neoliberal family configuration that progressive or gender-equitable-professing fathers (and others) can be proud to support. It is important, then, that everyone recognize, first, that neotraditional families are hegemonic, and that this family type also re-entrenches mothering and caretaking *as women's work* in the private sphere and outside the purview of the public sphere.

Moreover, it is also important to recognize that neotraditional families are also especially dangerous for contemporary women because this family configuration reveals that, while the second wave brought unencumbered women's liberation, there has *not been a mothers' liberation*. Indeed, as Peskowitz puts it: "the gains for women in the past decades have not meant a similar gain for mothers" (66). In other words, while unencumbered women have benefited in real and important ways from second wave feminism, especially in the public sphere, the analysis of both the new momism and the profiles reveal just how stalled we continue to be in terms of household labor and caregiving in the private sphere. Thus, in new and complex ways, while contemporary women's lives have been freed from a *domestic destiny* as mothers, women's lives have not been freed from *domestic responsibility and post-second wave neoliberal maternal choice* as mothers; and the new structure and norms that make the maternal body the central feature of the celebrity mom profiles thoroughly reinforce and normalize both, while also erasing the difference maternity continues to make in women's lives.

As a result, the analysis also reveals that motherhood is a new/old hegemonic barrier to mothers' lives because, as the third shift of body work becomes more and more integrated into celebrity mom profiles and the new momism, the third shift works rhetorically to continue to position women as primary, albeit even-more energized, productive, and stress-free, caregivers of children. As such, the new momism now resolves the post-second wave crisis in femininity by suggesting *it is an individual and privatized* problem that "only" requires individual body work by women in the private sphere rather than large-scale institutional change in the public sphere and/or changes in family-life formations that might include more equitable parenting between mothers and fathers. Consequently, at minimum, it is crucial that future scholarship about contemporary motherhood recognizes that a new, more-specific solution is being offered to contemporary mothers about how they must manage any work-life balance issues on their own via body work and within a seemingly progressive but still-hegemonic family configuration. Moreover, because that body work is now also entangled with even-more exacting feminine beauty norms, the now-required body work also further reinforces hegemonic beauty ideals. As such, it is also crucial that future scholarship recognize just how much beauty ideals have become entangled with the third-shift solution. And, again at minimum, feminist motherhood scholars interested in beginning the work of theorizing a mothers' revolution must begin to try to detangle this connection as they work toward gender justice for mothers.

An important caveat, however, is in order. To suggest that celebrity mom profiles and the new momism are continuing to be refined in ways that make motherhood a new/old barrier to women's empowerment *is not to suggest* that the desire to be a mother or to mother are problematic. To the contrary, what I am suggesting is that *that* desire and mothering itself are still primarily shaped by an institution of motherhood[2] rather than by women themselves. Consequently, I am proposing that, as motherhood scholars continue to explore and unpack the rhetorical dimensions of the new momism and the celebrity mom profiles that reinforce its ongoing refinement, we need the kind of analysis done here to recognize and explore contemporary women's post-second wave crisis in femininity in relation to *how* and *why* the new momism and celebrity mom profiles work rhetorically as a sophisticated postfeminist-neoliberal backlash ideology and media reinforcement of both that backlash and hegemonic family configurations.

The New Momism: Recognizing the New Fourth Principle

In terms of future exploration of the new momism, while I am not the first scholar to suggest that the new momism has intensified, I am the first scholar to argue that that intensification now includes a new and fourth core principle and value: the third shift of body. There are many reasons why recognizing this new fourth principle is important—it further entrenches and intensifies "old" gender assumptions about the importance of beauty to "successful" femininity, albeit successful maternal femininity; it demands intensive body work as the specific, privatized solution to any work-life balance struggles, to name two—but I believe that the most important reason is that the new fourth principle, as both the theoretical work in chapter 1 and the analysis chapters show, reveals just how entangled the post-second wave and neoliberal turns are in relation to contemporary motherhood. Indeed, as more and more privileged women take advantage of post-second wave gender change, they *also* do so within the neoliberal turn toward privatized and individualized solutions for all social issues and/or problems. And, above all else, I believe that the analysis and theoretical work done in this book reveal that this neoliberal regime is also becoming more and more embedded in cultural understandings of contemporary motherhood. As a result, the addition of this new fourth principle reveals how deeply entangled neoliberal ideas and sensibilities are now embedded and entangled with post-second wave ideas and sensibilities in ways, ultimately, that make mothers even more responsible rather than less responsible for parenting and family-life management in the private sphere, even though mothers are also mothering within a post-second wave context that seems to cultivate, even encourage post-second wave gender change in the public sphere. Consequently, any future work that does not recognize the addition of this new core value and principle would not fully comprehend how the new momism has been redesigned in response to the contemporary context.

That future scholarship recognize the new fourth core principle within the new momism is also important for several other reasons. Most significant is the fact that this fourth principle now offers a very specific, privatized, and energizing solution to mothers' difficulty having it all, and this solution is now being laid out in a two-step process via the profiles. By doing so, this fourth principle not only further entrenches the idea that parenting is mothers' work, it also reinforces the idea that that work *must begin* as a woman prepares for her future motherhood, and, once she is prepared and a mother, that work must be done alone and in the private sphere. As such, this new principle further reinforces neoliberal privatized solutions, while also serving as a "foil and a shield" for mothers asking for and receiving any support—from others and the larger society—for their mothering work.

Equally important, this new fourth principle is redesigning the new momism such that mothers are not only doing it all alone and in the private sphere, this fourth core value "tells" mothers *how* they must do it all alone: via energizing body work. In short, this new core value not only keeps mothers in their place, it shows mothers how to do it all alone, while also cultivating self-blame if they fail to manage it all or to juggle it all. And because this new principle also cultivates body work as the specific solution, I contend that this new principle also plays a pivotal role in intensifying feminine maternal—both pregnant and postpartum—beauty ideals, ideals that are getting harder and even more demanding, while also making the maternal body the new management tool for managing the post-second wave crisis in femininity. Consequently, scholars must also make sure that their work on the new momism now acknowledges the pivotal role the new fourth principle plays in making both the maternal body and body work central to the new momism and the "accepted" management tool for work-life struggles. And as they do so, feminist motherhood studies scholars must deconstruct and detangle the solution that maternal body work offers for women's contemporary struggles from any scholarship that aims to theorize a mothers' revolution.

Mother Blame

Another key theoretical finding is a new kind of privatized self-mothering blame. Historically, feminist scholars have explored *mother blame* as an issue in relation to mothers being blamed for any problem, issue, and or challenge that their children face. While I believe that the new momism continues to encourage mother blame, I also believe that another fruitful awareness that this book reveals is the various and insidious ways that the intensified new momism and celebrity mom profiles entrench and reinforce mothers' self-blame. Indeed, I believe scholars must also recognize that one of the most pernicious components of the new momism is that it set ups all women to fail with its impossible and now even-more intensive demands on mothers, and we need to recognize the various and insidious ways that the new momism and the profiles do so, especially in relation to cultivating and encouraging neoliberal self-blame among mothers. That scholars do so is crucial because the issue is not will mothers fail but how and when.

Moreover, appearing to be unencumbered and having a quickly slender body is a crucial job requirement for celebrity moms, so having celebrity moms held up as the norm also places even more unrealistic demands on "normal," noncelebrity mothers most especially nonprivileged mothers. Suggesting that managing the post-second wave crisis in femininity is a problem that individual women must solve via their own "good maternal choices"—choices that seemingly appear to be fully free post-second wave and empowered choices—and a third shift of body work, then, also encourage women to blame themselves for their "failures" as women and/or mothers. And, by doing so, the profiles now also clearly link post-second wave empowerment with the neoliberal approach of always holding individuals responsible for their circumstances. Clearly, as the analysis reveals, celebrity mom profiles are now so entangled with a kind of post-second wave neoliberal gender empowerment that those profiles now cultivate the idea that individual mothers are now "blameworthy" for any difficulty that they are having either adhering to the new maternal body ideals, as was Kardashian most obviously, and for any difficulty that any particular mother has juggling it all.

Indeed, when any individual woman is unable to juggle it all with cellulite-free ease, return quickly to an even better postpartum body, and/or does not have the means required to engage in the third shift of body work, this iteration of celebrity mom profiles make it much more likely that that woman will internalize the responsibility for the failure and experience even more guilt, self-recrimination, and/or anger at themselves. As such, the new profiles also work to keep women "in their place," suffering in the private sphere, separate from other women, and blaming themselves for the struggle they experience having it all by doing it all. Moreover, as celebrity mom profiles further entrench the neoliberal approach to blaming mothers for their circumstances, the profiles also further entrench and position nonprivileged mothers as even more blameworthy for their bad mothering rather than recognizing that larger structures of inequality—particularly in terms of race, class, sexuality, and cisgender—also play a key role in how well any particular mother can become and be a good or bad bikini-ready mom.

Or, alternatively, if they are heterosexual, mothers who adopt neotraditional families may find that this "solution" can also leave them chronically angry at and/or resentful of their husbands for having to do it all by themselves. This is especially true for mothers who are partnered with post-second wave men who profess their own commitment to gender-equitable families and parenting, while these same men also continue to live comfortably within and benefit from a neotraditional family configuration that they believe mothers are choosing freely. In other words, the profiles not only support neoliberalism—self-management in the private sphere to create individual solutions for larger social issues in the public sphere—they also support a new post-second wave neoliberal hegemonic family formation as a private-sphere solution to women's post-second wave crisis in femininity, while also encouraging women to blame themselves or, if they are heterosexual, only their husbands rather than the larger society for their post-second wave crisis in femininity. Thus, any work done to begin to theorize a mothers' revolution must also work toward consciousness raising that deconstructs the various dynamics that ultimately encourage mothers to blame themselves and/or their husbands rather than larger institutional structures for their struggle to have it all, while also working to challenge the exacting beauty ideals now associated with the "call" to be and become "hot mamas" via the now-required third shift of body work.

*Recognizing the Intersection of the
Post-Second Wave and Neoliberal Turns*

Equally important, future work must recognize that contemporary motherhood is now at the crosscurrents of the post-second wave and neoliberal turns, which means that we need to employ approaches that account for this intersection. While motherhood scholars are beginning to recognize that neoliberalism is shaping contemporary motherhood in profound ways, with the exception of Melinda Vandenbeld Gile's edited collection, *Mothering in the Age of Neoliberalism*, most of this recent scholarship only attends to neoliberalism. As the work done here reveals, attending only to neoliberalism, while still important, is incomplete because contemporary motherhood now sits at the epicenter of the post-second wave and neoliberalism turns. Moreover, because the approach in this book accounts for this intersection, I suggest that that approach sharpens and clarifies how contemporary motherhood is now being reshaped and reconstructed by *both* neoliberal and post-second wave gender sensibilities in novel ways. Thus, I believe that future work must also employ approaches to analysis that recognize and work from within this intersection in order to understand more fully how contemporary motherhood works today.

Exploring motherhood at this intersection also requires scholars to recognize and continue to analyze the ways mothers' lives are founded on a split-subject position that ultimately leads to a post-second wave crisis in femininity once women become mothers. Failure to recognize this split subjectivity is problematic because, as the work here reveals, two things are "true" simultaneously for privileged mothers: as unencumbered women, women's lives are more and more like unencumbered men's lives in the public sphere *and*, once they become mothers, women's lives remain very different from men's lives in the private sphere due to mothers' ongoing responsibility for childrearing, caregiving, and family-life management, all of which create difficulties for mothers that many men do not face; and even more problematic, these difficulties are also now denied and/or made invisible. Thus, it is crucial that scholars employ approaches that can recognize these two simultaneous truths that shape contemporary mothers' maternal subject position, both to make that split subjectivity more visible and to begin to eradicate it.

Doing so is also important theoretically to resist the new iron-clad relation that exists between post-second wave femininity and motherhood. While motherhood is no longer women's destiny—the pre-second wave iron-clad relationship between femininity and motherhood—as the analysis here shows, motherhood is now considered post-second wave women's maternal choice. And, because motherhood is now women's choice, a new iron-clad connection has emerged between femininity and motherhood: femininity and motherhood are now viewed such that motherhood is now a fully "free" maternal choice for women. As a result, the logic of this new connection is as follows: because women now have a choice—they can now choose to become mothers or not—mothers have responsibility for those seemingly free individual and seemingly empowered choices. In many ways, this new iron-clad connection is especially dangerous—possibly even more insidious—because, as the analysis here shows, in complex but seemingly progressive ways, mothers are now mothering within a neoliberal context that continues to decrease any state support for family life, while mothers are simultaneously held even more responsible for any difficulty they might have juggling it all because, after all, they choose to be mothers.

As such, it is imperative that future scholarship recognizes this new iron-clad connection between post-second wave femininity and motherhood, while fundamentally working to decouple this connection. At minimum, then, this means that motherhood scholars must begin to untangle or detangle the crosscurrents that work to promote this new but still problematic iron-clad connection, while also recognizing that this is not the same iron-clad connection that existed prior to second wave feminism. Failure to do so will create analyses that are incomplete because they will not appreciate just how much post-second wave gender change is being incorporated within and ultimately used to keep mothers primarily responsible for parenting, while also blaming those mothers for any difficulty they have by "reminding" them that they chose the situation they found themselves in when they chose to become mothers, as did "TS."

Related, it is also important that contemporary scholarship recognize and more fully attend to the post-second wave crisis in femininity. In other words, in the same way that "the post-second wave crisis in masculinity" rightfully received much scholarly attention—even, many would argue, initiating what is now commonly referred to as *Masculinity Studies*—it is now time to explore in much more detail the post-second wave crisis in femininity. Doing so requires that we use the language and idea of a *post-second wave crisis* to signal a new feminist agenda—to theorize and participate in a mothers' revolution—while also recognizing the actual rhetorical situation and context in which contemporary mothers mother; that is, this is a context that *simultaneously* recognizes that privileged women's lives have changed in the public sphere, while women's ongoing responsibility for rearing and raising children in the private sphere has not only not changed, these responsibilities have become even more intensive and hegemonic because they are now considered mothers' fully free and empowered choice. Thus, this context suggests that we also must employ women's post-second wave split subjectivity in our understanding and theorizing about contemporary motherhood and celebrity mom profiles. That we do so is imperative, because if not, our future work in motherhood studies will not fully understand mothers' contemporary struggles nor will that work fully understand why and how it is so tricky today for mothers first to articulate their struggle, and second, to ask for help from others without experiencing self-blame.

The Importance of Employing a Rhetorical Focus

Because much scholarship that now falls under the rubric of *Motherhood Studies* is being done by a variety of different scholars in different fields, motherhood studies is interdisciplinary. The interdisciplinary nature of motherhood studies is one of its most important strengths because, as a growing and new field, motherhood studies is taking a variety of different approaches to comprehending how contemporary motherhood is being reshaped today. Even so, I believe that taking the kind of rhetorical approach that has been employed in this book is especially important, because at its core a rhetorical approach explores *how* mothers are being persuaded to internalize the new rules and norms of contemporary motherhood as motherhood is being reshaped as a new/old hegemonic gender ideology. Equally important, future work also must recognize how the hegemonic beauty ideals now embedded in contemporary motherhood *work rhetorically* to simultaneously discipline mothers and then blame mothers for adhering to those more intensive maternal beauty ideals. Doing so is important because when an ideology is hegemonic, it functions as a form of social control because hegemonic ideologies shape what counts as normal or good in culture. Moreover, when hegemonic gender ideologies become deeply embedded in culture, they become so internalized that ideological tenets can then be attributed to women, even if they might not have created the ideology. So, for example, because women have been so well trained to buy into beauty ideals, these ideals seem normal, natural, or common sense to everyone, including the many women who engage in the body practices required to sustain those ideals.

Once gender ideals become normalized, often, rather than recognizing that those ideals are ideological and women have been trained into them, many attribute women's concern with beauty ideals as something only women have created. Even more insidious is, often, when a woman is "being a normal woman" and quite concerned about her beauty and body image, again, as examples, rather than rewarding her for being a good woman, others, including media, over and over again critique and blame that very woman for "caring too much" about her body and how she looks. Thus, normalizing women in this way into hegemonic gender ideals is a tricky and insidious *rhetorical device* that disciplines women into hegemonic beauty ideals that repeatedly oppresses them, while ultimately those oppressive ideals and practices are attributed to the women, as if they freely choose to make them the most important component of who they are as women: the very same dynamic at work in both post-second wave neoliberal maternal choice and the feminine maternal body ideals today. Thus, I believe motherhood studies would benefit from more attention to and analysis of *how contemporary motherhood works rhetorically* generally and specifically in relation to the hegemonic beauty ideals now embedded within the new momism.

Moreover, attending to the rhetorical dimensions of contemporary motherhood is also important because I believe this same tricky and dangerous rhetorical device is also at work when media describe the maternal body as "the new weapon of choice" *among women*. Indeed, as the opening vignette of this book showed, after Norwegian celebrity Caroline Berg Eriksen posted a three-days postpartum selfie posing in a bra and underwear reminiscent of a bikini, which highlighted her already-flat six-pack abs three days after giving birth, the picture engendered much controversy, including an online article by Beth Greenfield about Eriksen that begins with the following question: "Is the postpregnancy body the new weapon of choice among superfit women?" (par. 1). Greenfield's opening line makes this rhetorical device clear: when a woman like Eriksen buys into the maternal body ideals embedded and promoted in celebrity mom profiles and then provides the "required" bikini proof for her normalization into those quickly slender postpartum maternal body ideals, rather than celebrating Eriksen, Greenfield's question makes clear that Eriksen's selfie might be evidence of women enacting these maternal body standards *against one another* (because, are not all women always in competition with one another in terms of beauty?). Implied are two other assumptions: first, this is a weapon of choice that women have created, and second, it is a weapon of choice women use to fight one another (rather than a hegemonic rhetorical device being *used against women* to keep them in their place and mothering alone in the private sphere).

Because the maternal body as the new weapon of choice among women works in this way rhetorically, this is why I have been so insistent throughout this book to argue that this is the new weapon of choice *that celebrity mom profiles use* to train and discipline mothers into the new and even more exacting and demanding beauty ideals associated with the maternal body and contemporary motherhood today. And, because I believe that framing it as Greenfield does is so problematic and that that framing invokes and then uses a post-second wave but also neoliberal notion of choice, I also believe that it is not an accident that, as the maternal body has become more and more central to shaping what counts as good and bad future and current mothering, the maternal body has become the new weapon of postfeminist-neoliberal choice in disciplining mothers. And, as such, this is why raising consciousness about how and why the maternal body has become the weapon of choice within the profiles and the accompanying seven rules to keep mothers in their place in the private sphere is so important to the kinds of consciousness raising that I believe must be the hallmark of future work and theorizing about the now-necessary mothers' revolution. Finally, because this new weapon of choice works rhetorically in the ways just described, this is yet another reason why I believe employing rhetorical approaches to understanding how contemporary motherhood is being reshaped today is so important to future scholarship.

A caveat is in order: it may be the case that women who have internalized the slender-pregnant and quickly slender, even bikini-ready, maternal body ideals and practices are using their maternal body as a weapon of choice against other mothers, as Greenfield suggests; some women and mothers do want to compete against other women. However, until mothers' consciousness is raised about both *how* and *why* the maternal body is functioning rhetorically as it is today within celebrity mom profiles and contemporary motherhood, it will be hard to know how much any particular woman's participation in third-shift practices are due to her own interest in doing so or are due to a fully mediated commitment to the hegemonic "superfit" pregnant and postpartum ideals. Consequently, it is also now time for feminist maternal scholars to raise consciousness about the fact that the maternal body has become the weapon of choice within the now-intensified and hegemonic ideology of contemporary mothering to keep women in their place as mothers and mothering within neotraditional families configurations.

Additionally, while the analysis here reconfirms that the new momism "rose out of the ashes of feminism," as Douglas and Michaels first suggested, the work here also suggests that the contemporary intensified new momism is more than just a postfeminist repudiation of second wave feminism; it is now a postfeminist neoliberal denial of any need for feminism and the difference maternity continues to make in contemporary mothers' lives. Indeed, as the analysis in both chapter 2 and chapter 3 suggest, today the new momism is continuing to develop in more complex and sophisticated ways such that the new momism has become an even more powerful post-second wave neoliberal backlash ideology. In fact, by integrating a new fourth core principle of body work, the new momism is promoting an even-more intensive and insidious neoliberal post-feminism: one that simultaneously recognizes feminist gains, while also denying any need for ongoing feminist action by cultivating self-blame and an individualized, privatized solution when mothers find it difficult to juggle and do it all. Thus, if we hope to understand and explore how mothers' lives are being shaped today by postfeminism, then future work must both recognize the ways postfeminism has also continued to be redesigned and reshaped in terms of neoliberal sensibilities and how this reshaping of postfeminism also now works within contemporary motherhood and the celebrity mom profiles that reinforce what counts as good motherhood today.

Finally, if we hope to begin to theorize a mothers' revolution, we also must engage in analysis that recognizes the complex and sophisticated ways the contemporary ideology of good mothering continues to offer inadequate—even ridiculous and sometimes dangerous—solutions to women's post-second wave crisis in femininity. Moreover, as the quickly slender, even bikini-ready, body continues to work rhetorically to entrench the third shift of body work in the new momism and to support neotraditional family formations, it is imperative that scholars in particular but women in general understand *how and why* celebrity mom profiles are being refined in response to women's contemporary split subjectivity if we hope to continue to advocate for ongoing social justice for families and not just for women. In this way, both encumbered men and women can understand and make family-life decisions that resist placing the onus of responsibility for caregiving on women, while simultaneously engaging in the kinds of cultural critique and work within their families that make family life a gender issue for both mothers and fathers in the public sphere.

As a way to start conversations about how mothers might ask for changes that might make family life more equitable and to resist celebrity mom profiles in everyday ways, then it is also important to think through specific strategies of resistance that emerge as a result of the theoretical and analytic work done here. To do so, in the next chapter I close this book by proposing five strategies of resistance mothers might employ to resist the new/old hegemonic good mothering ideology and neotraditional families that celebrity mom profiles reinforce and support, resist the seven rules and ideological messages embedded in them, and begin conversations that, first and foremost, suggest that family life *is and should be* a gender issue for both encumbered men and women.

5

Resisting Being Bikini-Ready Moms

Five Strategies of Resistance

But the feminist historians agreed that what was truly necessary to the new momism's demise was a change in consciousness among women themselves. . . . They [mothers] became convinced that motherhood remained the unfinished business of the women's movement.
—Susan J. Douglas and Meredith Michaels, 336

Young fathers today know that they will have working wives. Their wives are likely to be at least as well if not better educated, just as ambitious as they are, and make more money than they do. More importantly, these men feel that being a father is not about being a hands-off economic provider. It's about paying attention, nurturing, listening, mentoring, coaching, and most of all, being present. It's also about changing diapers, making dinner, doing drop-offs and pick-ups, and housecleaning.
—Brad Harrington, Fred Van Deusen, and Beth Huberd,
"The New Dad: Caring Committed and Conflicted," 4

The idea that fathers have radically changed—they they are now intimately involved in raising their children—qualifies as a folk belief.
—Ralph LaRossa, 379

Mothers interested in resisting being bikini-ready moms must work to challenge the ideological messages and practices tied to the seven new rules of celebrity mom profiles and the even-more intensive new momism the profiles reinforce. While the last chapter explored some academic strategies of resistance, in this chapter I propose five everyday strategies of resistance. To do so, I return to Douglas and Michaels' thinking about a future beyond the new momism. In their Epilogue, titled, "Exorcising the New Momism," Douglas and Michaels playfully imagine what the future might look like five years after they published their book. In doing so, they dream of a Reality TV show titled, "Survivor: Motherhood Island," where fathers are deposited "into a house with a two-day-old infant, a four-year-old, and thirteen-year-old" (331). The winner will get a "million bucks" if he and the children survive until the end of the series. The dad must "always smile at the kids, never lose his temper, listen closely and be ever understanding, and always put himself last" (231). In short, a dad can only win if he adheres to the same new momism principles moms do. Douglas and Michaels then detail how no man ever wins because he quits over the fact that it is impossible "do it all." This then leads to the new momism becoming "an object of study in the academy, with feminist scholars tracing its rise and fall"; groups rising up to "exorcise momism," an awareness of how other institutions start to fall apart when everyone refuses to engage the tenets of the new momism, and eventually parents become "sick and tired of the huge gap between people's need and desire for decent day care the government's refusal to provide it" (335–336). Finally, Douglas and Michaels speculate, "But the feminist historians agreed that was truly necessary to the new momism's demise was a change in consciousness among women themselves. . . . They [mothers] became convinced that motherhood remained the unfinished business of the women's movement" (336).

Ten years later, in 2014, the publication of their landmark book in tandem with the growing field of motherhood studies has made some parts of their future fantasy real today: the new momism has become an object of study among feminist and motherhood scholars, and these scholars are detailing the various ways that the new momism continues to shape contemporary motherhood. Currently, however, as I showed in chapter 1, these scholars are only able to detail the continued, intensified rise of the new momism. Moreover, as I have argued throughout this book, rather than rising up and then falling as a result of scholarly and popular critique as Douglas and Michaels imagined, celebrity mom profiles have changed to entrench an even-more intensive mothering ideology, while also incorporating a new core fourth principle: a third shift of body work as the specific privatized solution to mothers' struggle to have it all.

However, because there is a growing body of scholarly work on the new momism, including this book, the growing academic literature is beginning to lay the groundwork for challenges to the new momism. In fact, I believe books like this one can began to trace strategies of resistance against the now-intensified new momism, the celebrity mom profiles that support that new momism, and the privatized and individual solutions offered via the celebrity mom profiles when contemporary mothers struggle to do it all. Thus, I end by proposing five strategies of resistance suggested by both the theoretical and analytical work done in this book.

Strategy One: Consciousness Raising

If a core component of second wave feminism was to raise women's consciousness about gender-based oppression against women generally, contemporary feminism must begin to raise consciousness about women's post-second wave split subjectivity and its role in gender-based oppression in the context of motherhood today. This means recognizing the real gains unencumbered women have enjoyed *and* women's ongoing and almost exclusive responsibility for childrearing and family-life management; both of which celebrity mom profiles and the accompanying seven rules recognize and use in the service of keeping women almost exclusively responsible for childrearing and family-life management in the private sphere. Most important, contemporary mothers must resist adopting and embracing the post-second wave subject position that undergirds contemporary motherhood once they become mothers. This means, at the most basic level, women must refuse to accept, even embrace their post-second wave split subjectivity when they become mothers because, when they do so, it is mostly to their detriment. Therefore, I believe that understanding how and why post-second wave beneficiaries' split subjectivity emerges once they become mothers must be at the center of consciousness raising today, a theoretical argument I also made in the previous chapter. Of utmost importance, however, is uncovering the various and entangled gender assumptions that undergird this subjectivity in ways that position women to be the primary caregivers.

That consciousness raising can be an effective strategy has already been proven. When second wave feminism raised women's (and men's) consciousness about how gender roles and assumptions shaped women's and men's lives differently, the strategy became a powerful strategy for initiating the changes we currently enjoy. I suggest, then, that strategy one can employ the same kind of consciousness raising in the context of contemporary motherhood to help women (and men) understand better how gender roles and assumptions continue to shape women's lives in problematic ways, especially in relation to the post-second wave split subjectivity and the now-intensified new momism. This means that, in addition to raising consciousness about women's split subjectivity, mothers who want to resist this split subjectivity must also understand the various and insidious ways that celebrity mom profiles are continuing to develop and change. Related, contemporary mothers also must resist internalizing post-second wave neoliberal maternal choice, even though reproductive choice has transformed many women's lives such that they can mostly control reproduction and when to bear children. However, bearing and rearing children are parental and societal responsibilities, regardless of what mediated images of motherhood, current public policy (or lack thereof), and everyday conversations suggest. Thus, mothers' consciousness about the insidious nature of post-second wave neoliberal maternal choice must be raised so that contemporary mothers can begin refusing to buy into maternal choice as the raison d'être for why they are primarily responsible for childrearing.

The first strategy, then, also encourages the idea of "awareness as resistance." In their interviewed-based work on women's strategies of resistance against normative slender body ideals, Lisa R. Rubin, Carol J. Nemeroff, and Nancy Felipe Russo argue that "awareness as resistance" is the most used strategy by feminist women in resisting ideological messages about normative body ideals. As they put it, "Rational resistance: Examining culture with a feminist scrutiny. Maintaining a critical awareness was one of the most commonly used strategies for resisting cultural messages about women's bodies" (33). In the same way, I suggest that awareness as resistance can be a viable strategy for mothers to resist, even challenge, both the con-temporary new momism and the celebrity mom profiles that rein-force it and the underlying split subjectivity that undergirds the new momism. Even though it has its limits, critical awareness can also be a strategy for also "talking back" to the profiles.

Strategy Two: Resist Maternal Body Norms

Given the new centrality of the maternal body in both the profiles and seven rules, critical awareness of and resistance to the profiles also requires resisting the maternal body norms and practices pro-moted and reinforced in the profiles. This would also entail employ-ing critical awareness about the maternal body; a strategy that Rubin et al.'s work suggests is already an effective first strategy for resisting normative feminine body ideals. There is no reason to believe that it would not also be an effective strategy in the context of the maternal body. However, because beauty ideals and the ongoing and power-ful link between femininity and those beauty ideals are even more intensified in the context of the maternal body, resisting the ideo-logical messages and practices promoted in celebrity mom profiles will be difficult. Women and mothers are not cultural dupes, but, given the even-more intensive and demanding feminine beauty ide-als now associated with the maternal body, it is not easy to simply resist or reject these imperatives. Additionally, as the analysis in both chapter 2 and chapter 3 revealed, when a woman fails to meet those standards, as Kardashian did initially, then, mothers are disciplined into maternal body norms through fat shaming and possibly viscous attacks. Even so, it is important that mothers begin to understand *why* and *how* beauty ideals have become so much more demand-ing and intensive in relation to the maternal body. Raising critical awareness about both seems to me to be an important first step in resisting and ultimately refusing to participate in the maternal body ideals promoted in celebrity mom profiles.

That critical awareness about the new postpartum body stan-dards can lead to resistance against those standards was demon-strated recently. Tary Brumfitt, a thirty-five-year-old Australian photographer and mother of three, has a Kickstarter campaign to fund a documentary, "Embrace," about women's postpartum body acceptance. She first got media attention in May 2012 after she had her third child. Elise Solé reports, "Brumfitt became a self-described 'obsessive' about getting her prepregnancy shape back, working out constantly and even contemplating breast implants and a tummy tuck" (par. 2). After dieting and working out, she entered a body-building contest. Solé reports that after four months Brumfitt looked fantastic; however, Brumfitt realized "'Nothing had changed about how I felt about my body'" (par. 4). In May 2013, she became an Internet sensation when she "made a photo composite of her-self—one photo featured her wearing a bikini during her bodybuild-ing days, and the other taken of her body at the time, 20 pounds heavier. She labeled the fitter picture 'before' and the heavier picture 'after,' although both were taken post-pregnancy" (par. 5). Brumfitt is not alone in adopting this tactic.

Another new mother, Neghar Fonooni, also posted a before picture of herself in a bikini, with a superfit body and "washboard abs," and an after photo of herself in another bikini about 14 pounds heavier. In an interview about the photos, Fonooni says, "'In the pic-ture on the left [before picture] I was miserable, and today I am free as a bird,' writes Neghar. 'I've chosen not to let my body fat % dictate how I feel about myself, and fully accepted my body and all of its beautiful imperfections. I hope you will too'" (quoted in Wurzburger par. 8). Andrea Wurzburger also reports about Fonooni, "Although she has gained roughly 14 pounds, she writes, 'I call this "reverse progress" but I actually think it's real progress. I'm happier now'" (par. 9). Both women have created the so-called reverse progress fit-ness movement. Wurzburger describes this movement in the follow-ing way: "New moms and fitness buffs Tara Brumfitt and Neghar Fonooni have taken to the Internet to share their not-so-typical before-and-after fitness photos. They're part of the reverse progress fitness movement, which is meant to help women realize that weight fluctuation is completely normal and sometimes even a good thing" (par. 2).

Clearly, as the analysis in chapter 3 revealed, the before-and-after format is a key and powerful rhetorical device in postpartum profiles that promotes the quickly slender ideal. Thus, by invert-ing the "order" and "argument" embedded within that device, both Brumfitt and Fonooni are raising awareness about the power of the rhetorical device and challenging it via their inversion and reverse progress fitness movement. Moreover, when both Brumfitt and Fonooni challenge postpartum maternal body ideals by refusing to buy into them, they also refuse to allow themselves to be blamed for their earlier attempts to meet those problematic ideals. As a result, both women also resist the insidious and rhetorically tricky maternal body ideals at work in both the new momism and celebrity mom profiles that I noted in the last chapter: hegemonic maternal gender ideologies that work rhetorically to simultaneously discipline women and then blame women for practicing those hegemonic gender ideologies. Finally, due to the support she received after the photos went viral, Brumfitt also started the "Body Image Movement" online in May 2013, which is an online community and website that hopes to redefine and rewrite beauty ideals, and "to harness and facilitate positive body image activism by encouraging women to be more accepting of who they are, to use positive language regarding their bodies and others, and to prioritise health before beauty" (Brumfitt par. 1). As such, both Brumfitt and Fonooni reveal how "real" mothers can employ critical awareness to resist the maternal beauty ideals embedded in contemporary motherhood today, while also talking back to the profiles that cultivate those ideals.

Thinking Critically about So-Called Mommy Makeovers

A related and additional tactic to resist the pressure to internalize the new maternal body norms and practices is to think critically about and possibly refuse to have a so-called mommy makeover postpartum, if a mother believes that doing so well necessarily make her feel better about herself, as Brumfitt did. As I noted in the last chapter, there is no doubt that mommy makeovers and celebrity mom profiles are mutually reinforcing in that they promote the same ideological messages about the importance of a particular slender, sexy postpartum body ideal for women that also appears like a reproductive-free body. Unfortunately, it appears that mommy makeovers have increased at the same time that the structure, norms, and rules have changed in celebrity mom profiles; and, I believe that the two are at least mutually reinforcing if not interconnected. Exact statistics about how many mothers get mommy makeovers, however, are hard to know, in part because many mothers are unwilling to acknowledge them and because they are elective medical procedures. Finally, because the term *mommy makeover* is a marketing term rather than a medical term, it is also hard to know just how many mothers have them.

Even so, there is some evidence that they are on the rise. So, for example, Annabelle Robertson, writing for *WebMD* under the title, "Mommy Makeover: A Plastic Surgery Trend," reveals: "While it's difficult to come by exact numbers for mommy makeovers because it's a marketing term, not a surgical one, Douglas Mackenzie, MD, a board-certified plastic surgeon in Santa Barbara, Calif., says that mothers are by far his largest demographic. He attributes the trend to our obsession with youth as well as the public's acceptance of plastic surgery. Even the numerous television makeover shows, he says, are merely an indication of a boom that began awhile back" (par. 6). Robertson also reveals:

> According to the American Society of Plastic Surgery (ASPS), 36% of the 9.9 million surgical and minimally-invasive cosmetic procedures performed in 2006 were on patients between the ages of 30 and 39; 29% of them were aged 20 to 29. Breast augmentations increased 55% from 2000 to 2006, going from 212,500 procedures to 329,326. Breast lifts—another favorite among the mommy makeover crowd—went up 96% during the past six years, with the total number of procedures going from 52,836 to 103,788. Tummy tucks jumped a whopping 4,384% and buttock lifts increased 174%. (pars. 8–9)

At the most basic level, these statistics confirm and further reinforce the newfound importance of erasing the signs of pregnancy from the maternal body for women, the intensified focus on doing so that celebrity mom profiles suggest, and the even-more exacting postpartum standards for "hot" and "sexy" postpartum bodies. Indeed, this *WebMD* report and the *Today Show* report I noted in chapter 3, also both suggest that mommy makeovers have increased at the same time that celebrity mom profiles have made the maternal body the primary focus. Thus, these statistics also confirm that contemporary mothers who opt for mommy makeovers understand the messages embedded in celebrity mom profiles: they must remain sexy postpartum, while also erasing any lingering signs of maternity.

Finally, if there is any doubt that the ideological messages promoted in celebrity mom profiles are now linked to mommy makeovers, all one has to do is look online at websites advertising them to see the connection between the profiles and, equally important, the newfound notion that the "proof is in the bikini." So, for example, in terms of the bikini as proof of postpartum sexiness and success, at "Mommy Makeover," which is a website for a plastic surgeon who performs the makeover, readers learn, "Women shouldn't have to sacrifice the way they look and feel once they become a mom" (Halperin par. 1). Moreover, under the heading, "Am I a good candidate for a Mommy Makeover?," readers also learn, "If you are not planning on having anymore children and have finished breast feeding then yes, you could be a good candidate for a *Mommy Makeover in Boston*. . . . If lowering the impact of pregnancy on your body would increase self esteem or make you feel great in a bikini, you may be a good candidate for a *mommy makeover*" (italics in original, Halperin par. 3).

Even though resisting the messages about the maternal body may be the hardest part of resisting celebrity mom profiles, as Rubin et al. suggest, critical awareness is the first step to resisting these messages. Moreover, if mothers simply refused to participate in both the third shift and mommy makeovers, this would be a small victory. It is also important to point out that there is nothing inherently wrong with a mother wanting to feel and be attractive; most of us want to be both. The problem with the maternal body promoted in celebrity mom profiles is that the ideals are so exacting and demanding that they can lead postpartum women to believe that a mommy makeover is the best solution to "her failure." And, as I noted in the previous chapter, everyone is doomed to fail, even the celebrities profiled because the standards are so exacting and demanding. So, what I am suggesting is, at minimum, mothers can resist buying into these exacting and more intensified standards by employing critical awareness when they find themselves feeling bad about their maternal body or like they are somehow failures. And, like Brumfitt, that critical awareness might mean working for and with women rather than against them via superfit postpartum body "battles" *and* shifting focus to accepting, even celebrating the changed maternal body rather than only doing intensive body work and/or opting for potentially dangerous plastic surgery.[1] By doing so, I hope that one consequence is the decrease in mommy makeovers rather than the ever-increasing number of mothers believing that they must do so to make their maternal body conform to the new, exacting standards for the postpartum maternal body, to feel better about themselves, and to embody the new and problematic maternal body norms today.

Strategy Three: Participate in the Now-Necessary Mothers' Movement

I have already suggested that I concur with Douglas and Michaels' hope that motherhood becomes the unfinished business of the women's movement. I believe that this means that contemporary feminism must do so by engaging in both new kinds of conversations about motherhood within feminism and feminist maternal scholarship, while participating in the now-necessary mothers' movement, strategies three and four. And I believe that these two strategies are interconnected; however, I separate the two strategies below to make it easier to clarify how and why I believe both strategies are important now.

I begin with a call to participate in the now-necessary mothers' revolution without denigrating second wave feminism. As a committed feminist thinker and scholar, in fact, I believe that we must not denigrate second wave feminism as we participate in this revolution. Beginning with a call to not denigrate second wave feminism is important, because some contemporary feminists characterize second wave feminism as "anti-motherhood" or describe second wave feminism as "having gotten it wrong" by focusing on advocating for women rather than mothers, as my earlier work reveals (*White Feminists*). As I argued in that work, rather than being anti-motherhood, many white second wave feminists were primarily silent about mothering. In terms of having gotten it wrong—having had the "wrong" focus in terms focusing on advocating gender change for women and "sisters" rather than for mothers—as I also argued (*White Feminists*), for many complicated reasons, this focus made sense within the rhetorical context of the time. Now, however, as this book reveals, women are mothering within a very different rhetorical context, and it is now time to no longer be silent about mothering and to begin to think through the ways feminism specifically can play a central role in theorizing and engaging in a mothers' revolution without grounding the conversation or the need for feminist action now in the notion that second wave feminism got it wrong.

Moreover and fortunately, because some feminist maternal scholars and women's activists have begun to recognize the pervasiveness of the new momism, the kinds of activism required of a mothers' revolution has already begun. In fact, there is a small but growing mothers' revolution occurring both within academia and in popular culture, especially online. Within academia, the interdisciplinary study of motherhood has grown in both Canada and the United States, and much of this work has been noted and utilized in this book. A significant amount of that groundbreaking work in motherhood studies is being published through the *Motherhood Initiative for Research and Community Involvement* and *Demeter Press*, which is the only peer-reviewed press devoted to the study of motherhood. Presses like *Demeter* must be supported both at the grassroots and institutional levels, as should academic presses that are also publishing books like this one in the area of feminist and women's studies. Moreover, at the grassroots level, supporting the presses that are publishing books about motherhood, while also acquiring and reading the books published, can become a vehicle for mothers to support both the presses and one another.

Another resource at the grassroots level is the online motherhood movement. Indeed, the *Mothers Movement Online*, which is "Resources and reporting for mothers and others who think about social change" (http://www.mothersmovement.org) is flourishing. The *Museum of Motherhood*, which "focuses specifically on the roles of women in the sphere of motherhood and generally on the topic of birth and caregiving," can be another resource for women to resist mothering in isolation, while also gaining more critical awareness about how motherhood shapes women's lives today (http://www. mommuseum.org/about/ par. 11). And, as I noted earlier, a related online resource devoted specifically to challenging maternal body ideals is the "Body Image Movement" (http://bodyimagemovement. com.au/). Finally, so-called mommy bloggers, while not all devoted to motherhood activism, are a growing presence online. Academic work, in fact, has begun to explore the role of mommy bloggers in relation to understanding contemporary motherhood. May Friedman, for example, recently published *Mommyblogs and the Changing Face of Motherhood*, which explores how blogging allows mothers to be less concerned about what good mothers "should do," while also detailing what a diverse group of mothers actually says about mothering in their blogs. Thus, all of these resources allow mothers to engage and participate in the now-necessary mothers' revolution that is beginning to occur without denigrating past feminist work and activism.

Strategy Four: Begin New Feminist Conversations

Even though the previous strategic focus on advocating for women and sisters rather than mothers is now understandable, there are some lingering consequences of this focus and enduring concerns about what should ground conversations about contemporary motherhood. In particular, some folks might be worried that feminist conversations that recognize women's desire to mother, acknowledging that the care of young children requires much time and someone has to do it, and, acknowledging the difference maternity makes in women's lives might, inadvertently, further entrench the current connection between femininity and maternal choice. I believe otherwise and, in fact, contend that it is now time to have these conversations as crucial components of the now-necessary mothers' revolution. Moreover, that we do so is essential in order to detangle the previously problematic issues associated with each topic, while also reframing the contemporary conversation in ways that will ultimately be fruitful for mothers today.

Maternal Desire and Maternal Agency

In the last chapter, I argued that celebrity mom profiles and the new momism are continuing to be refined in ways that make motherhood a new/old barrier to women's empowerment, while also insisting that this does not mean that the desire to be a mother or to mother are problematic. Rather, this means that contemporary feminism must find a way to acknowledge maternal desire and maternal agency outside patriarchal understandings of both and in ways that are consistent with contemporary feminist understandings. In some ways, however, maternal desire and maternal are relatively new ideas in feminism. This is the case because feminist views on maternal desire and maternal agency have changed over the past forty years. As I have argued in my earlier work (*White Feminists*), 1960s and 1970s white second-wave feminists were concerned that mothering could not be a site of agency for women because the connection between maternal destiny and femininity was so pervasive. In fact, as I noted earlier, because women's reproductive capacity had been used to define and constrain women's lives, motherhood was seen as one of women's greatest sources of oppression. As a result, in their attempt to decouple the early iron-clad connection between femininity and motherhood as women's destiny, many white second-wave feminists chose to organize as sisters outside of motherhood in order to advocate for women's rights separate from mothering.

In 1976, however, Adrienne Rich wrote what is now considered the first feminist text on motherhood and mothering, *Of Woman Born: Motherhood as Experience and Institution*. In the book, Rich's most basic argument is that motherhood is a patriarchal institution that oppresses women and that mothering has the potential to be empowering to women if they are allowed to define and practice mothering for themselves. As such, Rich made an all-important distinction between the institution of motherhood and the potential empowered relations in mothering. As Rich argued, "I try to distinguish two meanings of motherhood, one superimposed on the other: the *potential relationship* of any woman to her powers of reproduction and to children; and the *institution*, which aims at ensuring that that potential—and all women—shall remain under male control" (13). Based on this groundbreaking distinction, Rich viewed the institution of motherhood as male-defined, male-controlled, and as deeply oppressive to women, while she viewed the experience of mothering as a potential source of power for both women and children, if women were allowed to define mothering themselves. While Rich wrote the book in 1976 and Douglas and Michaels describe the book as having been widely read at the time, it was not until the 1990s that these ideas begin to be used by writers who are now described as *motherhood scholars* (O'Brien Hallstein *White Feminists*). Thus, thinking through both maternal desire and maternal agency are relatively new but have begun within some feminist and motherhood studies circles.

In terms of maternal desire, I ground my initial thinking in Daphne de Marneffe's work, *Maternal Desire: On Children, Love, and the Inner Life*, which also recognizes Rich's all-important distinction in de Marneffe's exploration of the "potential relationship" that can and does exist between mothers and children. In doing so, de Marneffe theorizes mothers' relatedness to their children and defines *maternal desire* as a mother's desire to care for and relate to her children. As a feminist, de Marneffe is also interested in theorizing maternal desire in ways that are consistent with feminism and free from sentimentality and clichés. Most importantly, however, de Marneffe challenges the idea that women who desire to care for children are powerless and without agency, without the ability to influence their own lives. I concur with de Marneffe; and, as a result, I am suggesting that we must recognize that maternal desire can include maternal agency, while also being empowering to mothers.

In this context, then, I view maternal agency as the notion that mothering can be a site of empowerment and a location for social change for women. Maternal agency draws on the idea of agency—the ability to influence one's life, to have power to control one's life—and explores how women can have agency in mothers' efforts to challenge and act against the aspects of institutionalized motherhood—including the celebrity mom profiles that support it—that constrain and limit women's lives and power as mothers. My thinking about maternal agency also draws on the work of other feminist scholars (Green; Horowitz; *Mother Outlaws* O'Reilly; Podnieks) who view mothering as empowering for women when mothering is a female-defined and centered experience for women. As a result, agentic power is practicing mothering with a sense of personal agency, which often includes the characteristics of critical thinking, thinking reflectively about dominant motherhood discourses, and making choices that benefit both mothers and children.

Maternal agency also requires empowered mothering. In theorizing empowered mothering, feminist maternal scholars (Green; Horowitz; *Mother Outlaws* O'Reilly; Podnieks) recognize that both mothers and children benefit when a mother lives her life and practices mothering from a position of agency—has the power to influence her own life, her children's, and the larger culture. Again drawing on a key and original insight by Rich, these contemporary feminist scholars also argue, for mothers to instill agency, authority, and authenticity in their growing children (but especially for daughters), mothers must model these same attributes in their own daily lives. Thus, rather than only focus on empowered mothering to benefit children's lives, it is also necessary to advocate for empowered mothering as necessary and essential to benefit mothers' lives and as a means to advocate for continued social change for women's lives. Thus, I suggest that the first part of strategy four entails having a contemporary conversation within feminism that is grounded first and foremost in the kind of maternal desire and maternal agency that open the space for mothers to engage in motherwork that is empowering to both them and their children and resists the institutionalized perspective embedded in the now-intensified new momism and the celebrity mom profiles that promote it.

Children Require Time and Energy

The second part of the new conversation that must unfold is that we must not be afraid to have an honest conversation about the fact that children, especially young children, need and require much time and care. And, as a result, whomever is the primary caregiver of children, especially young children, will need to devote substantial time to caregiving. Equally important is the fact that, especially in the early years, this caregiving does make it difficult for caregivers to participate in the public sphere as if they are unencumbered by family responsibilities. Some women and feminists, understandably, are afraid to have this second conversation because they believe, if we acknowledge that caregiving requires much energy and time, then doing so will encourage both the resurgence of the notion that maternity is women's destiny and give professional institutions "ammunition" to continue to penalize women for their difficulty meeting ideal worker norms in professional institutions. These worries are reasonable concerns; clearly, as I noted in the last chapter, celebrity mom profiles and the larger culture have reworked the iron-clad connection between femininity and maternity such that femininity is now viewed as women's maternal choice. However, if we continue to decouple femininity and maternal choice by redefining maternal desire and maternal agency within the context of empowered mothering, while also reframing how and what the contemporary conversations are about, then we can acknowledge that caregiving does require much time and attention without necessarily further entrenching maternal choice or further reinforcing professional barriers against mothers in professional institutions.

Of most importance, we have to reframe the problem that exists in relation to the fact that the care of young children *requires much of any caregiver*. Indeed, the care of children does require much time, and this fact is not the problem; rather, it is a biological fact. Or, as O'Reilly (*Mother Outlaws*) puts it, quoting Petra Buskins, "'Infancy and early childhood *are* periods of high emotional and physical dependency and, moreover, this is not a pure invention of patriarchal science . . . *The problem is not the fact of this requirement but rather that meeting this need has come to rest exclusively, and in isolation, on the shoulders of biological mothers*'" (emphasis in original 11). As such, as O'Reilly continues, intensive mothering, "becomes oppressive not because children have needs, but because we, as a culture, dictate that only the biological mother is capable of fulfilling them; that children's needs must always come before those of the mother; and, that children's needs must be responded to around the clock and with extensive time, money, and energy" (11). What needs to be reframed, then, is the solution to the fact rather than the fact itself. In other words, if we acknowledge the fact that children do require time and attention, while also simultaneously making clear that the "real problem" is the fact that the responsibility for that care is exclusively assigned to women within the context of an intensive mothering ideology that has intensified rather than decreased, then not only we would we insist on reframing the conversation to address the "real" problem, we would also lay the groundwork for making the difference maternity makes in mothers' lives visible; the third necessary part of the new conversation. Thus, I believe that acknowledging these facts are also the first step in talking openly about the difference maternity continues to make in women's lives today.

Quit Denying the Difference Maternity Makes

A complicating factor with the fact that children, especially young children, need much care, even outside the demands of intensive mothering and within empowered mothering, is that after women are assigned primary responsibility for that care, if they work they must continue to work in the public sphere that now assumes that men and women have gender equity and that all workers, especially professional workers, are unencumbered with family responsibilities, as are many fathers who are encumbered with children but without most of the same time-demanding and intensive family-life and childrearing responsibilities of mothers. Thus and finally, if we have honest conversations about how much time children require, then we can also begin to quit denying the difference maternity makes specifically for mothers by making caregiving visible, while also resisting assigning exclusive responsibility for caregiving to women. In addition to doing so by participating in the growing mothers' revolution, we must also ask post-second wave fathers to do more of what they say they believe about post-second wave fatherhood, which is strategy five.

Strategy Five: Ask Post-Second Wave Fathers To Do What They Say They Believe

Participating in the growing mothers' revolution in the public sphere must be accompanied with making real and significant changes in the private sphere and to neotraditional families now. That we do so is crucial because, as I have maintained throughout this book, the intensified new momism now resolves the post-second wave crisis in femininity by suggesting *it is an individual and privatized* problem that "only" requires individual body work by women in the private sphere rather than large-scale institutional change in the public sphere and/or changes in family-life formations that might include more equitable parenting between mothers and fathers. If a woman is heterosexual, as I noted in the previous chapter, this solution can leave her chronically angry at and/or resentful of her husband for having to do it all by herself. This is especially true for heterosexual mothers who are partnered with post-second wave men who profess their own commitment to gender-equitable families and parenting, while these same men also continue to live comfortably within and benefit from a neotraditional family configuration that they believe mothers are choosing freely. Thus, the post-second wave crisis in femininity is not just a feminist problem or a gender-studies problem; rather, this is a family-life problem that both men and women need to address. Hence, while I argue that mothers must implement strategy five, this strategy is as much for fathers as it is for mothers.

As I show next, enacting strategy five requires five interrelated steps. To begin laying out those steps, however, I start with a very simple point that is often forgotten in families and especially in celebrity mom profiles and its seven rules: when children are born, *all new parents become encumbered.* That fact is also indisputable. The problem today is that "encumberedness" is still built on problematic and entangled gender-based assumptions, and being encumbered is still different between mothers and fathers because, for a variety of reasons already detailed here, society still believes mothers still should and need to do the majority of parenting. To put it slightly differently: fathers' lives are encumbered also; they just get a "pass on" participating in that encumberedness via the new momism, the celebrity mom profiles that support it, and institutionalized professional norms that assume that ideal workers are unencumbered workers. This fact is especially ironic because contemporary men have also been raised within the same post-second wave context of contemporary women. Many fathers, especially well-educated privileged fathers, in fact, report that they believe in and support post-second wave gender equality and that they want to be much more involved fathers. Thus, in many ways, we no longer need to focus on changing fathers' ideas about family life; rather, *we need to ask those fathers to do more of what they say that they already believe.*

Post-Second Wave Fathers' Changed Ideas about Gender and Their Aspirations for Parenting

What is it that many contemporary men believe having also been raised within a post-second wave neoliberal context? Many contemporary fathers also recognize that young women today have educational and career expectations in addition to family aspirations and, as a result, many heterosexual men have different expectations and aspirations in relation to partnership and fatherhood. In fact, authors Brad Harrington, Fred Van Deusen, and Beth Huberd, co-authors of the Boston College (BC) study of 1,000 professional men titled, "The New Dad: Caring Committed and Conflicted," write:

Young fathers today know that they will have working wives. Their wives are likely to be at least as well if not better educated, just as ambitious as they are, and make more money than they do. More importantly, these men feel that being a father is not about being a hands-off economic provider. It's about paying attention, nurturing, listening, mentoring, coaching, and most of all, being present. It's also about changing diapers, making dinner, doing drop-offs and pickups, and housecleaning. (4)

Harrington et al.'s description of contemporary men is also consistent with Ralph LaRossa's 1997 description of "modern" or "involved" fatherhood. As LaRossa noted: there is a cultural belief that fathers have radically changed; that is, fathers "now are intimately involved in raising their children" (379).

LaRossa continues, however, by also suggesting that this cultural belief is out of sync with the reality of how much fathers actually participate in caregiving; in fact, he notes that "the idea that fathers have radically changed—they they are now intimately involved in raising their children—qualifies as a folk belief" (379). The BC study, published in 2011, also found that men's aspirations for fatherhood were out of sync with the reality of their actual parenting. As Harrington et al. suggest:

65% of the fathers believe that both partners SHOULD provide equal amounts of care while 30% feel that their spouse should provide more care. However, when asked to report on how caregiving IS divided, only 30% of fathers reported that caregiving is divided equally, while 64% reported that their spouse provides more care. This highlights a large and noteworthy gap between aspirations and reality for the majority of fathers in this study. (capitalization in original 23)

Clearly, this aspiration-reality gap is yet another way that neotraditional family configurations are reinforced, while seeming to be progressive: these men say they are committed to both gender equity with women and as fathers, but they *do not practice* parenting equality and instead their wives do far more parenting. In short, today there is a gap between what men like the BC men say they believe and what they do. Thus, I want to conclude this book by proposing this fifth strategy as a final strategy to intervene squarely in this aspiration-reality gap to resist neotraditional family configurations.

Implementing a specific strategy of resistance within families now may be the most important strategy to resist celebrity mom profiles that promote neotraditional family configurations, because having the right kind of parenting partnerships may be even more crucial for women's long-term success and ability to be both a mother and a professional than structural or institutional changes. This is the case because, as O'Reilly (*I Should Have*) argues specifically about the women she interviewed, who are both academics and mothers, but is also relevant to all mothers: "if the findings of my interviews are any indication, the type of relationship a woman has with her life partner is a crucial, though largely overlooked, variable, that hugely determines, arguably more so than workplace policies or practices, women's ability to successfully combine an academic career with motherhood" (98).

Moreover, historian Jodi Vandenberg-Davis also suggests that non-normative family structures "may prove to be more important than the rather minimal institutional adaptations" to challenge ongoing gender inequality and secure maternal empowerment for mothers (quoted in O'Brien Hallstein and O'Reilly 38). Roseanna Hertz also argues that resisting gender inequality at home is vital, when she suggests, "Unless something drastic changes [in professional expectations], the more difficult battle for gender equality will be found not in the nation's factories and corporate high-rises but in its private homes" (243). Finally, a May 2014 NPR report titled, "Plenty Of Women Enter Academic Science. They Just Don't Stay," explored why, even though men and women tend to enter scientific fields in relatively equal numbers, women scientists have difficulty getting to the top echelons of science, especially in academia. Near the end of the report, NPR science correspondent Joe Palca, reported, "But the other thing that's going to have to happen, it seems to me and from the people I've talked to, is that the women who've had the biggest success in their careers have done so because they have a partner who carries a lot of the load in terms of having a family. And so it's going to be either men who are going to have to share the load or take on more of it. In some cases, that's going to make it possible for women to reach the top" (par. 20). Focusing on how our family lives are configured and pushing back against inequitable parenting partnerships within our families, then, are crucial to helping mothers resist neotraditional family structures and get better, possibly more satisfying, solutions and support for the post-second wave crisis in femininity, while also asking male partners to do what they say they believe.

When "It Just Isn't Working" and the Hegemony of the Male Career

Others scholars[2] address further the challenges ideal worker norms and intensive mothering raise for two-career families with children and the barriers to mothers' empowerment. What needs more attention, however, is how men's felt entitlement to work acts to reinforce the hegemony of the male career, even though many of these same men say they believe in gender equality, have different expectations of women, and say they want to be engaged and involved fathers. Men's "felt entitlement" to work originates from the hegemony of the male career. Indeed, Karen Pyke argues that upper-class men in particular benefit from what she calls *the hegemony of the male career*. Drawing on the early work of Arlie Hochschild, Pyke argues, as does Joan Williams, that the supremacy of the male career is founded on a patriarchal notion of gender differences, which "provides a rationale for husbands' entitlements that obscures the underlying gendered-power structure. The logic is this: Because husbands are the main providers in their families, they ought to have certain privileges and rights that enable them to perform their duties" (533).

As a result, men's careers are often privileged and prioritized over women's careers in heterosexual relations. Pyke argues, "The supremacy of the male career is most apparent in the marital arrangements of the middle to upper classes" because men are generally freed from the day-to-day responsibilities of childrearing and care (533). Additionally, although Pyke was writing in 1996, Stone's work in 2007 also confirms that contemporary research "consistently reveals another pervasive pattern: in addition to shouldering the work of family, women defer to or accord privilege and priority to their husbands' careers over their own (and by extension often shield or exempt their husbands from household responsibilities)" (64). And this shielding also further reinforces the privatization of work-life struggles[3] and encourages the kind of everyday common-sense neotraditional family configuration that both the new momism and celebrity mom profiles cultivate and reinforce.

Stone's work also explicitly notes the role of post-second wave neoliberal maternal choice in women's decision making about how to structure their family life and the ways that this configuration also supports the hegemony of the male career. In doing so, Stone recognizes that the "choices" women make are not "free" choices but are choices within gender constraints, male organizing systems in professional life, the privileging of men's careers, and women's caregiving responsibilities, even though the women with whom she spoke do not fully recognize these gender-power structures. As Stone puts it:

> While they couch them in the language of choice and privilege, the stories they tell reveal not the expression of choice, but rather the existence of a choice gap, a gap that is a function of a double bind created primarily by the conditions of work in the gilded cages of elite professions. Married to fellow professionals, who face the same pressures at work that they do, women are home alone, and go home because they have been unsuccessful in their efforts to obtain flexibility [at work] or, for those who were able to, because they found themselves marginalized and stigmatized, negatively reinforced to trying to hold on to their careers after becoming mothers. (19)

Consequently, in detailing why high-achieving privileged women "opt out" of their professional career in two-career couples, Stone suggests "The fact that men's careers came first was the underlying and unspoken 'reason' women quit, but men's careers almost always come first; they come first in couples in which women continue working" (78).

Significantly, then, the conflicting crosscurrents that constitute post-second wave neoliberal maternal choices today also reinforce and further entrench the hegemony of the male career. Or, as Stone concludes, "Women's own understanding of their decisions as implementing choice was further reinforced, as we saw earlier, by their husbands, who spoke repeatedly of giving their wives the 'choice' to decide whether or not to quit" (113). Although Stone does not say so specifically, this understanding of choice further entrenches the neotraditional family structure because neither the hegemony of the male career nor women's caregiving responsibilities are ever questioned; both are "second nature" or are "commonsense," everyday experiences built on gender-assumptions about childrearing and family-life responsibilities. As such, "when it just isn't working," the only "questions" revolve around a woman's maternal choices: Should she have a career and have primary responsibility for childcare and household labor? Should she quit work and be home full time to meet her ongoing private sphere responsibilities? Should she interrupt her career for some length of time to focus on her family responsibilities and then try to return to work when the "children are older"? Clearly, celebrity mom profiles also make these questions normal or common sense by entrenching the privatized solution and focus on a third shift of maternal body work as the energizing solution to the crisis in femininity, and ultimately, the answers to these questions.

When work-life decisions are framed around women's maternal choices, the hegemony of the male career—with its hidden privileges and ongoing gender-power inequalities—also becomes invisible in ways that further erase family-life struggles in both the public sphere and within our families and, as a result, also works to erase the difference maternity continues to make in women's lives today. Thus, I am suggesting the invisibility of the hegemony of the male career as the ongoing norm in privileged heterosexual parenting relationships, marriages, and neotraditional family configurations is yet another postfeminist neoliberal idea that encourages the belief that gender oppression no longer exists both outside and inside our families and, equally important, reinforces the folk belief or myth that contemporary fathers and fatherhood have changed such that fathers are intimately involved in parenting because many fathers say they are committed to post-second wave gender equality and that they want to be more involved fathers.

The BC Study: Making the Invisible Visible

While the hegemony of the male career is still largely invisible, the BC study makes visible how it works in relation to the heterosexual men's reports about their actual practices of fathering and how these fathers manage work-life issues in ways that reinforce their family-life privilege that celebrity mom profiles and the new momism grant them. In terms of background, the BC study is a two-phase study of almost 1,000 married, well-educated, privileged, heterosexual professional men. Phase one entailed in-depth interviews with new fathers, while Harrington et al. report that "The New Dad: Caring Committed and Conflicted," "presents the results of the second phase of our research on fatherhood, a survey completed by nearly 1000 [963] fathers who are 'white collar workers' in large corporations" (5). The authors also note: "The report presents a portrait of fathers who strive for professional growth in the workplace as they also strive for equality in their home life, although they openly admit they have not yet achieved it [equality in their home life]" (Harrington et al. 11). While, clearly, these fathers do not represent "all" fathers and, in fact, are clearly privileged, their responses reveal interesting data about how this group of men and fathers represent the aspiration-reality gap that fuels the hegemony of the male career.

One of the most important findings in terms of the hegemony of the male career and subsequent neotraditional family configuration is a chart on page 13 of the report. The chart, titled "Six Aspects of Being a Good Father," reports both the six characteristics of good fathering and reveals how the fathers prioritize those characteristics. Each aspect was rated on a 5-point scale and in order of importance. The findings are as follows in order of importance: provide love and emotional support (4.7/5); be involved and present in your child's life (4.6/5); be a good teacher, guide, and coach (4.5ish/5); provide discipline (4/5); provide financial security (4/5); do your part in the day-to-day childcare tasks (3.9/5) (13).

Three key findings of this data in relation to strategy five are as follows: first and positively, these fathers report that they strive for gender equality in their home life, and, second, they aspire to be emotionally supportive and present in their children's lives, while they place providing financial security lower. Clearly, this is evidence of a different kind of post-second wave fathering than these men probably received from their own fathers where providing financial security was the hallmark of previous generations of fathers' parenting, as was more pronounced and visible gender inequity at home. Third and problematic, however, is that these men rank "do your

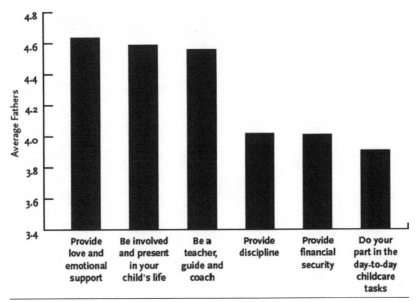

Six Aspects of Being a Good Father
Harrington et al. (13). Used with permission.

part in the day-to-day childcare tasks" as the least important charac-teristic of good fathering. Even Harrington et al. note this particu-lar finding as follows: "Interestingly, 'do your part in the day-to-day childcare tasks' was the lowest rated attribute of being a good father" (13). Thus, even though 65 percent of these men believe both part-ners should provide equal amounts of care, this belief is contradicted by the importance these men place on the actual doing of daily fathering/parenting; there is a gap between what these men believe and what they do; and this gap fuels mothers' primary responsibil-ity for childrearing and family-life management that celebrity mom profiles promote and reinforce.

The findings also reveal another gap in terms of the men's rela-tionship to their own ambitions and how they manage work-life conflict after becoming fathers. First, these men did not take sig-nificant time off with the birth of their children. As the BC study reveals, "more than three-quarters of our sample took off one week or less and 16% did not take any time off at all following the birth of their most recent child" (15). Harrington et al. also report: "Further,

	Never	Rarely	Sometimes	Quite Often	Very Often
How often do you interrupt your time at home or away from the workplace outside "official" work hours to address work-related issues?	2%	26%	43%	21%	8%
How often do you interrupt your time at work to address family-related issues?	2%	40%	52%	6%	<1%

It is clear from the above responses that while interruptions occurred in both directions, fathers' time at home was more than four times as likely to be interrupted quite often or very often by work than fathers' time at work was interrupted by family matters.

More specifically, as illustrated by the questions in the table below, fathers reported that time spent with their children was much more likely to get interrupted (by work-related matters), than time with managers was likely to get interrupted (by family-related matters).

	Never	Rarely	Sometimes	Quite Often	Very Often
How often do you interrupt your time with your children to address work-related issues?	7%	32%	42%	13%	6%
How often do you interrupt time with your manager or supervisor to address family-related issues?	35%	54%	10%	1%	0.1%

Harrington et al. (18). Used with permission.

we found that fathers made few, if any, adjustments to their work after the birth of their children. Virtually all of the fathers (98%) returned to the same jobs (which is not surprising given their time off much more closely resembled a vacation than a leave)" (15). In short, these men were freed to continue "life-as-it-was-before children"—life as if they are unencumbered with family responsibilities—after becoming fathers and seem, as Stone might say, "shielded from day-to-day responsibilities" of childcare. And implicitly, this makes it easier for men to continue to rank "do your part in day-to-day tasks" as the sixth characteristic of good fathering while also allowing them to continue to prioritize their careers after becoming fathers, even if these men say they want to be engaged fathers and do not see being the financial provider as the most important characteristic of good fathers.

Moreover, the report also reveals some very interesting data about how these men managed the relationship between work and childcare in *practice*. In fact, in response to the question, "How often do you interrupt your time with your children to address work-related issues?," the answers were as follows: Never: 7 percent;

Rarely: 32 percent; Sometimes: 42 percent; Quite Often: 13 percent; Very often: 6 percent. These findings suggest that 61 percent of these men interrupt their time with their children to address work-related issues, while 92 percent of these men rarely or sometimes interrupt their time at work to address family-related issues. Additionally, when asked "How often do you interrupt time with your manager or supervisor to address family-related issues?," the fathers reported: Never: 35 percent; Rarely: 54 percent; Sometimes: 10 percent; Quite Often: 1 percent; Very Often: 0.1 percent (18). These responses mean that 89 percent of fathers never or rarely interrupt work time with their managers or supervisor to address family issues. Clearly, both of these findings suggest that, in addition to not engaging in the material practices of daily childcare, these men also rarely engage in any family-life management while they are at work. This indicates that for these fathers, even when home, parenting is secondary to work rather than primary. In short, when these men are at work, they are at work; and when they are at home, they are at home and often working professionally. Thus, the BC data provide more specific detail about how the aspiration-reality gap works in practice: even though these men aspire to parenting equality, *they neither prioritize the daily doing of parenting nor do they actually prioritize children when at work*; rather, they invoke their right to privilege work over parenting at almost every turn of their life at work and at home, privileges very few mothers currently enjoy under the now-intensive new momism regime that celebrity mom profiles promote.

Within this post-second wave context for fathers and in light of the BC findings, I now turn to proposing steps to enact strategy five. At the core of each step is two key assumptions: first, that fathers do believe in gender equity—as they report that they do in the study and Crittenden notes privileged men tend to practice before the arrival of children—and, as a result, second, rather than trying to change men's minds, *we need to change what they actually do*. Therefore, all the steps are geared toward asking partners and/or husbands to do what they say they believe, while also pushing back against the hegemony of the male career, and closing the aspiration-reality gap that both reinforces and encourages neotraditional family configurations, while also allowing mothers to refuse to keep the difference maternity makes in their lives invisible, both in their professional lives and, most importantly, at home.

Step One: Mothers Must Not Give Up on Their Own Ambitions

At the 2012 "What do Mothers Need? Empowering Mothers/
Maternal Empowerment" conference last year and in the chapter
(*What do Mothers Need?* O'Brien Hallstein) I wrote from that talk,
I argued that maternal empowerment can only begin when mothers
refuse to give up on their own professional ambitions after becoming
mothers. I still believe that this is a foundational step to create more
gender equity at home, so I reiterate but not belabor this point. This
must be the foundation for challenging the hegemony of the male
career, neotraditional family configurations, and making the difference maternity makes in mothers' lives visible because, if mothers do
not believe they have the right to their own career and aspirations,
even after becoming mothers, then they will not advocate for themselves. To put it in the context of accepting, even embracing, the
post-second wave split subjectivity that celebrity mom profiles cultivate and reinforce after women become mothers, post-second wave
women must resist giving up on their own ambitions in order also to
resist the underlying post-feminist neoliberal split subject position
that undergirds and supports both the post-second wave crisis in
femininity and neotraditional family structures. Therefore, just like
the women Stone interviewed and probably like the partners and
wives of the BC respondents, I am arguing that if mothers give up
their own right to maintain their ambitions after becoming mothers,
especially first-time mothers, then they will continue to grant their
partners' and husbands' careers privilege over their own, and they
will continue to participate in and reinforce a gender-power structure that makes the hegemony of the male career primary and wom-
en's own aspirations secondary, while also further entrenching rather
than challenging our post-second wave split subjectivity.

As a result, mothers must reassert their right *to be both* success-
ful/ambitious at work and successful mothers. This means that when
contemporary mothers refuse to give up their own right to want to
be both a good mother and a good and/or dedicated professional or
worker—when they refuse to give up their desire to have success in
both the encumbered and unencumbered world in which *both mothers and fathers move in and out of every day*—they also refuse to give
up their status as both post-second wave beneficiaries and, possibly,

empowered mothers. As a result, for the mothers who O'Reilly (*Mother Outlaws*) notes—women who lay the foundation of a career before having children—and those whom Douglas and Michaels describe as wanting to be both good mothers and good professionals (12), these women must allow themselves the ambition that they once felt when they were younger and, equally important, must allow themselves to enact and practice the aspirations that their husbands continue to enact after becoming a parent.

That the men did not give up their professional aspirations after becoming fathers was made clear when the BC respondents revealed that they allowed work to interrupt their fathering but not vice versa. The BC study also reveals additional information about fathers' aspirations after becoming fathers. In fact, another finding of the BC study was that fathers continued to have "strong" aspirations, even after they became fathers. As Harrington et al. report: "fathers had strong aspirations to advance in their careers: 76% of respondents wished to advance to a position with greater responsibility; 58% of respondents had a strong desire to be in senior management" (9). This data suggest fathers' aspirations and ambitions continued, even flourished after fatherhood; mothers have the same right to both also.

Aging usually comes with more wisdom, so mothers' aspirations may be different from fathers and a mother's ambition may be different from her younger self's ambition. But, most importantly, I argue that, as with men, women have the right to maintain their own ambitions after children—even when it gets hard and difficult, when "it just isn't working" and they face the post-second wave crisis in femininity—and must persist in securing what they need at home to realize their right to continue to be high-achieving women and mothers. Moreover and related, remembering that the personal is political in relation to securing partnerships at home is especially important *now* because ongoing gender divisions of labor at home continue to be tied to gender inequalities in the public sphere. As Hertz suggests, "Gender inequalities in the labor market are intimately tied to gender inequalities in the home because the time women spend in unpaid work—particularly child care—reduces their availability for employment" (241). Thus, pushing back against the hegemony of the male career at home and making the

difference maternity makes visible will also play key roles in pushing back against the ongoing gender inequality that undergirds both
neotraditional family configurations and the labor market. Finally, I
believe that when mothers insist that they too have a right to maintain their own ambitions, then they will be more likely to resist the
third-shift solution offered in celebrity mom profiles because they
will recognize that they do not need to do more; someone else needs
to do more. And, what better solution than to ask male partners to
do what they say they believe?

Step Two: Resist Maternal Choices

As I noted earlier, "when it just isn't working," the only problem-
solving "questions" revolve around a woman's maternal choices.
In step two, I suggest that we need to "intervene" squarely in the
gap that currently exists between what many men say they believe
about gender equality in parenting and what these men actually do
by refusing to make family-life problem solving only about mothers' choices. And, no matter how much any particular mother resists
the new momism by engaging in empowered mothering, children
require much care, time, and attention. Consequently, much problem
solving will always be required. Thus, rather than have the problem
solving revolve around questions about mothers' choices, we need
to insist on shifting the ground to parental questions that ask men
to enact what they say are their own beliefs, while mothers begin to
refuse to participate in the intensification of women's work in the
private sphere. To do so, instead of focusing on mothers' choices,
the kinds of questions that we must insist on asking and answering instead are the following: How can each of us have a career and
actually do our part in childcare and household labor? Can we each
make career changes to accommodate family life? Is it possible to
take turns prioritizing career over family, at least when the children are young and have so many needs? And, equally important,
when there is any resistance to this shift in grounding, we must be
clear that these are the kinds of questions that must be addressed by
anyone who believes in more equitable family partnerships and to
ensure that our ideas about parenting and the "doing" of parenting
are more in sync and more visible to all.

Step Three: Quit Being Normative

Both celebrity mom profiles and the intensified new momism assume and cultivate a normative "wife" role for mothers, and this role is an essential component of the hegemony of the male career and the neotraditional family configuration. As a result, third, we need to refuse the normative wife role. We must do so because the normative wife role entrenches the hegemony of the male career and neotraditional families, while also making it much easier for men like those who participated in the BC study to live comfortably within the aspiration-reality gap. Again, O'Reilly's work is helpful here to explain further why the normative wife role is so pivotal to reinforcing neotraditional family configurations. O'Reilly (*I Should Have*) writes and is worth quoting in length:

> The normative wife role assumes and expects that 1) the family will be organized around the career of the husband 2) that the career of the wife, should she have one, will be necessarily secondary to that of her husband 3) that the wife is to support her husband's career and its advancement 4) that the woman is responsible for and performs the many and varied tasks of maintaining the household and home making. (198)

Clearly, O'Reilly reveals how the normative wife role reproduces and regulates neotraditional families and women's ongoing caretaking responsibility for childrearing, while also requiring women to sidetrack their own ambition for their husband's. Equally important, as the analysis chapters also showed, celebrity mom profiles also reinforce problematic and entangled gender-based assumptions that further re-entrench the wife role: women still want a fairy-tale wedding; being a mother is still the most important role for women, regardless of any other success that they might have in the public sphere, and women must always command the male gaze. Thus, refusing the normative wife role and accompanying gender assumptions intertwined with that role also push back against the hegemony of the male career, while also helping to challenge neotraditional family structures.

Refusing to be good wives does not mean that women cannot be good partners or good mothers. Rather, being non-normative or bad wives creates the possibility for more equitable parenting partnerships and empowered mothering. Why do we need to be non-normative or bad wives to be empowered mothers? At the most basic level, being bad wives is an approach that can challenge the everyday commonsense experiences in the private sphere and the neotraditional family. In William Hanks' review of Pierre Bourdieu's work in relation to anthropology, Hanks argues, "the stability of the habitus is not expressed in rules, which Bourdieu rejects, but in habits, dispositions to act in certain ways, and schemes of perception that order individual perspectives along socially defined lines" (69). In other words, habitus is experienced in everyday life and practices and becomes, what Harvey would call, *commonsense ideologies*; people are formed through the kinds of everyday actions and practices the BC fathers reported when they placed "do your part in day-to-day childcare tasks" as the sixth most important characteristic of good fathering, while also reporting that 64 percent of them have spouses who provide more care. Clearly, regardless of what they say they believe, these men are "stably" ensconced in a habitus that benefits fathers along inequitable and socially defined gender lines that also reinforce and cultivate the normative wife role and the new momism today. There is no doubt that both allow contemporary men to say they believe in being different kinds of fathers without actually doing what is necessary to be those kinds of fathers and more equitable parenting partners, while also continuing to keep the difference maternity makes in women's lives invisible. Thus, resisting the normative wife role, while also eroding the everyday habitus of the hegemony of the male career, are vital to make maternity visible and to challenge neotraditional family structures.

Step Four: Insist That Fathers Do More Mental Labor

One of the clearest findings of the BC study was that 92 percent of these men rarely or sometimes interrupt their time at work to address family-related issues. At the most basic level this means that, when at work these men are at work and not doing any of the mental labor of parenting. Moreover, the BC data also revealed that more than three-quarters of the men took off one week or less after the birth of their most recent child. In her own work, Susan Walzer suggests that women must "make men think about the baby," as early as possible, because this mental labor is a necessary but often avoided and ignored component of parenting by many men, and, if not done with the birth of a first child, then this labor is unlikely to ever be done later. Walzer suggests mental labor "is meant to distinguish the thinking, feeling, and interpersonal work that accompany the care of babies from physical tasks" (219). This is the kind of work that Hochschild refers to as the "invisible" labor of family life or what Sara Ruddick calls "maternal thinking." In other words, this is the managerial work of family life: the worrying, scheduling, and organizational work required to keep a family running and working.

I and O'Reilly (*Academic Motherhood*) have argued the following tasks are involved in this kind of maternal thinking: remembering to buy the milk, managing all communication between the family and a child's school, managing, scheduling, and taking a child to a doctor appointment, planning the birthday parties, and/or worrying that the daughter's recent loss of appetite may be indicative of anorexia. Although the father may sign the field-trip permission form or buy the diapers, it is the mother in neotraditional households who reminds him to do so. Delegation does not make equality and, equally important, delegation also continues to require that mothers have the psychological responsibility for remembering, managing, and executing the household, family life, and childrearing. And this kind of work is never-ending, and difficult for many women to simply turn off at work, especially when those women are the only parent doing this kind of mental labor. Clearly, however, the BC study reveals an important related finding: this mental labor can be turned off—the BC fathers turn off parenting while at work. So, in step four, I suggest that we must insist that fathers do more of the mental labor—starting with the birth of their first child—rather than simply just being delegated to, and that we should also get the chance, as fathers do, to turn off this mental labor of family work when doing our professional work.

Difficulty Turning off the Mental Labor. It is true that, even though the mental labor of family is onerous, enacting step four might be very hard for many mothers to actually do. This is the case because step four also requires that mothers allow fathers to do the mental labor as the fathers might want to do so, not necessarily the

way that mothers might do it. Indeed, in my everyday life, I regularly hear mothers complain that they finally insisted that their husbands do some family-life task, and their husbands "did not do it
correctly"; that is, the fathers did not do it exactly the same way as
the mothers would do. I also hear fathers make the related but con-
verse complaint: they are trying to do more, but they can never do
it "right"; that is, if they do not do it the way their wives do it, then
what they do is wrong. Recently, for example, a mother friend of
mine insisted that her husband needed to take over the "backpack"
responsibilities: the unpacking of the children's school backpacks,
the signing of the permission slips for various school-related activities, and the nightly signing of the "reading log."

When this was her job, she did the job like clockwork: every
evening, she unpacked the bags, asked the children to get the school
paperwork, and she signed everything after dinner and returned it to
the backpacks. When her husband took over the responsibilities, he
did it very differently: he did it every morning as part of the getting-
ready-for-school activities. Moreover, in the beginning, he often
forgot to complete the job. And especially in the beginning, when
he often forgot to do it, the children came home from school upset
because they had arrived at school "unsigned." All of this made my
friend crazy and at first she insisted that her husband should do it at
night as she did. She also soothed her children's upset about arriving at school without all the paperwork signed. My friend and her
husband had many fights about this small change in their routine
and change in mental-labor responsibilities, and it took some time
to make it run smoothly for all involved.

Asking fathers to do more mental labor and day-to-day tasks,
then, can be a very tricky dynamic between mothers and fathers, and
it is especially hard for mothers who have primarily been in charge
to suddenly let go of how things should be done, even if they genu-
inely wish to do so. Even so, especially in the context of the mental
labor of family life, if mothers want to have less of this work, not
only do they have to insist that fathers do more of it, they also have
to let go of their own assumptions that only they know how best to
do it. Eventually, my friend had to let go of her sense of the right
way to do things and had to allow her husband to soothe the children when they were upset about arriving at school unsigned, while
her husband had to learn to remember this work and actually do

it. This means, then, that even though step four might actually be difficult for some mothers to do, mothers must do so. They cannot have it both ways; they cannot insist on doing less mental labor, while also insisting that fathers must do that labor exactly as they do, because believing that there is only one way to do things or that men are incompetent, only benefits men and keeps women doing all the work. As a result, enacting strategy four may be difficult, but it is a necessary step to challenge fathers to do more of what they actually say they believe.

Step Five: Ask Fathers to Make the Conduct of Fatherhood Primary

Clearly, the aspiration-reality gap that the BC study reveals suggests a significant disparity between what the men say about how they want to father and what they actually do. Step five also intervenes in this gap by asking fathers to make the conduct of fatherhood primary rather than secondary. To explain this strategy, I borrow more from LaRossa's writing. LaRossa argues that the institution of fatherhood "includes two related but still distinct elements. There is the *culture of fatherhood* (specifically the shared norms, values, and beliefs surrounding men's parenting), and there is the *conduct of fatherhood* (what fathers do, their parental behaviors)" (377). Writing in 1988, as LaRossa noted, often these two are out of sync. Clearly, the BC study reveals that the contemporary culture of fatherhood is currently out of sync with the conduct of fatherhood, particularly in terms of men's expressed aspirations and the reality of their parenting. As a result, both at the time LaRossa was writing and now, there is an asynchrony between what we—men and women—say about contemporary fatherhood and many men's conduct of it.

LaRossa suggests that the primary solution to correcting this asynchrony is to "force" men to examine their professed commitments to fatherhood. Indeed, he argues, "Only when men are forced to seriously examine their commitments to fatherhood (vs. their commitment to their jobs and avocations) can we hope to bring about the kinds of changes that will be required to alter the division of child care in this country" (383). I also suggest the same: we must insist that our male partners and husbands make the conduct of fatherhood primary rather than secondary by making what they do more consistent with what they say they believe. Moreover, making the conduct of fatherhood primary will also encourage men to make their caregiving visible in ways that challenge both neotraditional family structures and the celebrity mom profiles that make fathers invisible in caregiving. Thus, step five is the final step to enacting strategy five—asking men to do what they say that they believe— because making the conduct of fatherhood primary rather than secondary requires men to practice what they say they believe, while also making fathering visible, too.

In conclusion, I understand that the five strategies are demanding and may be difficult to employ in each and every situation or parenting moment. As a result, I offer them as possibilities and potential strategies to: be used sometimes individually and sometimes together, especially when we find ourselves recognizing that it just isn't working, inspire post-second wave fathers to practice what they say they already believe, and encourage mothers to push back against the hegemony of the male career in ways that might grant mothers more space to ease some of the difficulties of having to do it all, while also allowing mothers to continue to meet their own career aspirations after becoming parents. Moreover, as I noted earlier, because contemporary motherhood sits at the epicenter of conflicting and contradictory cultural and gender change, my hope is that these five initial strategies of resistance might also be used together to fuel the now-necessary mothers' revolution in ways that resist and challenge the now even-more-intensified new mothering ideology, the celebrity mom profiles and accompanying rules that support those profiles, and the neotraditional family configurations that are currently being offered to contemporary women when they face the post-second wave crisis in femininity when they become *both post-second wave beneficiaries and mothers.*

NOTES

Introduction

1. Mothers are judged even more harshly if they "fail" to have the forms of privilege promoted by the profiles.
2. Although academia is viewed as liberal and progressive, academic mothers also continue to have primary responsibility for caregiving within neotraditional family configurations and, as a result, also are not immune from the ideological messages and practices reinforced in the profiles. Moreover, academic mothers also suffer penalties at work because of their caregiving responsibilities. Recent studies of both academic women and mothers (Mason and Goulden, "Do Babies Matter?"; Mason and Goulden, "Do Babies Matter (II)?"; Wolfinger, Mason, and Goulden) reveal that gender discrimination more generally and specifically against academic mothers continues to be widespread in academia, primarily due to women's ongoing caregiving responsibilities. Indeed, even though more and more women are completing PhDs and are entering the academic "pipeline," academic mothers do not have gender equity with male academics, including male academics who also have children. Goulden and Mason ("Do Babies (II)"), for example, argue that "Even though women make up nearly half of the PhD population, they are not advancing at the same rate as men to the upper ranks of the professoriate; many are dropping out of the race" (11).

The primary reason women are dropping out or "leaking out of the pipeline" is because having children penalizes academic mothers far more than it does academic fathers, while sometimes having children even benefits academic fathers. Mason and Goulden ("Do Babies (II)") even wryly argue "'Married with children' is the success formula for men, but the opposite is true for women, for whom there is a serious 'baby gap'" (11). More pointedly, in their earlier essay, Mason and Goulden also note "there is a consistent and large gap in achieving tenure between women who have early babies and men who have early babies [having a baby prior to five years after a parent completes his or her PhD], and this gap is surprisingly uniform across the disciplines and across types of institutions" ("Do Babies Matter?" 24). They also note, "surprisingly, having early babies seems to help men; men who have early babies achieve tenure at slightly higher rates than people who do not have early babies" (24). The opposite is the case for women who have early babies. Consequently, Mason and Goulden ("Do Babies Matter?") find that women with early babies often "do not get as far as ladder-rank jobs" and often make family–work choices that "force them to leave the academy or put them into the second tier of faculty: the lecturers, adjuncts, and part-time faculty" (24). Thus, even though academic institutions are primarily progressive and liberal institutions, academic motherhood also continues to be replete with discrimination based on motherhood.

3. While the exact year that the second iteration of profiles emerged is hard to pinpoint exactly, I began to notice them first in 2009, but by 2010, this new kind of profile was the "new normal." And, once bikini profiles began, the number has only increased since then.

4. When I tracked down some of the profiles that Douglas and Michaels analyzed, almost all them were one- to two-years postpartum. Thus, it is clear that the timeline for the first iteration of profiles was later than they are today.

5. By employing the term *post-second wave*, I mean to suggest "after second wave feminism" or "as a result of second wave feminism." Consequently, unlike much popular writing, I do not employ the term to mean that we live in a postfeminist context,

implying that all gender problems have been solved via second wave feminism.

6. From the early days of the celebrity mom profiles, women of privilege—economic, racial, and heterosexual—were and continue to be the focus of the profiles.

7. Equally important, key topics in *Bikini-Ready Moms* were not addressed in any sustained way in *The Mommy Myth*: neoliberalism, the maternal body, and the post-second wave crisis in femininity, all of which are becoming more and more entangled with both celebrity mom profiles and contemporary motherhood.

8. The initial scholarship on "post-feminism" hyphenated the word. However, many scholars, including myself and Douglas and Michaels, have now dropped the hyphen. When quoting McRobbie directly here, I will hyphenate the word as she does; however, here and elsewhere in the book, I follow the more contemporary convention of dropping the hyphen.

9. Because I draw on and concur with Benita Roth's recent argument in *Roads to Feminism* that it is essential to recognize second wave feminisms were organized along racial/ethnic lines, my definition of white second wave feminism is founded in Roth's writings. As Roth argues, "The second wave has to be understood as a group of feminisms, movements made by activist women that were largely organizationally distinct from one another, and from the beginning, largely organized along racial/ethnic lines" (3). By *white second-wave feminism*, then, I mean white feminism of the 1960s and through the 1970s that was organized primarily, but not exclusively, by and around white middle-class women and is generally marked as ending with the failure of the Equal Rights Amendment (Dow; Evans). Thus, from this point on, I will use *white second-wave feminism* and *second-wave feminism* interchangeably. And I will suggest that recognizing that race was central in terms of how second-wave feminisms organized is also important to challenge the conventional narrative that racism was the sole reason that there was a paucity of women of color in white second-wave feminisms. Moreover, as Roth also suggests, this conventional narrative "is an inaccurate conception that negates the agency of feminists of color. Different contexts for doing politics influenced how

feminists situated in Black, Chicano/a, and white oppositional communities were able to relate to their movements of origin, and to one another" (6).

I also view white second wave feminism as a historical phenomenon that continues to be a part of contemporary feminism's history. Viewing all feminisms of the second wave as history, as Bonnie J. Dow recently argued, allows feminist rhetoricians to recognize the second wave as a historical phenomenon without necessarily suggesting that the second wave is done or over. Rather, it simply means that the "second wave has receded far enough into the past that it has become suitable for treatment as an historical phenomenon" (89). As such, rereading the second wave as a historical phenomenon allows us to build on the second wave rather than break from it. Or, as Sara Evans also argues in the introduction of *Tidal Wave*, her book is intended "to affirm for future generations that they do indeed have a history, by turns glorious and distressing, on which they can build" (17). Finally, situating second wave feminism historically is important because, as Dow suggests, rereading the second wave of feminism can reveal "the renewed importance of understanding its [feminism's] problems and possibilities during a period when many of its gains are simultaneously taken for granted and under attack" (91).

10. Specifically, I also follow Condit and Lawrence Grossberg who argue hegemonic ideologies function as a form of social control when they shape what counts as "normal" or "good" in culture. Moreover, these communication scholars and Cloud also argue media can be a primary tool for entrenching rather than challenging hegemonic ideologies.

Chapter 1. Contemporary Motherhood at the Epicenter of Intersecting Cultural Changes

1. Describing major moments of economic and social change as a *turn* has precedent within academic writing. Indeed, Harvey (2005) was the first to use the term *neoliberal turn*, while Steven

Best and Douglas Kellner used the term *postmodern turn* in their landmark work on the advent of postmodernism. I mirror this thinking and convention when I use the language of *post-second wave turn*. Moreover, as do Best and Kellner, in doing so, I use the term to suggest that the current "turn" sits at the intersection of the old and new, that is, the modern and postmodern for Best and Kellner. I take this to mean that the post-second wave turn includes both the "new" and the "old" in relation to gender, that is, to include post-second wave gender equity in the public sphere and pre-second wave gender inequity in the private sphere.

2. In the Introduction, to distinguish between "previous" and "new" profiles, I employed the language of *first- and second-iteration of celebrity mom profiles* to distinguish between the previous profile structure, rules, and norms that Douglas and Michaels' first noted and the new profile structure, rules, and norms of contemporary profiles. From this point on, when I say *new celebrity mom profiles,* I mean the new, second iteration of profiles.

3. The popular press often refers to mothers who engage in this kind of child surveillance and micro-management as *helicopter mothers* or as *hover mothers*. Although different scholars and popular writers all disagree about which is the best label, they all agree that mothering has intensified recently.

4. White describes Foucault's original ideas about the body as follows: "The body is directly involved in a political field: power relations have an immediate hold upon it; they invest it, mark it, train it, torture it, force it to carry out tasks to perform ceremonies, to emit signs'" (270). Moreover, White suggests, caught in neoliberal power relations, then, "good" neoliberal subjects discipline and train their bodies to be consistent with "expert" discourses, especially medical discourses associated with healthism. White, in fact, argues, "The discourses produced by these disciplines are also internalized individual practices, in the 'technologies of the self.' These are the practices whereby individuals constitute themselves as subjects, internalizing the discourses of the medical and helping professions, through self-appraisal, monitoring their feelings and emotions and constructing their bodies" (270).

Chapter 2. Step One—Becoming First-Time Mothers

1. The moment that Middleton's second pregnancy became public—early September 2014—again, reluctantly due to Middleton's struggle with hyperemesis gravidarum, media immediately
   linked Middleton to Kardashian, even though there was no confirmation that Kardashian was actually pregnant. On September
   22, 2014, *Star* magazine, for example, had a cover story titled,
   "It's Official! Kim & Kate Two Babies!" Inside the cover story,
   readers learn that Middleton's second pregnancy is described
   as a "happy accident" (39), while Kardashian is reported to be
   unhappy and worried about her maternal body and pregnancy
   weight gain. As the article reveals, "In early August, Kim went
   on a Twitter rant about the baby weight she hasn't been able to
   shed since giving birth. 'Kim's biggest fear is putting on as much
   weight while carrying her second baby as she did with Nori,'
   says the source, pointing to the whopping 65 lbs. Kim gained
   during her first pregnancy" (41). Thus, even though they are no
   longer first-time mothers, linking these two women is so important to slender-pregnancy profiles that they were immediately
   relinked and compared in relation to one another, with the Middleton coverage being "positive" and the Kardashian coverage as
   a "warning," again, about pregnancy weight gain, even though
   there was no confirmation that Kardashian was also pregnant
   for the second time.
2. It is true that Simpson's second pregnancy was covered more
   than Philipp's pregnancy, and much of that coverage focused
   on Simpson's weight gain and struggle with that weight gain.
   Simpson, in fact, as I note in the next chapter, has had her own
   weight struggles and fat shaming throughout her career. Even
   so, Simpson's pregnancy was still secondary to the coverage of
   the Middleton-Kardashian battle in the media.
3. Ess is mistaken here: Middleton and Kardashian both married
   in 2011. As a result, these were the two most popular weddings
   of 2011.
4. Clearly, this report had it wrong: Kardashian and Humphries
   separated 72 days after the marriage rather than divorced 72
   days later.
5. "Pregorexia" is also used to describe pregnant women's preoc-
   cupation with weight control through extreme dieting and

exercise while pregnant. In a *CBS Early Show* report on Pregorexia, "'Pregorexia' Inspired by Thin Celebs?" the link between
celebrity moms and dieting during pregnancy was made clear.
The report suggests, "And some of those women may get started
on the path to 'pregorexia' by images of celebrities who look
thin while pregnant and immediately after giving birth, observ-
ers agree" (par. 2). The report also suggests, "Some women get
so obsessed with keeping their weight in check while pregnant that they go overboard on dieting and exercise and put
their baby's health at some risk, some experts say" (par. 1). In
an ABC News report, both women and their mothering were
indicted in a report about pregorexia. Dr. Robert Zurawin, an
associate professor at the department of obstetrics and gynecology at Huston's Baylor College of Medicine, said "Women
who are pregorexic—or don't eat when they're pregnant because
they're afraid of gaining weight—need to think about their
baby" (quoted in Friedman par. 10). He went on to say, "There
are so many fad diets out there with no carbs and women are so
obsessed with body image that they don't want to gain weight
during their pregnancy because they're afraid of not being able
to lose it afterward" (in Friedman par. 11). Interestingly, then,
while pregorexia is the "logical" outcome of messages women
receive about trying to remain attractive and fit when pregnant,
pregorexia is blamed on the very women who try to meet these
ideological imperatives. This blaming is also yet another example of the tricky and insidious rhetorical device that disciplines
women into beauty standards that, repeatedly, oppresses them,
while, ultimately, these oppressive ideals and practices are attributed to the women, as if they freely choose to make beauty the
most important component of who they are as women (the very
same dynamic at work in post-second wave neoliberal maternal
choice today) that I discuss in chapter 4.

6. While there was some nuanced discussion about the fact that
Middleton and Kardashian have different body types, for the
most part that was ignored and both women's maternal bodies
were compared to one another and in relation to the slender-
pregnant ideal. So, for example, quoting a fitness expert, Sandra Clark also argues, "'Kim and Kate have different body types,'
pregnancy fitness expert and celebrity nutritionist, Lisa DeFazio,
MS, RD tells *Holly Baby.com* exclusively. 'Kim is more full

figured, standing 5'2", whereas Kate has a smaller frame, standing 5'10. That's a big difference and as a result they are going to
carry their babies differently'" (par. 3). Even so, as noted next,
DeFazio also quickly moved to a discussion about Kardashian
gaining too much weight too soon.

Chapter 3. Step Two—Being Bikini-Ready Moms

1. From the early days of the celebrity mom profiles, women of
   privilege—economic, racial, and heterosexual—were and continue to be the focus of the profiles.
2. In fact, the *Popeater* story suggests that these quickly slender
   post-baby reveals are so important now that magazines are even
   willing to photo shop mothers' postpartum bodies to get the
   quickly slender story first.
3. For brevity, in the remainder of this chapter, I use *quickly slender
   profiles, bikini-ready profiles,* and *postpartum profiles* interchangeably when discussing quickly slender, even bikini-ready, postpartum celebrity mom profiles.
4. In terms of the images that accompany the profiles, Douglas
   and Michaels argue "the celebrity had to be photographed dis-
   playing a board toothy grin, her child in her lap or lifted with
   outstretched arms above her head, an accessory who made her
   look especially good on her sofa or balcony. Celebrity mothers
   are invariably surrounded by pastels and suffused in white light;
   the rooms we often see them in feature white or pastel furniture"
   (113). Consequently, celebrity mom profiles reveal the joy celebrity moms have found as privileged fit mothers as they intensively juggle work, family, and childcare. Moreover, in looking
   at the celebrity mom profiles in Douglas and Michaels' book, it
   is clear that many of the moms were profiled with much older
   babies, that is, the babies all appear to be closer to a year old
   or older (toddlers). In other words, even though babies appear
   far less frequently in the quickly slender profiles, when they do
   appear, the babies are also much younger than those shown in
   the profiles that Douglas and Michaels detail. Thus, it is also
   clear that celebrity mom postpartum profiles appeared much
   later than they do now in the quickly slender profiles.

5. The focus on Wikinson-Baskett's postpartum body continued a few months later when *People Online* describes Wilkinson-Baskett in the following way: "Kendra Wilkinson shows off her svelte body-after-baby at Moorea Beach Club at Mondalay Bay in Las Vegas on Saturday" ("Kendra Wikinson" par. 1).

6. This cover first came to my attention in Meredith Nash's book, *Making "Postmodern" Mothers*, 171.

7. Michaels did become a mother after this interview. With her partner, she adopted a two-year-old girl from Haiti and her partner gave birth to a boy; both events happened in the same week.

8. I thank an anonymous reviewer in the previously published version of this analysis for pointing out this changed understanding of women's bodies.

9. It is this cover of Kourtney Khardashian that was the impetus for the *Popeater* article. Khardashian also protested the cover, arguing that she never gave an interview and insisting that her postpartum body did not look like the cover. Indeed, she insisted that the picture was photo shopped. Even though the image was photo shopped, the messages contained in the cover story are consistent with the discourse of quickly slender postpartum bodies in other celebrity mom profiles.

10. A second "logical" outcome of the demand for a quickly slender body is not just being fit during pregnancy but also trying to stay thin during pregnancy, an issue I addressed in chapter 2 via the analysis of Middleton. Another example of the connection between slender pregnancy and trying to "stay thin" during pregnancy is supermodel Giselle Bundchen when she was pregnant with her first child. The *omg!* website reveals "Supermodel Gisele Bundchen stayed so thin while pregnant with baby Benjamin, she didn't need to wear maternity clothes" ("Gisele Bundchen Didn't Wear" par. 1). After admitting that she has not exercised since giving birth, Bundchen, who posed for Brazilian fashion line Colcci just six-and-a-half weeks after giving birth, goes on to say "But little by little I recovered the form. It helps that I have not gained much, have had natural childbirth, and breastfeeding" (par. 6). While Bundchen challenges the imperative to immediately return to exercise, she clearly recognizes that staying thin during pregnancy can be a "preemptive

strategy" for a quick recovery. Moreover, Bundchen also seems to suggest that being the best, most "natural" mother—being an intensively laboring birthing mother—also played a part in her quickly slender body. And, ironically, she did return to exercise to enhance her postpartum body. A few months after giving birth, *People Online* had a picture of Bundchen in workout clothes with the following copy, "After recently unveiling her enviable, post-baby body, Gisele Bundchen intends to keep it that way with a workout Tuesday in Studio City, Calif." ("Feel the Burn" par. 1).

11. Ekberg reported this about Fox in the context of lauding Middleton for being willing to proudly display her mummy tummy when she left the hospital after giving birth. Directly after her report about Fox, Ekberg concludes: "So there's one more good reason to applaud Kate's perfectly normal pregnancy belly" (par. 7).

12. There is no doubt that celebrity moms are women of privilege in terms of economic, racial, and sexuality privilege. Indeed, almost all the women profiled are white, heterosexual, and have the economic means to hire both the childcare and domestic help necessary to engage in the kind of rigorous dieting and exercise required of the quickly slender body. As noted in the Introduction, this invisible privilege is almost never acknowledged by celebrity moms nor the profiles of them.

13. In a follow-up footnote, Gremillion also points out "Wellness at Work" programs are on the increase, and they focus on worker productivity as well as stress reduction. Moreover, citing Rippe's article, "CEO Fitness: The Performance Plus" that suggests that CEOs who "manage stress" through exercise "feel pressure" at work "but have learned to live with it—perhaps even thrive on it. They're what researchers call 'contented hard workers, not harried, Type-A workaholics' (53)" (Gremillion 398).

14. MILF means "mother I would like to fuck." It tends to be used by teenage boys and young men to describe their friends' mothers and/or attractive "older" mothers.

15. In her essay, Bordo ("Reading") does suggest that the slender body is a denial of reproduction. By arguing that the quickly slender body does not deny reproduction but now denies pregnancy and maternity, I am updating Bordo's work for our

contemporary context rather than challenging her initial claims. Seventeen years later, I believe that the slender body ideal is being refined in the same ways that the new momism continues to be refined. Thus, I do not disagree with Bordo's early work; rather, I simply suggest an update to her landmark ideas here.

Chapter 4. Consequences, Rules, and Conclusions about Bikini-Ready Moms

1. There is nothing inherently problematic with the number of rules staying the same as the structure, rules, and norms change. Moreover, because I am not arguing that the entire structure, format, and rules have completely changed—indeed, this second iteration of profiles still has the same ultimate goal and remains the most important media format to sell the new momism— it also makes sense that the number of rules remain the same, while the actual imperatives of the rules change along with the focus, structure, and norms.

2. In making this argument about the institution of motherhood versus the potential of mothering to be empowering to women if they can define mothering for themselves, I am drawing on Adrienne Rich's landmark work in *Of Women Born*. I also elaborate further the impact of this all-important distinction in chapter 5 in my discussion of empowered mothering. For now, however, it is important to note that Rich's most basic argument is that motherhood is a patriarchal institution that oppresses women and that mothering has the potential to be empowering to women if they are allowed to define and practice mothering for themselves. In doing so, Rich was the first feminist scholar to introduce the idea that motherhood was ideological and, as a result, also political. Rich culms the history of pregnancy, childbirth, and mothering in the first five chapters of her book to argue that the institution of motherhood exercises control over women as they bear and rear children to serve the interests of men. As Rich puts it: "the mother serves the interests of patriarchy: she exemplifies in one person religion, social conscience, and nationalism. Institutional motherhood revives and renews all other institutions" (45). Even though Rich did not

have the language of "social construction" yet, Rich made one of the first social constructionist arguments when she claimed: "The patriarchal institution of motherhood is not the 'human condition' any more than rape, prostitution, and slavery are . . . motherhood has a history, an ideology" (33). Thus, first and foremost, Rich views the institution of motherhood as a patriarchal form of social control, while she also views the experience of mothering as potentially empowering if women are allowed to define mothering for themselves outside of the institution of motherhood.

As such, Rich made an all-important distinction between the institution of motherhood and the potential empowered relations in mothering. As Rich argued, "I try to distinguish two meanings of motherhood, one superimposed on the other: the *potential relationship* of any woman to her powers of reproduction and to children; and the *institution*, which aims at ensuring that that potential—and all women—shall remain under male control" (italics in original 13). Based on this groundbreaking distinction, Rich views the institution of motherhood as male-defined, male-controlled, and as deeply oppressive to women, while she views the experience of mothering as a potentially empowering relationship for both women and children.

Chapter 5. Resisting Being Bikini-Ready Moms

1. I am well aware that the elective plastic surgery that mommy makeovers entail could be empowering for a mother if she elects to have the surgery performed after careful and critical thinking. Victoria Pitts-Taylor's work on why women engage in plastic surgery, for example, suggests that women who opt for plastic surgery after careful reflection and to "fix" problems rather than to "fix" the woman, can be empowering. Even so, even elective plastic surgery comes with real potential physical risks. So, what I am suggesting in strategy two is that my hope is that, with critical reflection, mothers may shift to resisting these procedures to fix themselves or to fix the problem of having it all, and instead to opt for resisting the ideological messages that suggest this fix.

2. See Douglas and Michaels; Hays; O'Brien Hallstein and O'Reilly; *Mother Outlaws* O'Reilly; and Warner.

3. By advocating for change within families, it might appear that I, too, like "TS" and "Ann Ingram" seem to be suggesting that solving the post-second wave crisis is only a family problem that families need to work out rather than society. Indeed, as I noted in chapter 1: In addition to being grounded in the rhetoric of choice, "TS" (June 12, 2012, comment 3), for example, suggests, "If women want more successful careers, they should demand partners who will equally share domestic responsibilities. Dividing the burden of childcare is a personal choice made between the parents, and if one assumes more responsibility than the other, that parent's career will likely suffer. Why should any employer or coworker have to make up for that?" A grammatically incorrect comment by Anne Ingram also concurs that, because motherhood is a choice, professional institutions need not support working mothers. As she (June 12, 2012, comment 16) puts it: "My feeling is that if you have kids, [sic] that is your business. don't [sic] bring it into the workplace and make other people compensate for you. it's [sic] your choice and your problem." I believe, however, that I am advocating something very different from what "TS" and Ingram suggest because strategy five is the fifth strategy of five strategies that all work together to try to change both the public and private spheres. Moreover, strategy five is not grounded in mothers' maternal choices; rather, strategy five is, first and foremost, grounded in what contemporary fathers' report that they believe. As a result, while strategy five might look similar to what is now the everyday commonsense solution that "TS" and Ingram both articulate, it is founded in a very different set of principles, values, and ideas and, as a result, works differently than what they advocate.

WORKS CITED

Abrahamson, Rachel Paula. "Teen Mom Monsters." *US Weekly*, issue 952, May 13, 2013, 72–75.

Adams, Jeanne. "Is Kate Middelton Still Anorexis and Can She Put Baby Before Body Insecurities?" *celebdirtylaundry.com*, December 8, 2012. http://www.celebdirtylaundry.com/2012/is-kate-middleton-still-anorexic-and-can-she-put-baby-before-body-insecurities-1208/

Adams, Rebecca. "Royal Wedding vs. Kim Kardashian's Wedding: By The Numbers (PHOTOS)." *huffingtonpost.com*, April 28, 2012. http://www.huffingtonpost.com/2012/04/27/royal-wedding-vs-kardashian_n_1459827.html

———. "Duchess Kate's Bump Looks Lovely In Erdem During Manchester Visit (PHOTOS)." *huffingtonpost.com*, February 23, 2014. http://www.huffingtonpost.com/2013/04/23/duchess-kate-bump-photos-pictures_n_3138267.html?utm_hp_ref=kate-middleton-pregnant

Anderson, Eric. "It's All Greek to Them!" *US Weekly*, issue 952, May 13, 2013, 70–71.

Anthony, Stacie, and Molly McGonigle. "Celebs Bodies after Babies." *wonderwallmsn.com*. n.d. Web. March 23, 2014. http://wonderwall.msn.com/movies/reveal-body-after-baby-21401.gallery

"Baby Mama." *Urban Dictionary.com*. Web. June 10, 2013. http://www.urbandictionary.com/define.php?term=baby%20mama

"Baby Mama." *Wicktionary.org.* n.d. Web. June 10, 2013. http://en.wiktionary.org/wiki/baby_mama

Baez, Jenn. "Kate Middleton: Glowing Beauty As New Mom Leaves Hospital." *hollywoodlife.com.* July 23, 2013. http://hollywoodlife.com/2013/07/23/kate-middleton-after-birth-royal-baby-leaving-hospital-hair-makeup/

Bass, Shauna. "My Body after Baby. Kendra Wilkinson Exclusive." *OK Weekly*, February 22, 2010, 32–39.

"Battle of the Bumps! Kate the Waif vs. Kim the Whale." *You.* May 09, 2013.

Beetham, Richard. "Jessica Simpson. How I Got My Body Back!" *OK! USA*, December 9, 2013, 4–7.

Belanger, Larissa. "Emily Blunt Debuts Slender Post-Baby Body One Month After Daughter Hazel's Birth." *pregnancytips.org,* April 8, 2014. http:/pregnancytips.org/baby/your-newborn/emily-blunt-debuts-slender-post-baby-body-one-month-after-daughter-hazels-birth/

Best, Steven, and Douglas Kellner. *Postmodern Theory: Critical Interrogations.* New York: Guilford Press, 1991.

Bezanson, Kate, and Meg Luxton. "Child Care Delivered Through the Mailbox: Social Reproduction, Choice, and Neoliberalism in a Theo-Conservative Canada." *Social Reproduction: Feminist Political Economy Challenges Neo-Liberalism.* Edited by Meg Luxton and Kate Bezanson. Montreal: McGill-Queens University Press, 2006, 90–112.

———. "Introduction: Social Reproduction and Feminist Political Economy." *Social Reproduction: Feminist Political Economy Challenges Neo-Liberalism.* Edited by Meg Luxton and Kate Bezason. Montreal: McGill-Queens University Press, 2006, 3–11.

Bianchi, Suzanne M., John P. Robinson, and Melissa A. Milkie. *Changing Rhythms of American Life.* London: Russell Sage, 2006.

Bishop, Mardia J. "The Mommy Lift: Cutting Mothers Down to Size." *Mommy Angst: Motherhood in American Culture.* Edited by Ann C. Hall and Mardia J. Bishop. Santa Barbara, CA: Praeger, 2009.

Blickley, Leigh. "Kate Middleton vs. Kim Kardashian: It's Time For A Pregnancy Battle." *huffingtonpost.com.* n.d. Web. December 3,

2013. http://www.huffingtonpost.com/2013/03/06/kate-middleton-kim-kardashian-pregnancy_n_2814304.html

"Body After Baby. At What Cost?" *Disney Family.com*, June 18, 2010. http://www.celebrityparents.com/articles/6030.php

"Body After Baby: Star Moms Who Bounced Right Back Go figure! See how quickly Kate Winslet, Halle Berry, Jessica Simpson and more Returned to their Fab Physiques." *people.com*. n.d. Web. March 27, 2014. http://www.people.com/people/celebritybabies/gallery/0,,20781628,00.html#30123916

"Body after Twins." *usmagazine.com*. n.d. Web. March 24, 2014. http://www.usmagazine.com/celebrity-news/pictures/body-after-twins-2009278/2462

"Body Image Movement." http://bodyimagemovement.com.au/

"Body Moments of the Year." "Most Talked about Bodies 2014." *People*, June 2, 2014.

Bordo, Susan. "Reading the Slender Body." *Feminism and Philosophy: Essential Readings in Theory, Reinterpretation, and Application.* Edited by Nancy Tuana and Rosemarie Tong. Boulder, CO: Westview Press, 1995, 467–488.

———. *Unbearable Weight: Feminism, Western Culture, and the Body.* Berkeley: University of CA Press, 2004.

Braedley, Susan, and Meg Luxton. "Competing Philosophies: Neoliberalism and Challenges of Everyday Life." *Neoliberalism and Everyday Life*. Edited by Susan Braedley and Meg Luxton. Montreal: McGill-Queens University Press, 2010, 1–22.

Braithwaite, Ann. "Politics of/and Backlash." *Journal of International Women's Studies* 5.5 (June 2004): 18–33.

Brooks, Gary R. *Beyond the Crisis in Masculinity: A Transtheoretical Model for Male-Friendly Therapy.* Washington DC: APA Press, 2009.

Brown, Wendy. "Neo-liberalism and the End of Liberal Democracy." *Theory & Event* 7.1 (2003), October 1, 2014. http://muse.jhu.edu.ezproxy.bu.edu/journals/theory_and_event/v007/7.1brown.html

Brumberg, Joan Jacobs. *The Body Project: An Intimate History of American Girls.* New York: Random House, 1997.

Brumfitt, Taryn. "Body Image Movement." n.d. Web. May 12, 2013. http://bodyimagemovement.com.au/about-taryn-brumfitt/

Burton, Cinya. "Kim Kardashian Reveals Her Biggest Pregnancy Craving, Favorite Junk Food." *eonline.com*, December 16, 2013. http://www.eonline.com/news/491360/kim-kardashian-reveals-her-biggest-pregnancy-craving-favorite-junk-food

"Busy Philipps shows off burgeoning belly in floral dress . . . and claims Kim Kardashian's pregnancy 'takes all the heat off' of hers." *dailymail.co.uk*, April 3, 2013. http://www.dailymail.co.uk/tvshowbiz/article-2303745/Busy-Philipps-shows-burgeoning-belly-floral-dress--claims-Kim-Kardashians-pregnancy-takes-heat-hers.html

Byrne, Suzy. "Mom-to-Be Ivanka Trump's 3 Delivery Room Essentials." *Yahoo! Celebrity*, October 1, 2013. https://celebrity.yahoo.com/blogs/celeb-news/mom-ivanka-trump-3-delivery-room-essentials-112941447.html

"Celebrity Bikini Bodies after Babies. Stars Looking Fit, Healthy And Fab Post Kids." *huffingtonpost.com*. n.d. Web. March 21, 2014. http://www.huffingtonpost.com/2013/04/12/celebrity-bikini-bodies-after-baby-photos_n_3071740.html

"Celebrity Post-Baby Bods." *Yahoo! Celebrity*. n.d. Web. July 19, 2013. https://celebrity.yahoo.com/photos/celebrities-post-baby-bodies-1374172956-slideshow/

"Celebs Flaunt Their Amazing Transformations." *Abcnews.go.com*. n.d. Web. March 21, 2014. http://abcnews.go.com/Entertainment/photos/ups-downs-celebrity-weight-3094935/image-kate-winslet-reveals-slim-post-baby-body-22953307

Chávez Karma R., and Cindy L. Griffin, eds. *Standing in the Intersection: Feminist Voices, Feminist Practices in Communication Studies*. Albany: State University of New York Press, 2012.

Christopher, Karen, and Avery Kolers. "Halving It Both Ways: Co-Parenting in an Academic Couple." *Contemporary Motherhood in a Post- Second Wave Context: Challenges, Strategies, and Possibilities*. Edited by D. Lynn O'Brien Hallstein and Andrea O'Reilly. Toronto: Demeter Press, 2012, 298–308.

Clark, Sandra. "Pregnant Kim Kardashian Vs. Kate Middleton—Baby Bumps & Bangs." *hollywoodlife.com*, February 5, 2013. http://hollywoodlife.com/2013/02/05/pregnant-kim-kardashian-kate-middleton-baby-bump-bangs-pics/

Cloud, Dana. L. "Hegemony or Concordance?: The Rhetoric of

Tokenism in Oprah Winfrey's Rags-to-Riches Biography." *Critical Studies in Mass Communication* (1996): 115–137.

Collins, Patricia Hill, "Forward: Emerging Intersections—Building Knowledge and Transforming Institutions." In *Emerging Intersections: Race, Class, and Gender in Theory, Policy, and Practice*, edited by Bonnie Thornton Dill and Ruth Enid Zambrama. New Brunswick, NJ: Rutgers University Press, 2009, vii–xiii.

Condit, Celeste Michelle. "Hegemony in a Mass-mediated Society: Concordance about Reproductive Technologies." *Critical Studies in Mass Communication* 11 (1994): 205–230.

———. *The Meaning of the Gene: Public Debates about Human Heredity*. Madison: University of Wisconsin Press, 1999.

Coontz, Stephanie. "The Family Revolution." *greatergood.berkeley.edu*, September 1, 2007. http://greatergood.berkeley.edu/article/item/the_family_revolution

Craven, Christa. "A 'Consumer's Right' to Choose a Midwife: Shifting Meanings for Reproductive Rights under Neoliberalism." *American Anthropologist* 109.4 (2007): 701–712.

Crenshaw, Kimberle. "Mapping the Margins: Intersectionality, Identity Politics and Violence against Women of Color." *Stanford Law Review* 43 (1991): 1241–1299.

Crittenden, Ann. *The Price of Motherhood: Why the Most Important Job the World is Still the Least Valued*. New York: Holt, 2001.

Crompton, Rosemary, and Clare Lyonette. "Work-Life 'Balance' in Europe." *ACTA SOCIOLOGICA* 49.4 (2006): 379–393.

Cronin, Melissa. "Exclusive Octomom: One Year Later. My New Bikini Body!" *Star*, February 1, 2010, 52–59.

Cunningham, Hilary. "Prodigal Bodies: Pop Culture and Post-Pregnancy." *Michigan Quarterly Review* 41.3 (2002): 429–454.

Davies, Caroline. "Duke and Duchess of Cambridge announce they are expecting first baby." *theguardian.com*, December 3, 2012. http://www.theguardian.com/uk/2012/dec/03/duke-and-duchess-of-cambridge-expecting-baby

de Marneffe, Daphne. *Maternal Desire: On Children, Love, and the Inner Life*. New York: Little, Brown, 2004.

Douglas, Susan J., and Michaels, Meredith. *The Mommy Myth: The Idealization of Motherhood and How It Has Undermined Women*. New York: Free Press, 2004.

Dow, Bonnie J. "Review Essay: Reading the Second Wave." *Quarterly Journal of Speech* 91.1 (February 2005): 89–107.

Dworkin, Shari L., and Faye Linda Wachs. *Body Panic: Gender, Health, and the Selling of Fitness*. New York: New York University Press, 2009.

Earle, Sarah. "Bumps and Boobs: Fatness and Women's Experiences of Pregnancy." *Women's Studies International Forum* 26.3 (2003): 245–252.

Edwards, Leigh H. *Triumph of Reality TV: The Revolution in American Television*. Santa Barbara, CA: Praeger, 2013.

Edwards, Tim. *Cultures of Masculinity*. New York: Routledge, 2005.

Eggenberger, Nicole. "Busy Philipps to Chelsea Handler: Kim Kardashian's Pregnancy 'Takes All The Heat' Off Mine." *usmagazine.com*, April 3, 2013. http://www.usmagazine.com/celebrity-moms/news/busy-philipps-to-chelsea-handler-kim-kardashians-pregnancy-takes-all-the-heat-off-mine-201334

Ekberg, Aida. "Kate Middleton and Other Celebs Feel Pressure to Lose the 'Mummy Tummy' Fast." *Yahoo! Celebrity*. n.d. Web. March 24, 2014. http://celebrity.yahoo.com/news/kate-middleton-other-celebs-feel-pressure-lose-mummy-185200580.html

English, Rebecca. "So Proud to Show off her Mummy Tummy: Mothers Hail Kate's Decision Not to Hide Her Post-Baby Bump." *dailymail online*, July 23, 2013. http://www.dailymail.co.uk/news/article-2375634/Kate-Middleton-proud-post-Royal-baby-bump.html

Ess, Amy. "Is Kim Kardashian competing with Kate Middleton for Fame?" *Yahoo! Voices*, May 20, 2013. http://voices.yahoo.com/is-kim-kardashian-competing-kate-middleton-for-12145046.html

Evans, Sara. *Tidal Wave: How Women Changed America at Century's End*. New York: Free Press, 2003.

"FAQs about 'Mommy Makeover' Surgery—What Women Need to Know." *medicine.stonybrookmedicine.edu*, January 10, 2010. http://medicine.stonybrookmedicine.edu/surgery/blog/faqs-about-mommy-makeover-surgery-what-women-need-to-know

"Feel the Burn." *people.com*, July 1, 2010. http://www.people.com/people/gallery/0,,20398382_20806152,00.html

Folbre, Nancy. *Who Pays for the Kids? Gender and Structures of Constraint*. London: 27 Routledge, 1994.

Foss, Sonja. K. *Rhetorical Criticism: Exploration and Practice*. 4th ed. Long Grove, IL: Waveland Press, 2009.

Frazier, Kevin. "Invanka Trump Fearless in Slinky Pregnancy Dress." *omg! Insider Update*. n.d. Web. October 2, 2013. https://screen.yahoo.com/ivanka-trump-fearless-slinky-pregnancy-223617704.html

Friedman, Emily. "Anorexia and Pregnancy Don't Mix, Docs Say." *abcnews.go.com*, June 8, 2009. http://abcnews.go.com/Health/ReproductiveHealth/story?id=7768530&page=1

Friedman, May. *Mommyblogs and the Changing Face of Motherhood*. Toronto: University of Toronto Press, 2013.

Galinsky, Ellen. "The Ongoing Struggle to Balance Career and Family." *The Diane Rehm Show*. Transcript. http://the-dianerehmshow.org/shows/2012–06–25/ongoing-struggle-balance-career-and-family/transcript

Gershon, Ilana. "Neoliberal Agency." *Current Anthropology* 52.4 (August 2011): 537–547.

Giantis, Kat. "Beyonce Makes her Post-Blue Debut!" *wonderwall. com*. n.d. Web. June 2, 2014. http://www.wonderwall.com/music/gossip-beyonce-makes-her-post-blue-debut-17941. gallery

Giles, Melinda Vandenbeld, ed. *Mothering in the Age of Neoliberalism*. Bradford, ON: Demeter Press, 2014, 297–314.

Gimlin, Debra. "The Absent Body Project: Cosmetic Surgery as a Response to Bodily Dys-appearance." *Sociology* 40.4 (2006): 699–716.

Gipson, Brooklyne. "Mommies with Great Snapback." *Juicy*, Fall 2010, 50–51.

"Gisele Bundchen Didn't Wear Maternity Clothes." *omg!* February 1, 2010. http://omg!.yahoo.com/news/gisele-bundchen-didn-t-wear-maternity-clothes/35086

Glickman, Rose L. *Daughters of Feminists: Young Women with Feminist Mothers Talk about Their Lives*. New York: St. Martin's Press, 1993.

Glines, Carole. "Kourtney's Body after Baby: Exclusive." *US Weekly*, February 1, 2010, 32–35.

Glynn, Kevin. *Tabloid Culture: Trash Taste, Popular Power, and the Transformation of American Television*. Durham and London: Duke University Press, 2000.

Gornstein, Leslie. "Kim Kardashian's Pregnant World Travels—Is It OK to Be Flying in Her Third Trimester?" *Yahoo! Celebrity*, May 29, 2013. https://celebrity.yahoo.com/blogs/celeb-news/kim-kardashian-pregnant-world-travels-ok-flying-her-004155825.html

Green, Fiona. "Empowered Mothering." In *Encyclopedia of Motherhood Volume One*. Edited by Andrea O'Reilly. Thousand Oaks, CA: Sage, 2010, 347–348.

Greenfield, Beth. "New Mom Under Fire for Post-Baby Body Selfie. *Yahoo! Shine*, December 2, 2013. https://shine.yahoo.com/parenting/new-mom-under-fire-for-post-baby-body-selfie-195830521.html

Gremillion, Helen. "In Fitness and in Health: Crafting Bodies in the Treatment of Anorexia Nervosa." *Signs* 27.2 (Winter 2002): 381–414.

Grossbart, Sarah. "How Stars Get Thin." *US Weekly*, January 25, 2010, 44–49.

———"Battle of the Bumps!" *US Weekly*, June 24, 2013, 52–57.

Grossberg, Lawrence. "Cultural Studies and/in New Worlds." *Critical Studies in Mass Communication* 10 (1993): 1–12.

Hall, Stuart. "The March of the Neoliberals." *Guardian Online*, September 12, 2011. http://www.guardian.co.uk/politics/2011/sep/12/march-of-the-neoliberals

Halperin, Terri. "Mommy Makeover." *drterrihalperin.com*. n.d. Web. September 27, 2013. http://drterrihalperin.com/mommy-makeover/

Hanks, William F. "Pierre Bourdieu and the Practices of Language." *Annual Review of Anthropology* 34 (2005): 67–83.

Hanson, Teri. "The Secret to Getting Your Body Back Fast." *Fit Pregnancy* (April/May 2013): 58–63.

Harrington, Brad, Fred Van Deusen, and Beth Humberd. "The New Dad: Caring Committed and Conflicted." Boston: Boston College Center for Work & Family, 2011.

Harvey, David. *A Brief History of Neoliberalism*. Oxford: Oxford University Press, 2005.

Hasan, Lama. "Kate Middleton is Pregnant." ABC News. *abcnews.go.com*, December 3, 2012. http://abcnews.go.com/Entertainment/kate-middleton-pregnant/story?id=17041409#.UbYdivmsiSo

"Have the Baby, Keep the Body (And make it better)." Cover. Australian *Women's Health Bump*, January 2011.

Hays, Sharon. *The Cultural Contradictions of Motherhood*. New Haven: Yale University Press, 1996.

Hefferman, Kristin, Paula Nicolson, and Rebekah Fox. "The Next Generation of Pregnant Women: More Freedom in the Public Sphere or Just an Illusion?" *Journal of Gender Studies* 20.4 (December 2011): 321–332.

Hertz, Rosanna. "Book Review: The Contemporary Myth of Choice." *American Academy of Political and Social Science* 596 (November 2004): 232–244.

Hill, Emily, and Emily Kent Smith. "It's Kate v Kim . . . The bump off! One's an English duchess. The other is Hollywood royalty. And when it comes to maternity wear, they really ARE oceans apart." *dailymail.co.uk*, April 6, 2013. http://www.dailymail.co.uk/femail/article-2305066/Kate-Middleton-v-Kim-Kadashian-baby-bump-Duchess-Cambridges-maternity-style-oceans-apart.html

Hirsch, Marianne, and Evelyn Fox Keller. "Introduction: January 04, 1990." In *Conflicts in Feminism*, edited by Marianne Hirsch and Evelyn Fox Keller. New York: Routledge, 1990, 1–5.

Hirshman, Linda R. *Get to Work: A Manifesto for Women of the World*. New York: Viking, 2006.

Hochschild, Arlie. *The Second Shift: Working Parents and the Revolution at Home*. New York: Viking, 1989.

"Holly Madison Shows Off Slim Post-Baby Body Three Weeks After Giving Birth to Daughter Rainbow: Picture" *Yahoo! Celebrity*, March 23, 2013. https://celebrity.yahoo.com/news/holly-madison-shows-off-slim-post-baby-body-214500470-us-weekly.html

"Holly's Amazing Post-Baby Body!" *OK*, May 27, 2013, 22.

Holmes, Su. "'All you've got to Worry about is the Task, having a Cup of Tea, and doing a Bit of Sunbathing,': Approaching celebrity in *Big Brother*. *Understanding Reality Television*. Edited by Su Holmes and Deborah Jermyn. New York: Routledge, 2004, 111–135.

Holmes, Su, and Deborah Jermyn. "Introduction: Understanding Reality TV." *Understanding Reality Television*. Edited by Su Holmes and Deborah Jermyn. New York: Routledge, 2004, 1–32.

Horowitz, Erika. "Resistance as a Site of Empowerment: The Journey away from Maternal Sacrifice." *Mother Outlaws: Theories and Practices of Empowered Mothering*. Edited by Andrea O'Reilly. Toronto: Women's Press, 2004, 43–58.

"Ingram, Anne." "Comment 16." "Motherhood Still a Cause of Pay Inequality." *New York Times*, June 12, 2012. http://www.nytimes.com/2012/06/13/business/economy/motherhood-still-a-cause-of-pay-inequality.html?_r=1&emc=eta1

"It's Official! Kim & Kate Two Babies!" *Star*, September 22, 2014, 38–41.

James, Amber. "Magazines Photoshop Stars' Post-Baby Pounds Away." *Popeater*, February 11, 2010. http://www.popeater.com/2010/02/11mgazines-photoshop-celebrities/

James, Jennifer Hauver. "Re-Writing the Script." In *Contemporary Motherhood in a Post-Second Wave Context: Challenges, Strategies, and Possibilities*, edited by D. Lynn O'Brien Hallstein and Andrea O'Reilly. Toronto: Demeter Press, 2012, 269–278.

"Jennifer Garner." *Yahoo!.com.* n.d. Web. June 17, 2010. http://omg!.yahoo.com/news/jennifer-garner-debuts-post-baby-body/17893

"Jennifer Lopez Shows Off Bikini Bod." *Yahoo!.com.* Web. July 6, 2010. http://omg!.yahoo.com/news/jennifer-lopez-shows-off-bikini-bod/25986/print

"Jennifer Lopez Shows Off Bikini Bod." *usmagazine.com*, September 3, 2010. http://www.usmagazine.com/healthylifestyle/news/jennifer-lopez-shows-off-bikini-bod-200948

Jermyn, Deborah. "Still Something Else Besides a Mother? Negotiating Celebrity Motherhood in Sarah Jessica Parker's Star Story." *Social Semiotics*, 18.2 (June 2008): 163–176.

"Jessica Simpson: How I Got My Body Back." *OK USA* 09 (December 2013): 4–7.

Jette, Shannon. "Fit for Two? A Critical Discourse Analysis of *Oxygen* Fitness Magazine." *Sociology of Sport Journal* 23 (2006): 331–351.

Johnson, Zack. "Kim Kardashian on Pregnancy Curves: "How the F-ck Did I Get Like This?" *usmagazine.com.* Web. May 23, 2013. http://www.usmagazine.com/entertainment/news/kim-kardashian-on-pregnancy-curves-how-the-f-ck-did-i-get-like-this-2013225?stop_mobi=yes

Kardashian, Kourtney, Kim, and Khloe. *Kardashian Konfidential.* New York: St. Martin's Press, 2010.

"Kate Gosslin Flaunts Bikini Bod." *usmagazine.com*, May 31,

2009. http://www.usmagazine.com/healthylifestyle/news/kate-gosselin-flaunts-bikini-body-2009315

"Kate Gosslin Shows Off Bikini Bod, Short Hair." *usmagazine.com*, May 21, 2010. http://www.usmagazine.com/healthylifestyle/news/pic-kate-gosselin-shows-off-bikini-bod-shorter-haircut-1970241

"Kate Middleton Flashes Flat Stomach 3 Months After Baby!" *toofab.com*, October 18, 2013. http://www.toofab.com/2013/10/18/kate-middleton-stomach-after-baby-photos/#sthash.0Wed2NFW.dpuf

"Kate Middleton's Pregnant Bikini Pics Published In United States." *hollywoodlife.com*, February 13, 2013. http://hollywoodlife.com/2013/02/13/kate-middleton-baby-bump-bikini-pictures-america/

"Kate Middleton Vs. Kim Kardashian In Pretty Dresses—Whose Look Is Best?" *hollywoodlife.com*, April 29, 2013. http://hollywoodlife.com/2013/04/29/kim-kardashian-kate-middleton-pregnancy-style-pics/

"Kate Shows Off Baby Bump!" *starmagazineonline.com*, February 13, 2013. https://www.google.com/search?q=star+magazine+february+2013&espv=2&biw=1366&bih=643&tbm=isch&tbo=u&source=univ&sa=X&ei=rD1eVKn-oqsyASD0IHQDA&ved=0CB0QsAQ

Katz, Jason. "Tough Guise: Violence, Media, and The Crisis in Masculinity." Media Education Foundation. Northampton, MA: Media Education Foundation, 1999.

Katzenstein, Mary Fainsod. "Feminism within American Institutions: Unobtrusive Mobilization in the 1980s." *Signs: Journal of Women in Culture and Society* 16.1 (Autumn 1990): 27–54.

Kauppinen, Kati. "Managing Motherhood: Empowerment and Neoliberalism in a Postfeminist Women's Magazine." *Proceedings of the 5th Biennial International Gender and Language Association Conference IGALA*. Victoria, University of Wellington, July 2008, 83–95. http://www.victoria.ac.nz/igala5/igala-proceedings-book.pdf

"Kendra Wilkinson Show Off her Svelte Body-after-Baby" *people.com*. n.d. Web. July 6, 2010. http://www.people.com/people/gallery/0,,20399186,00.html#20807217

"Kim Kardashian Baby Bump Fashion Disasters." *youtube.com*, March 25, 2013. http://www.youtube.com/watch?v=HR08RzhOO2A

"Kim Kardashian Baby Bump Wardrobe Malfunction Vs. Kate

Middleton." *youtube.com*, April 5, 2013. http://www.youtube.com/watch?v=lPdwAwFMc6Y

"Kim Kardashian Dons A Bikini For The Cover Of *Us Weekly*." *huffingtonpost.com*, December 11, 2013. http://www.huffingtonpost.com/2013/12/11/kim-kardashian-bikini-us-weekly_n_4424673.html?utm_hp_ref=email_share

"Kim Kardashian finally gives into her pregnancy cravings as she chows down 1,000 calories on a burger and cheese fries." *mailonline.com*, March 28, 2013. http://www.dailymail.co.uk/tvshowbiz/article-2300374/Kim-Kardashian-gives-pregnancy-cravings-chows-burger-cheese-fries.html

"Kim Kardashian Had 'No Idea' Kanye Was Revealing Pregnancy." *tmz.com*, December 31, 2012. http://www.tmz.com/2012/12/31/kim-kardashian-had-no-idea-kanye-west-was-announcing-pregnancy/

"Kim Kardashian vs. Kate Middleton Pregnant Fashion Style." *youtube.com*, April 24, 2014. http://www.youtube.com/watch?v=9WYkzVTTmwg

"Kim Kardashian Vs A Killer Whale: Who Wore it Better?" *memecollection.net*, March 4, 2013. http://memecollection.net/?s=Kim+kardashian+vs+shamu

Kimmel, Michael. *Manhood in America: A Cultural History*. Oxford: Oxford University Press, 2000.

Kirby, Iona and Jade Watkins. "Suffering for Style! Heavily Pregnant Kim Kardashian Squeeze[sic] her Swollen Feet into Perspex Stilettos." *dailymailonline*. Web. February 23, 2014. http://www.dailymail.co.uk/tvshowbiz/article-2325813/Kim-Kardashians-swollen-feet-severely-pinched-squeezes-sky-high-perspex-stilettos.html

"Kris Humphries' Family Kim K should admit . . . Marriage was a Sham." *tmz.com*, October 3, 2013. http://www.tmz.com/2013/03/10/kris-humphries-family-kim-kardashian-divorce-marriage-sham/

Langan, Debra. "Mothering in the Middle and Self Care: Just One More Thing to Do." *Mediated Moms: Mothers in Popular Culture*. Edited by Elizabeth Podnieks. Montreal: McGill-Queen's University Press, 2012, 268–283.

Lareau, Annette. *Unequal Childhoods: Class, Race, and Family Life*. Berkeley: University of California Press, 2003.

LaRossa, Ralph. "The Culture and Conduct of Fatherhood." *Families in the U.S.: Kinship and Domestic Politics*. Edited by Karen V. Hansen and Anita Ilta Garey. Philadelphia: Temple University Press, 1998, 377–386.

Lee, Allyssa. "Winner Takes All." *Women's Health* (May 2010): 42–45.

Lee, Esther. "Emily Blunt Debuts Slender Post-Baby Body One Month After Daughter Hazel's Birth:" *usmagazine.com*, March 19, 2014. http://www.usmagazine.com/celebrity-body/news/emily-blunt-debuts-slender-post-baby-body-one-month-after-daughter-hazels-birth-picture-2014193

Lee, Sharon Heijin. "The (Geo)politics of Beauty: Race, Transnationalism, and Neoliberalism in South Korean Beauty Culture." University of Michigan, 2012. *Diss. ProQuest Dissertations and Theses*. Web. May 12, 2013. http://search.proquest.com.ezproxy.bu.edu/pqdtft/docview/1222054979/previewPDF/C7A520AB6F6248DDPQ/3?accountid=9676

Leibowitz, Lauren. "Kate Middleton Outfit Repeats, Might Have An Official Due Date (PHOTOS)." *huffingtonpost.com*, May 12, 2013. http://www.huffingtonpost.com/2013/05/12/kate-middleton-repeats-due-date_n_3262806.html

Lennon, Christine. "BETTER BODY AFTER BABY: Legions of alpha moms are emerging from their post-pregnancy figure slimmer and trimmer than ever." *harparsbazaar.com*, October 2, 2012. http://www.harpersbazaar.com/beauty/health-wellness-articles/better-body-after-baby-1012

Lewis, Raha. "Laila Ali: How I Got my Bikini Body Back." *people.com*, May 27, 2013. http://celebritybabies.people.com/2013/05/27/laila-ali-bikini-body/

Ley, Rebecca. "How do our bumps compare to Kate's? The nation's agog over the Duchess's blossoming baby bump. So what do other women due at the same time look like . . ." *dailymail.co.uk*, May 14, 2013. http://www.dailymail.co.uk/femail/article-2324586/Kate-Middletons-baby-bump-photos-How-pregnant-bellies-compare-Duchess-Cambridges.html

Lovejoy, Meg, and Pamela Stone. "Opting Back In: The Influence of Time at Home on Professional Women's Career Redirection after Opting Out." *Gender, Work and Organization* 19.6 (November 2012): 631–653.

Luxton, Meg. Doing Neoliberalism: "Perverse Individualism in Personal Life." *Neoliberalism and Everyday Life*. Edited by Susan Braedley and Meg Luxton. Montreal: McGill-Queens University Press, 2010, 163–183.

Malin, Brenton, J. *American Masculinity under Clinton: Popular Media and the Crisis in Masculinity*. New York: Peter Lang, 2005.

Mason, Mary Ann, and Marc Goulden. "Do Babies Matter?: The Effect of Family Formation on the Lifelong Careers of Academic Men and Women." *Academe*, 90.6 (November–December, 2002): 21–27.

———. "Do Babies Matter (Part II)?: Closing the Baby Gap." *Academe* 90.6 (November–December, 2004): 10–15.

McNally, Kelby. "The Duchess of Cambridge Claims Top Spot in Favourite Pregnant Celebrity Hairstyle Poll." *express.co.uk*, May 14, 2013. http://www.express.co.uk/news/royal/399576/The-Duchess-of-Cambridge-claims-top-spot-in-favourite-pregnant-celebrity-hairstyle-poll

McRobbie, Angela. "Post-Feminism and Popular Culture." *Feminist Media Studies* 4.3 (2004): 255–264.

———. "Yummy Mummies Leave a Bad Taste for Young Women." *theguardian.com*, March 1, 2006. http://www.theguardian.com/world/2006/mar/02/gender.comment

———. *The Aftermath of Feminism: Gender, Culture, and Social Change*. Los Angeles: Sage, 2009.

Melnick, Meredith. "Royal Wedding Weight Watch: Wispy Kate Middleton Spotlights 'Brideorexia'." *time.com*, April 18, 2011. http://healthland.time.com/2011/04/18/royal-wedding-weight-watch-wispy-kate-middleton-spotlights-brideorexia/

Messner, Michael A. *Power at Play: Sports and the Problem of Masculinity*. Boston: Beacon Press, 1992.

"MILF." *urbandictionary.com*. n.d. Web. June 18, 2010. http://www.urbandictionary.com/define.php?term=milf

Miller, Lee M., Robert J. Antonio, and Alessandro Bonanno. "Hazards of Neoliberalism: Delayed Electric Power Restoration after Hurricane Ike." *British Journal of Sociology* 62.3 (2011): 505–522.

Mitzeliotis, Katrina. "Kim Kardashian Flashes Thong: See-Through Wardrobe Malfunction." *hollywoodlife.com*, April 24, 2013. http://hollwoodlife.com/2013/04/24/kim-kardashian-thong-see-through-dress-pic/

"Most Talked about Bodies 2014." *People*, June 02, 2014.

"Motherhood Today: Tougher Challenges, Less Success." *Pew Research Center* (May 2, 2007). http://www.people-press.org/2007/05/02/motherhood-today-tougher-challenges-less-success/

"Mothers Movement Online." http://www.mothersmovement.org

Murray, Susan, and Laurie Ouellette, eds. *Reality TV: Remaking Television Culture*. New York: New York University Press, 2004.

"Museum of Motherhood." http://www.mommuseum.org/about/

Nash, Meredith. *Making "Postmodern" Mothers: Pregnant Embodiment, Baby Bumps, and Body Image*. New York: Palgrave Macmillan, 2012.

Nelson, Margaret K. *Parenting Out of Control: Anxious Parents in Uncertain Times*. New York: New York University Press, 2010.

"New Mom's Instagram of Chiseled Post-Baby Belly Causes Backlash." *abcnews.go.com*, December 2, 2013. http://abcnews.go.com/blogs/health/2013/12/02/new-moms-instagram-of-chiseled-post-baby-belly-causes-backlash/

Ng, Christina. "Kate Middleton is Pregnant." *abcnews.go.com*, December 3, 2012. http://abcnews.go.com/Entertainment/kate-middleton-pregnant/story?id=17041409#.UbYeOlhbZb8.email

"Nicole Richie." *Omg!* May 7, 2011. http://omg!.yahoo.com/news/nicole-richie-debuts-post-baby-body/28011

O'Brien Hallstein, D. Lynn. *White Feminists and Contemporary Maternity: Purging Matrophobia*. New York: Palgrave Macmillan, March 2010.

———. "Public Choices, Private Control: How Mediated Mom Labels Work Rhetorically to Dismantle the Politics of Choice and White Second Wave Feminist Successes." *Contemplating Maternity in an Era of Choice: Explorations into Discourses of Reproduction*. Edited by Sara Hayden and D. Lynn O'Brien Hallstein. Lanham, MD: Lexington Books, 2010, 5–26.

———. Lecture titled, "What do Mothers Need?: Not to Give up on Their Own Ambitions and Persistence in Securing Partner Participation in Family Life." "What do Mothers Need? Empowering Mothers/Maternal Empowerment: The Motherhood Movement, Motherhood Studies, Perspectives and Possibilities across Activism and Scholarship," conference sponsored by the Motherhood Initiative for Research and Community Involvement, Toronto, Ontario, May 8–10, 2012.

————. "When Neoliberalism Intersects with Post-Second Wave Mothering: Reinforcing Neo-traditional American Family Configurations and Exacerbating the Post-second Wave Crisis in Femininity." *Mothering in the Age of Neoliberalism*. Edited by Melinda Vandenbeld Giles. Bradford, ON: Demeter Press, 2014, 297–314.

————, and Andrea O'Reilly. "Academic Motherhood in a Post-Second Wave Context." In *Contemporary Motherhood in a Post-Second Wave Context: Challenges, Strategies, and Possibilities*, edited by D. Lynn O'Brien Hallstein and Andrea O'Reilly. Toronto: Demeter Press, 2012, 1–48.

Oldenburg, Ann. "Gwen Stefani 'Bumps It' in Stilettos." *usatoday.com*, January 22, 2014. http://www.usatoday.com/story/life/2014/01/22/gwen-stefani-bumps-it-in-stilettos/4767523/

O'Leary, Kevin. "Kim Dares to Bare." *US Weekly* 953, May 13, 2013, 58–65.

————. "Tortured by her Body." *US Weekly*, August 26, 2013, 48–53.

————. "My Body is Back!" *US Weekly* 984, December 23, 2013, 52–57.

————, and Omid Scobie. "Countdown to Baby!" *US Weekly* 53, May 13, 2013, 62–68.

Olowokere-Rein, Shanelle. "Molly Sims Flaunts Fab Post-Baby Body in Bikini." *people.com*, February 2, 2013. http://www.people.com/people/article/0,,20670653,00.html

"100 Years of Maternity Fashion." *whattoexpect.com.* n.d. Web. September 12, 2012. http://www.whattoexpect.com/tools/photolist/100-years-of-maternity-fashion

O'Reilly, Andrea. "I Should Have Married Another Man; I Couldn't Do What I Do Without Him: Intimate Heterosexual Partnerships and their Impact on Mothers' Success in Academe." *Contemporary Motherhood in a Post–Second Wave Context: Challenges, Strategies, and Possibilities*. Edited by D. Lynn O'Brien Hallstein and Andrea O'Reilly. Toronto: Demeter Press, 2012, 197–213.

————, ed. *Mother Outlaws: Theories and Practices of Empowered Mothering*. Toronto: Women's Press, 2004.

Orenstein, Peggy. *Flux: Women on Sex, Work, Kids, Love, and Life in a Half-Changed World*. New York: Double Day, 2000.

Ouellette, Laurie. "'Take Responsibility for Yourself': *Judge Judy* and the Neoliberal Citizen." Edited by Susan Murray and Laurie Ouellette. *Reality TV: Remaking Television Culture*. New York: New York University Press, 2004, 231–250.

————, and Susan Murray. "Introduction." Edited by Susan Murray and Laurie Ouellette. *Reality TV: Remaking Television Culture*. New York: New York University Press, 2004, 1–18.

Palca, Joe. "Gender Imbalance in Academic Science." *wbur.org*. Transcript. May 11, 2014. http://www.wbur.org/npr/311521514/plenty-of-women-enter-academic-science-they-just-dont-stay

Parker West, Lauri. "Welfare Queens, Soccer Moms, and Working Mothers: The Socio-political Construction of State Child Care Policy." Unpublished doctoral dissertation, Emery University, Atlanta Georgia, 2004.

Peskowitz, Miriam. *The Truth Behind the Mommy Wars: Who Decides What Makes a Good Mother?* Emeryville, CA: Seal Press, 2005.

Pitts-Taylor, Victoria. *Surgery Junkies: Wellness and Pathology in Cosmetic Culture*. New Brunswick, NJ: Rutgers University Press, 2007.

Podnieks, Elizabeth. "Introduction: Popular Culture's Maternal Embrace." In *Mediated Moms: Mothers in Popular Culture*, edited by Elizabeth Podnieks. Montreal: McGill-Queen's University Press, 2012, 3–34.

———— "'The Bump is Back': Celebrity Moms, Entertainment Journalism, and the 'Media Mother Police.'" In *Mediated Moms: Mothers in Popular Culture*, edited by Elizabeth Podnieks. Montreal: McGill-Queen's University Press, 2012, 87–107.

Porter, Eduardo. "Motherhood Still a Cause of Pay Inequality." *newyorktimes.com*, June 6, 2013. http://www.nytimes.com/2012/06/13/business/economy/motherhood-still-a-cause-of-pay-inequality.html?_r=1&emc=eta1

"Pregnant Kim Kardashian Indulges in Cravings: Chicken and Waffles, Risotto, Decadent Desserts and More. intouchweekly.com, April 3, 2013. http://www.intouchweekly.com/posts/pregnant-kim-kardashian-indulges-in-cravings-chicken-and-waffles-risotto-decadent-desserts-and-more-25848

"'Pregorexia' Inspired By Thin Celebs?" *cbsnews.com*, August 11, 2008. http://www.cbsnews.com/stories/2008/08/11/earlyshow/health/main4337521.shtml

Pyke, Karen D. "Class-Based Masculinities: The Interdependence of Gender, Class, and Interpersonal Power." *Gender and Society* 10.5 (October 1996): 527–549.

Ravitz, Justin. "Kim Kardashian Wears Baggy Clothes on Latest Post-Baby Outing: Pictures." *usmagazine.com*, September 30, 2013. http://www.usmagazine.com/celebrity-body/news/kim-kardashian-wears-baggy-clothes-on-latest-post-baby-outing-pictures-2013209

Rich, Adrienne. *Of Woman Born: Motherhood as Experience and Institution.* 2nd ed. New York: Norton, 1986.

Robertson, Annabelle. "Mommy Makeover: A Plastic Surgery Trend." *webmd.com*. n.d. Web. September 27, 2013. http://www.webmd.com/beauty/treatments/mommy-makeover-a-plastic-surgery-trend?page=1

Rochman, Bonnie. "Is Kate Middleton Too Thin to Be Pregnant?" *time.com*, December 7, 2012. http://healthland.time.com/2012/12/07/is-kate-middleton-too-thin-to-be-pregnant/

Rogers, Christopher. "Kim Kardashian Pregnant—Kanye West Announces On Stage." *hollywoodLife.com*, October 31, 2012. http://hollywoodlife.com/2012/12/31/kim-kardashian-pregnant-kanye-west-concert/

Rose, Nikolas. "Governing 'Advanced' Liberal Democracies." In *Foucault and Political Reason: Liberalism, Neoliberalism, and Rationalities of Government,* edited by Andrew Barry, Thomas Osborne, and Nikolas Rose Chicago: University of Chicago Press, 1996, 37–65.

Rosenfeld, Alvin, and Nicole Wise. *The Over-Scheduled Child: Avoiding the Hyper-Parenting.* New York: St. Martin's Griffin, 2001.

Roth, Benita. *Separate Roads to Feminism: Black, Chicana, and White Feminist Movements in America's Second Wave.* Cambridge: Cambridge University Press, 2004.

Rubin, Lisa R., Carol J. Nemeroff, and Nancy Felipe Russo. "Exploring Feminist Women's Body Consciousness." *Psychology of Women Quarterly* 28 (2004): 27–37.

Ruddick, Sara. *Maternal Thinking: Toward a Politics of Peace.* Boston: Beacon Press, 1989.

Saunders, Louise. "'I really did love him': Pregnant Kim Kardashian hits back at claims she married Kris Humphries for publicity

. . . as she sits through NINE HOUR divorce deposition." *dailymail.co.uk*, March 21, 2013. http://www.dailymail.co.uk/tvshowbiz/article-2296845/Kim-Kardashian-hits-claims-married-Kris-Humphries-boost-TV-ratings-sits-NINE-HOUR-divorce-deposition.html

Schutte, Lauren. "Beyonce Reveals She Went from 195 Pounds to 130 Post-Pregnancy: See the Slimdown in Photos!" *omg!* n.d. Web. December 31 2012. https://celebrity.yahoo.com/blogs/celeb-news/beyonce-reveals-she-went-from-195-pounds-to-130-post-pregnancy--see-the-slimdown-in-photos--003027849.html?soc_src=mediacontentstory

———. "Holly Madison Shows Off Her Dramatic Weight Loss." *Yahoo! Celebrity*, May 3, 2013. https://celebrity.yahoo.com/blogs/celeb-news/holly-madison-shows-off-her-dramatic-weight-loss-233101648.html

Shewfelt, Raechal Leone. "Snooki Shows Off Fab Post-Baby Abs." *Yahoo! Celebrity*, May 28, 2013. https://celebrity.yahoo.com/blogs/celeb-news/snooki-shows-off-fab-post-baby-abs-230744716.html

———. "Kim Kardashian's Post-Pregnancy Style." *Yahoo! Celebrity*, September 20, 2013. https://celebrity.yahoo.com/blogs/celeb-news/kim-kardashian-post-pregnancy-style-235453878.html

Shilling, Chris. *The Body and Social Theory*. 2nd ed. Thousand Oaks, CA: Sage, 2003.

Shugart, Helene. "Consuming Citizen: Neoliberating the Obese Body." *Communication, Culture & Critique* 3 (2010): 105–126.

———. "Managing Masculinities: The Meterosexual Moment." *Communication and Critical/Cultural Studies* 5.3 (September 2008): 280–300.

———. "Crossing Over: Hybridity and Hegemony in the Popular Media. *Communication and Critical/Cultural Studies* 4.2 (June 2007): 115–141.

Sieczkowski, Caven. "Kanye West Baby Announcement: Kim Kardashian Had 'No Idea' Rapper Would Announce Pregnancy (VIDEO)." *huffingtonpost.com*, December 31, 2012. http://www.huffingtonpost.com/2012/12/31/kanye-west-baby-announcement-kim-kardashian-no-idea-announce-pregnancy-at-concert_n_2387621.html

Sitzer, Carly Jane. "Hot Mama Alert! Fergie Flaunts Post-Pregnancy

Figure: See 4 More Recent Impressive Bodies After Baby!" *intouchweekly.com*, January 31, 2014. http://www.intouchweekly. com/posts/hot-mama-alert-fergie-flaunts-post-pregnancy-fig-ure-see-4-more-recent-impressive-bodies-after-baby-27741

Skeggs, Beverley and Helen Wood. *Reacting to Reality Television: Performance, Audience and Value.* New York: Routledge, 2012.

———. "Introduction: Real Class." In *Reality Television and Class*, edited by Helen Wood and Beverley Skeggs. London: Palgrave Macmillan, 2011, 1–32.

Slaughter, Anne-Marie. "Why Women Still Can't Have It All." *Atlantic Monthly* (July/August 2012). http://www.theatlantic. com/magazine/archive/2012/07/why-women-still-cant-have-it-all/309020/#.T-ml9BYPrO4.email

Solé, Elise. "Mom's Body Image Documentary Will Make You Embrace Your Flaws." *Yahoo! She*, May 17, 2014. https:// ph.she.yahoo.com/blogs/healthy-living/taryn-brumfitt-body-image-180640278.html

"Stars, Style, Secrets!" *People*, January 21, 2014, 31.

Stephens, Hallie. "Shakira Flaunts Post-Baby Body in Skin-Tight Leather Pants." *Yahoo! Celebrity*, March 28, 2013. https://celeb-rity.yahoo.com/blogs/celeb-news/shakira-flaunts-post-baby-body-skin-tight-leather-012301458.html

Stiehl, Christina. "Kim Kardashian Reveals: I've Only Gained 20 Pounds While Pregnant." *hollywoodlife.com*, March 26, 2013. http://hollywoodlife.com/2013/03/26/kim-kardashian-weight-gain-pregnant-live-with-kelly-and-michael/

———. "Kim Kardashian Shows Off Fit Pregnant Body in Tiny Bikini – Pic." *hollywoodlife.com*, May 8, 2013. http:// hollywoodlife.com/2013/05/08/kim-kardashian-pregnant-bikini-pics-baby-bump-greece/

———. "Kim Kardashian: Showing Off Of Your Pregnant Body Is Empowering." *hollywoodlife.com*, May 9, 2013. http://hol-lywoodlife.com/2013/05/09/kim-kardashian-pregnant-body-bikini-baby-bump/

Stone, Pamela. *Opting Out?: Why Women Really Quit Careers and Head Home.* Berkeley: University of California Press, 2007.

suzy. "Kim K. Shares a Revealing Photo of Her Post-Baby Curves— to Kanye's Delight." *omg!* October 13, 2013. https://celebrity.

yahoo.com/blogs/celeb-news/kim-k-shares-revealing-photo-her-post-baby-120938600.html

Sweetman, Paul. "Modified Bodies: Texts, Projects and Process." *Routledge Handbook of Body Studies.* Edited by Bryan S. Turner. New York: Routledge, 2012, 347–361.

Sykes, Tom. "Pregorexia: Is Skinny Kate Too Thin For A Pregnant Woman?" *thedailybeast.com*, December 7, 2012. http://www.the-dailybeast.com/articles/2012/12/07/pregorexia-is-skinny-kate-too-thin-to-be-pregnant.html

Takeda, Allison, and Omid Scobie. "She's Glowing! Kate Middleton Shows Off Baby Bump in a Yellow Coat Dress." *usmagazine.com*, May 22, 2013. http://www.usmagazine.com/celebrity-moms/news/kate-middleton-plays-up-pregnant-bump-at-queen-elizabeths-garden-party-pictures-2013225

Tarkin, Laurie. "Mom Would you Erase the Signs of Pregnancy?" *Today Health.* n.d. Web. June 03, 2014. http://today.msnbc.msn.com/id/25583034

Tauber, Michelle, Simon Perry, Philip Boucher and Monique Jessen. "Kate Bounces Back!" *People*, November 3, 2014, 48–52.

Tesler, Michael. "The Spillover of Racialization into Health Care: How President Obama Polarized Public Opinion by Racial Attitudes and Race." *American Journal of Political Science* 56.3 (February 2012): 690–704.

Thompson, Mary. "Learn Something From This!: The Problem of Optional Ethnicity on American's Next Top Model." *Feminist Media Studies* 7.1 (2007): 47–63.

"TS." "Comment 3." "Motherhood Still a Cause of Pay Inequality." *New York Times* (June 12, 2012). http://www.nytimes.com/2012/06/13/business/economy/motherhood-still-a-cause-of-pay-inequality.html?_r=1&emc=eta1

Turner, Bryan S. "Introduction: The Turn of the Body." *Routledge Handbook of Body Studies.* Edited by Bryan S. Turner. New York: Routledge, 2012, 1–18.

Turner, Julia. "Where Do 'Baby-Daddies' Come From?" *www.slate.com*, May 7, 2006. http://www.slate.com/articles/life/the_good_word/2006/05/where_do_babydaddies_come_from.html

Tyree, Tia C.M. "Lovin' Momma and Hatin' on Baby Mama: A Comparison of Misogynistic and Stereotypical Representations in Songs about Rappers' Mothers and Baby Mamas." *Women & Language* 32.2 (Fall 2009): 50–58.

"Vanity Fair: Demi Moore Poses Nude while Pregnant, and Earlier with Paint." *latimes.com.* n.d. Web. February 2, 2014. http://www.latimes.com/entertainment/la-et-vanity-fair-demi-pix-photo.html#ixzz2sMqhJiES

Vavrus, Mary Douglas. "Opting Out Moms in the News: Selling New Traditionalism in the New Millennium." *Feminist Media Studies* 10.3 (2010): 335–352.

Villalobos, Ana. *Motherload: Making it All Better in Insecure Times.* Berkeley: University of California Press, 2014.

Vissar, Josh. "Kate and Prince William Announce Pregnancy Early amid Fears News Would Leak over Internet." *nationalpost.com*, December 3, 2012. http://news.nationalpost.com/2012/12/03/kate-middleton-pregnant-royal-couple-announce-they-are-having-a-baby/

Walzer, Susan. "Thinking about the Baby: Gender and Divisions of Infant Care." *Social Problems* 43.2 (May 1996): 219–234.

Warner, Judith. "Mommy Madness (excerpted from *Perfect Madness*): What Happened When the Girls Who Had It All Became Mothers? A New Book Explores Why This Generation Feels so Insane." *thedailybeast.com*, February 21, 2012. http://www.the-dailybeast.com/newsweek/2005/02/21/mommy-madness.print.html

Webber, Stephanie. "Thandi Newton Debuts Stunning Post-Baby Body Five Weeks After Giving Birth." *usmagazine.com*, April 10, 2014. http://www.usmagazine.com/celebrity-body/news/thandie-newton-debuts-stunning-post-baby-body-five-weeks-after-giving-birth-picture-2014104

Weiner, Julie. "The Top 10 Best-Dressed Pregnant Ladies." *vanity-fair.com*, April 19, 2013. http://www.vanityfair.com/style/2013/04/top-ten-best-dressed-pregnant-celebrities

Westcott, Kathryn. "The Bikini: Not a Brief Affair." *newsvote.bbc.co.uk.* n.d. Web. July 6, 2010. http://newsvote.bbc.co.uk/mpapps/pagetools/print/news.bbc.co.uk/2/hi/in_depth/5130460.stm

White, Kevin. "The Body, Social Inequality and Health." *Routledge Handbook of Body Studies.* Edited by Bryan S. Turner. New York: Routledge, 2012, 264–274.

Williams, Joan. *Unbending Gender: Why Family and Work Conflict and What To Do About It*. Oxford: Oxford University Press, 2000.

Willis, Jackie. "Mother-of-Six Kim Zolciak Flashes Slim Swimsuit Body." *Yahoo! Celebrity*, September 18, 2014. https://us-mg6. mail.yahoo.com/neo/launch?.rand=0eb2db0flga2k#8355756845

Wolf, Naomi. *Misconceptions: Truth, Lies, and the Unexpected on the Journey to Motherhood*. New York: Anchor Books, 2003.

Wolfinger, Nicholas H., Mary Ann Mason, and Marc Goulden. "Stay in the Game: Gender, Family Formation and Alternative Trajectories in the Academic Life Course." *Social Forces* 87.3 (2009): 1591–1621.

Wood, Julia T. *Gendered Lives: Communication, Gender, and Culture*. 7th ed. Belmont: Wadsworth, 2007.

Wurzburger, Andrea. "Everything You Need to Know About the 'Reverse Progress' Fitness Movement." *redbookmag.com*, June 12, 2014. http://www.redbookmag.com/health-wellness/body-blog/ reverse-fitness-progress-movement

Zuckerman, Suzanne, Simon Perry, Monique Jessen, and Philip Boucher. "Kate's Baby Bump Diary!" *People*, May 13, 2013, 62–66.

INDEX